THE CRIMES OF
DR GRAMSHAW

THE CRIMES OF DR GRAMSHAW

ROSEMARY COOK

Matador
9 Priory Business Park,
Wistow Road, Kibworth Beauchamp,
Leicestershire. LE8 0RX
Tel: 0116 279 2299
Email: books@troubador.co.uk
Web: www.troubador.co.uk/matador
Twitter: @matadorbooks

ISBN 978 1800460 287

British Library Cataloguing in Publication Data.
A catalogue record for this book is available from the British Library.

Printed and bound by CPI Group (UK) Ltd, Croydon, CR0 4YY
Typeset in 11pt Minion Pro by Troubador Publishing Ltd, Leicester, UK

Matador is an imprint of Troubador Publishing Ltd

Front cover photograh first appeared in the *Yorkshire Evening Post* on 9 May 1908.

For Alison, who has lived with
Dr Gramshaw for a long time now

Contents

PROLOGUE

After his death, the Yorkshire Evening Post published a photograph of the late Dr Farbrace Sidney Gramshaw. In this image, he looks like the archetypal Victorian criminal. His hair is shaved close to his scalp, though he has a bushy black beard. Pictured in quarter profile, he stares straight ahead, unsmiling, his eyes deeply shadowed under prominent brows. He even wears a striped shirt reminiscent of prison-issue clothing.

But Dr Gramshaw was never in prison. He was never even convicted of a serious crime. The origin of this photograph – apparently the only remaining image of the man who was a family doctor in Yorkshire for 35 years – is unknown. But he did have a lot of dealings with the justice system, as witness and as defendant. And it is likely that it was only his own death that saved him from finally experiencing the reality of prison life; and maybe even the ultimate sanction of capital punishment.

This is a true story. It is put together from newspaper accounts, official records and local sources. Although the litany of love and lust, success and deceit, crimes and lies, adultery, bigamy and insanity has all the ingredients of a gothic novel, for the Gramshaw family – sons and daughters as well as the man at the centre of the story – it was stark reality with tragic consequences. This is their story.

Chapter 1

'THE SENSATIONAL CASE AT YORK'

Dr Gramshaw spent the last day of his conscious life in court. It was 4 May 1908 and outside the imposing edifice of the Law Courts in York, the city was dank and cold after an unseasonably snowy and cold period at the end of April. Inside the courtroom, five doctors, two solicitors, the Town Clerk (representing the Chief Constable) and nine witnesses were due to give evidence in what the papers were calling 'the sensational case at York.' This was the second day of the proceedings, and Dr Gramshaw had already given his evidence in a long session on day one. Spectators in court for the second session noticed that he seemed distracted and listless; he was described as seeming 'more or less indifferent to the proceedings'.

He even appeared to doze at intervals: later it would be reported that he said he had not slept for days. At other times, he was seen to be drawing and writing in a red-covered notebook. His solicitor sat with him and consulted him when the court asked if the doctor wanted to add to his previous evidence. Dr Gramshaw declined.

The case they were attending was the inquest into the death of a 19-year old governess called Margaret Eleanor Brown. The first day's proceedings had taken place six days before, on 28 April, in front of the Coroner, Mr John Wood, the Chief Constable, the medical men and members of Margaret's family. Her sister Alison Brown, who was seven years older than Margaret and also a governess, told the Coroner that she and her sister had arranged a holiday in York for Easter. Alison was working in Hurstpierpoint in West Sussex, and Margaret had a post in Thornton Watlass in North Yorkshire. The sisters were to meet in York, as Margaret said she could not afford the trip down to Brighton. The family had previously lived in York for many years, so this was familiar territory. Margaret had been born in the city, and the rest of the family, including Margaret's two older sisters, had only left to move south in 1902. However, their plans for time together at Easter changed, when Alison wrote to say that she could not come up to York. So Margaret made the trip alone, travelling by train from North Yorkshire, with her luggage, so the proprietor of her hotel reported, in a Japanese basket.

Margaret's destination was the Glynn Temperance Hotel in the cobbled road called Micklegate, leading from one of the 'bars' or gates in the city walls across the river into the city centre. Elizabeth Dennison, the proprietor of the hotel, was only 29 years old. She had taken over the hotel with her husband Luke on 4 April, and the booking for Margaret and her sister's stay was made on 6 April, for their arrival on 15 April.

The booking was made by Dr Gramshaw, whom Mrs Dennison understood to be the young woman's guardian. He told the inquest that he had known the deceased and her sisters very well and had attended them all. Margaret had written to him, he said, wanting to consult him about her health. Dr Gramshaw had suggested that she come to York and invite her older sister, Alison, to come too. In fact, he wrote to Alison himself, suggesting the arrangement. He called Mrs Dennison and engaged rooms for two young ladies. When Alison wrote back to say that she could not come, Dr Gramshaw asked Mrs Dennison book a front room at the hotel for Margaret, and 'to be a mother to her' during her stay.

Margaret arrived in York on Wednesday 15 April. Dr Gramshaw visited her that evening and told the inquest that she did not look well and was particularly depressed. She feared that she was pregnant, though the doctor said that 'he very much doubted if she were.' Dr Gramshaw visited again on the Thursday, and the next day, which was Good Friday, the start of the Easter weekend. On that day, he said, he found that she was about to miscarry. He sent for his nephew, a fifth year medical student at Newcastle currently staying with his uncle in York, who brought a medical bag and chloroform to the hotel. Dr

Gramshaw also sent for nurses to attend to the girl and told Mrs Dennison that evening that Margaret had had a miscarriage. Over Easter weekend, Margaret's condition worsened. By Easter Sunday, her temperature was 104°, and Dr Gramshaw called another doctor, Dr Fell, who visited and advised on the case. Dr Gramshaw also wanted to call Margaret's parents but, he told the inquest, she 'absolutely refused' permission for him to do so.

On Easter Monday, Dr Gramshaw wrote to the family who employed Margaret as a governess in Thornton Watlass about her illness. In fact, he wrote twice. His first letter said that she had 'not much wrong with her' on her arrival in York, but that she was not so well on the Thursday. Later, he wrote, she had had 'a severe attack of blood poisoning' starting on Saturday, with a temperature of 105°, and he had had to get the services of three nurses. However, this letter said that 'he trusted she would be quite well in a few days.' His second letter spoke of a relapse, and that she was 'very ill.'

On Tuesday 21 April, Dr Gramshaw telegraphed Margaret's parents, and they and her sister Alison started the long journey from Sussex to Yorkshire. They arrived on the Thursday and endured a turbulent few days, with a stream of official and medical visitors coming in and out of the hotel bedroom. In spite of the best efforts of the doctors and nurses who attended, her family must have seen that the battle for the young girl's life was being lost. Margaret died from acute peritonitis on Sunday 26 April. It had been nine painful days since she lost her baby.

Perhaps Dr Gramshaw was reflecting on this failure as

he sat through the second day of the inquest, a week later. He was a well-known York doctor, a member of many medical and professional societies, who had practised his profession in the county for 35 years. At 54 years old he was in his prime, described by the papers as 'a tall, fine-looking man with a bushy beard and whiskers.' He was an impressive figure, accustomed to wearing a gold watch and chain, a plain gold ring, a signet ring and an engraved Indian ring. The only known photograph of him shows him with close-cropped hair but a full moustache and a beard down to his chest. He has a broad forehead and large nose, with close-set eyes under strong dark eyebrows. Over the course of the long second day of the inquest, he heard the statements of his nephew the medical student, Margaret's employer from Thornton Watlass and her former landlady in York. Dr Watson from Leeds, who had carried out the post-mortem, and the other doctors present at the examination gave their evidence, and the jury heard their views on the cause of death. Their evidence, added to that of the Chief Constable and the nurses given on day one, was supplemented, in a rare and poignant occurrence, by testimony recorded from Margaret herself three days before she died.

The papers were having a field day. So many details, so much probing into the lives of the people surrounding Margaret Brown in her last days: the case was reported across the country, with its 'startling revelations', 'sensational developments' and 'differences among the doctors', as the Coroner probed the 'mystery' of the girl's 'singular' death. At five thirty in the afternoon on 4 May, after a seven-hour sitting, the inquest was adjourned, with the intention of continuing the next day. But when the Coroner and jury did re-convene, on 19 May, Dr Gramshaw was not there. By then he too was dead, in circumstances that raised more questions for the Coroner to answer: so he never heard the verdict on the death of his patient Margaret Brown and his treatment of her.

Chapter 2

THE MAKING OF DR GRAMSHAW

Although he practised medicine in Yorkshire for more than 30 years, Dr Gramshaw was not a Yorkshireman. He was born on 26 October 1853 in Tettenhall in Staffordshire, and christened, the following January, Farbrace Sidney Gramshaw. In his adult life he was often referred to as 'F. Sidney Gramshaw', and he is listed in the 1861 Census, when he was at school in Ipswich at the age of seven, as 'Sidney Gramshaw'. His written signature was also 'F. Sidney Gramshaw'. So it is likely that he went by his middle name, at least within the family. His first name, Farbrace, was a family name: his grandfather William Gramshaw had it as a middle name.

William Farbrace Gramshaw was also a doctor, as his own father had been, practising as a surgeon in

Hinckley, Leicestershire. He had four children, two sons and two daughters. Both sons – James Henry the eldest, and Henry the youngest – also became doctors. When he died in 1843, William Gramshaw left his medical instruments, books and 'wearing apparel' to 'my dear son James Henry Gramshaw'. Young Henry Gramshaw inherited some of his father's other books, shared with his sisters Rosa and Fanny. It was the younger son, Henry Gramshaw, who married Jane Morgan and was Farbrace Sidney Gramshaw's father. Sidney was the eldest son: his brother Leonard was born three years later in 1856, and was followed by five sisters, Isabel, Cecilia, Lucy, Frances, Rosa and Norah.

Henry Gramshaw, Sidney's father, was a general practitioner in Tettenhall. He had studied medicine in London and qualified as a GP by virtue of being a Licentiate of the Society of Apothecaries in London. He was also a licentiate of the Royal College of Physicians as well as a Member of the Royal College of Surgeons. He had a medical degree from the University of St Andrews in Scotland. The family lived in Upper Green, Tettenhall in Staffordshire where Henry was practising, for the first three years of Sidney's life. The village, lying on the ancient route from London to Holyhead, is now part of the Borough of Wolverhampton in the West Midlands. In 1856, Henry sold the contents of his house there, including all the furniture and the contents of the kitchen and garden: the sale was advertised in the local paper 'by Henry Gramshaw Esq, surgeon, who is leaving the district.' The family moved south, to live in Laxfield Villa near Framlingham, a small market town in Suffolk. It was here that Sidney's sister Lucy was born in 1862; and three years later a brother, Charles Cecil, was born but died only 10 months later. The family moved on to Ampthill in Bedfordshire, though by this time, Sidney Gramshaw had left home to start his own medical training.

Meanwhile, Sidney's uncle, Dr James Henry Gramshaw, spent the whole of his professional life in Gravesend in Kent. He too had obtained a Doctorate in Medicine from the University of St Andrews, was a Member and later a Fellow of the Royal College of Surgeons, and a Licentiate of the Society of Apothecaries in London. He acted as medical officer to the Gravesend Union for more than 30 years. Though he was nine years older than Sidney's father Henry, James had outlived his younger brother by 12 years when he died in 1902.

When Sidney Gramshaw's father became a doctor, in around 1851, medical education was changing. Henry Gramshaw had trained in London, where medical training had evolved from informal arrangements between students and the physicians and surgeons at the hospitals, combined with occasional courses and private anatomy schools, to a more structured approach. Medical schools grew up around major hospitals in the big cities, with the practising surgeons and physicians acting also as lecturers and examiners. The licensing of doctors was in the hands of the Royal College of Physicians and the Royal College of Surgeons, while general practitioners were licensed by the Society of Apothecaries. The Apothecaries Act of 1815 had required more than just lectures on anatomy and dissection: it introduced compulsory apprenticeship and formal qualifications for apothecaries, who by this time combined diagnosis of disease with their traditional role of dispensing medicines. Students who did not hold a university degree were now bound by law to take the Licence of Apothecaries Hall in order to practice as a general practitioner.

The 1858 Medical Act marked a key moment in the history of the medical profession. It was based on the premise that 'it is expedient that Persons requiring Medical Aid should be enabled to distinguish qualified from unqualified Practitioners.' To that end, it created the General Medical Council to regulate all members of the medical profession – physicians, surgeons and apothecaries – by setting standards for their education, holding a Register of all qualified doctors, and removing doctors from the Register should they prove unfit to practise. Only doctors on the Register could be appointed to formal medical positions.

Before this, in Sidney's grandfather's time, the requirements for medical education were set solely by the Society of Apothecaries and the Royal College of Surgeons. Students began by apprenticing themselves to local practitioners, often the surgeons in the hospital, for a fee. Then they paid to attend a course of lectures, gathering certificates signed by the lecturer, before sitting their final examinations: four viva sessions lasting just 15 minutes each. Dissatisfaction in the 1820s with the costs to the student, the monopoly enjoyed by the 'College and Hall' – the Royal College of Surgeons and the Society of

Apothecaries – and the restrictive practices of the hospitals in this system led to a Select Committee inquiry being set up in 1833. Reformers hoped that the Government would legislate to establish a central body to conduct a national examination: but this did not happen at this point. The medical journal *The Lancet* continued to campaign for improvements in the system, including better clinical teaching, exams at intervals throughout the course, and free admission to the practice of the hospitals. The establishment of the General Medical Council in 1858, bringing together the various professional organisations into one central system of medical education, finally made it easier to modify and modernise the curriculum for medical training: removing, for example, the need for medical students to study outlandish and questionably relevant subjects such as the dentition of the mastodon as part of their course. Students were now also required to have some general education before embarking on medical training.

When the Council opened its Medical Register in January 1859, both Dr Henry Gramshaw, Sidney's father, and Dr James Henry Gramshaw, his uncle, were listed in it. Dr Farbrace Sidney Gramshaw would join the Register in September 1874, so the following year, all three Gramshaws were listed together. Sidney was the fourth generation of Gramshaw doctors, as his great-grandfather Samuel, grandfather William and father Henry (as well as his uncle) were all in the same profession.

Dr Sidney Gramshaw listed his first registrable qualification in the medical directory of 1875 – a

THE CRIMES OF DR GRAMSHAW

commercial publication, separate to the formal Medical Register – as 'Licentiate of Apothecaries Hall (LAH) Dublin 1873'. The role of the Company of Apothecaries Hall, established in 1791, was to examine candidates and qualify them to trade as apothecaries by awarding its licence. The LAH had become a registrable qualification when the General Medical Council was set up, so gaining this qualification would enable Gramshaw to qualify and practise as a doctor. However, the Hall itself did not provide education to candidates; they had to bring a portfolio of evidence to prove that they had undertaken the required educational courses and experiences before they could sit the Company's examinations. And the demands, set out in the Medical Directory of 1873, the year Gramshaw qualified, were considerable.

The evidence required consisted of a certificate showing that the candidate had passed an 'Examination in the Arts' before entering professional study; and that he was at least 21 years of age and 'of good moral character'. Certificates were also needed to show that the candidate had been apprenticed to a qualified apothecary for at least three years after passing the Examination in the Arts; and had spent at least four years in professional study. He must also have certificates showing attendance at courses in chemistry (one winter session), anatomy and physiology (two winter sessions), demonstrations and dissections (two winter sessions), botany and natural history (one summer session), 'materia medica' (knowledge about the therapeutic properties of medicines) and pharmacy, with instruction in a laboratory (three months), practical chemistry (three months), principles and practice of medicine (one winter session), midwifery and diseases of women and children (six months), practical midwifery at a recognised hospital, attendance upon 20 cases, surgery (one winter session), forensic medicine (one summer session), and instruction in the practice of vaccination.

Alongside this theoretical knowledge and practical experience, the candidate also needed 'to have attended, at a recognised Hospital or Hospitals, the Practice of Medicine and Clinical Lectures on Medicine during two winter and two summer sessions; also the Practice of Surgery and Clinical Lectures on Surgery during one winter and one summer session.' Finally, he had to 'have performed the operation of vaccination successfully under a recognised vaccinator.' Potential candidates had to lodge their 'Testimonials' with the Clerk of the Hall in Dublin a week before the date of the examinations.

The examination for the Licence came in two parts, one of which could be undertaken halfway through the candidate's professional studies, and one that had to be taken on completion. The exams were spread over three days: 'The first two hours of each day will be devoted to writing Answers, and after that two hours to an oral and practical examination.' It was a tough regime, very different from the four 15 minutes vivas of the old days; and the Society of Apothecaries warned that 'only Candidates who possess a proficiency in Medical knowledge in *all* the subjects will obtain the "Licence to Practise".' Exams had to be sat in Dublin, so Gramshaw must have made the journey to Ireland to do so in 1873. Later entries in the

Medical Directory give 'University College' as his place of training: this would have been University College in London, as University College Dublin did not take on that name until the beginning of the twentieth century. Why Gramshaw chose to sit his Licentiate exams in Dublin rather than at the Apothecaries Hall in London, after his education there, is a mystery. Both his father Henry and his uncle James Henry had obtained their Licentiates in London: but although he followed them into medicine, he did not follow their example in this.

His certificates and testimonials were however accepted by the Apothecaries Hall of Ireland and he must have demonstrated 'proficiency in Medical knowledge in *all* the subjects' when he sat their exams. Farbrace Sidney Gramshaw's name was added to the Register of Apothecaries Hall, Dublin on 11 September 1873. This qualification enabled him to join the General Medical Council's Medical Register in 1874.

At the time of joining the Apothecaries' Register, Gramshaw was living in Easingwold in the North Riding of Yorkshire and working as medical assistant to the local GP, Dr Frederick Hall. He had settled in Yorkshire after moving round the country to gain experience as a doctor's assistant. He had been a medical assistant to an apothecary in Nottingham, Dr Charles Huthwaite, in 1869. In April 1871, at the time of the Census, he was in Somerton, Devon, working as a medical assistant to Dr Edmund Valentine, a local GP. His time in Somerton, though brief, led to a major change in his life: he met Mary Rosabelle Poole, whose father William was a banker in the town. She was a West Country woman, born in Frome in Somerset. Gramshaw and Mary were married in St Michael's parish church in Somerton on Boxing Day, 26 December 1871. They returned to Easingwold, where Gramshaw was still an unqualified medical assistant. They would live in that area for more than thirty years.

Easingwold was a market town 13 miles from York, described in the local Directory as 'pleasantly situated in the Vale of York, on the Western side of the Howardian Hills ... although a market town it has the appearance of a rural village ... market is held every Friday and the trade in bacon and butter is important to York.' The Easingwold 'Union' – a collection of 29 parishes and townships, including Stillington, where the Gramshaws would move next – had a total population of just over 2,000 in 1871.

The Gramshaws moved to Stillington while he was still working as medical assistant to Dr Frederick Hall. The village was a little closer to York, which would be important for Gramshaw's later activities and hobbies; and numbered only 675 inhabitants. According to a local 19th century directory, Stillington was supposed to have taken its name from 'stelan', the stealing town, because it was said that 'the original settlers made a living by robbing the King's forest of its deer and the packmen of their merchandise, as they journeyed to the north along the Roman road which passed about a mile below the town.' When the Gramshaws arrived, the village had two schools, one National and one Wesleyan; a 15th century parish church named for St Nicholas; and a house called The Villa, on Main Street almost opposite the church, where the Gramshaws took up residence. The young couple and their baby son, Cecil, must have been a welcome addition to the village: they were soon involved in all the social activities of the community. And when Dr Hall retired, Dr Gramshaw – now qualified by his Licence from Apothecaries Hall of Dublin and entered on the Medical Register – took over the practice. The villagers must have thought they had been very lucky in their new doctor: and for a while at least, everything did seem perfect.

Chapter 3

THE GRAMSHAWS IN STILLINGTON

The Gramshaw family grew and flourished in Stillington. A second son, William, was born there to join Cecil, and followed by two sisters, Amy and Hilda. The fifth and last child was Guy, all five having been born within nine years. Their parents employed household servants to help look after the family and give them time to join local societies and to organise or take part in village social events.

Throwing himself into rural life, Gramshaw was elected a member of the Sherriff Hutton Agricultural club and of the Yorkshire Agricultural Society. He even ventured to give local farmers advice about agricultural products by writing to the Yorkshire Gazette. The paper reported:

'Mr Sydney F. Gramshaw [sic] of Stillington, Easingwold, writes as follows: Having observed in your paper mention made of the relative merits of Yorkshire and German moss litter, may I ask you to give the following details in the interest of both vendors and consumers as from an independent witness? I have tried both the home and imported article and my verdict must be in favour of the former both on the score of economy and practical utility. Charity commences at home, and in these days of depression all true Englishmen should foster home production where there is an identity of values, but in this case the home product is superior.'

Whether the farmers were inclined to take the 'independent' advice of a young country doctor on the matter of moss litter is open to speculation.

Both Sidney and Mary Gramshaw enjoyed music and drama, and much of their social life involved concerts and plays. On Valentine's day 1881, Gramshaw appeared in a concert in the school rooms at Brandsby, a village adjacent to Stillington, which was raising funds for the school. The doctor appeared in both halves of the concert. Before the interval, he gave a reading called 'A Thrilling Experience'; afterwards he gave another reading 'in Yorkshire dialect.' The York Herald reported that 'in spite of the inclement weather a large audience assembled and by their hearty encores seemed thoroughly to appreciate the efforts made.' Four pounds was raised by the concert and used for school expenses.

Another performance in aid of school funds took place in the Stillington National Schoolroom. This saw Gramshaw taking part in a farce called 'Apartments to Let', in which, it was reported, 'the characters were excellently sustained by Dr Gramshaw, Mr R Wood, Mr F Tenniswood and Mr J W Richardson.'

Mrs Gramshaw joined her husband on the concert programme at another event held at the National School. She opened the concert with a piano solo, and also sang in the first half of the event. During the interval, she accompanied a violinist, Miss Richards, from Newcastle, on the piano. The second part of the event was a dramatic piece called 'Our Bitterest Foe', recounting an incident from the Franco-German war. In it, the paper reported, 'characters were sustained with much ability by Miss W Richards [the violinist from Newcastle], Dr Gramshaw and Mr Allan and gave great satisfaction.' A vote of thanks was given at the end to the Gramshaws, who had been involved in organising the event.

Both the Gramshaws were also on the bill at another concert in Brandsby, this time in aid of the local cricket club. Gramshaw was trying out his Yorkshire accent again with a reading entitled 'T'Cuckoo Clock'; and he gave another reading called 'The Widow of Glencoe'. The newspaper report fails to say whether he assumed a Scottish accent for this one. Mrs Gramshaw and Miss Richards sang Il Trovatore, which was encored, and Mrs Gramshaw had a solo piece too. The concert raised £5 for the club.

In 1885, Gramshaw took on an ambitious musical project, arranging an 'entertainment' at the National

School in Stillington that would run for two nights over Easter Monday and Tuesday. He himself played in a dramatic sketch, gave a recitation, and closed the event with 'a very amusing sketch' with two other performers. His wife was part of a quartet singing an arrangement of the National Anthem and a song about summer roses. Mrs Gramshaw also sang 'The Maid of the Mill', reportedly 'in capital style'. The programme was repeated on the second night, 'after which a ball was held.'

It seems likely that Gramshaw was not a singer himself. His part in the concerts was usually acting, recitations and organising the events. He played 'Mr Spreadbrow, a faithful lover', and 'Mr Honeyton, an irascible husband', and took part in excerpts from The Merchant of Venice, playing opposite many young ladies from the village. So it was probably Mrs Gramshaw's musical abilities that were passed on to at least some of her children. In her teens, her eldest daughter Amy sang in a concert at Easingwold alongside pupils of the Longley House School, organised by their music master, Herr Oberhoffer. As well as music, Amy studied art and drawing. She received certificates from the York School of Art and Science for freehand drawing, drawing from light and shade, and model drawing. Perhaps inheriting her management ability (or desire to be in charge) from her father, Amy was also part of a committee of art students who organised the annual art school dance, at the Assembly Rooms in York.

Amy's younger brother Guy also had certificates from the Royal Drawing Society of Great Britain and Ireland, for subjects including dictated drawing, foreshortened curves, and plant drawing. He may have been artistic – or mischievous – in other ways too. At an invitation fancy dress ball organised by the Gramshaws, Guy 'was admirably got up as [one of] the Sisters Leavey, of music hall fame'. Alongside Miss Kate Summerscale, in the part of the other Sister Leavey, he caused 'a good deal of laughter and applause.' Amy attended that ball as 'Powder and Patches'; her older brother Cecil came as a Yorkshire Hussar; while Dr Gramshaw played it very safe by dressing up as a Doctor of Medicine.

The Gramshaw sons were possibly more interested in being sportsmen than singers or artists. Cecil Gramshaw, the eldest son, played cricket regularly for the village team; and his father was Vice President of the Stillington cricket club. William, the second son, was an angler. Guy Gramshaw, the youngest son, played football. He captained 'The Greens', the football team at St Martin's School in York, when it won the School Football Challenge Cup in the 1999/1900 season. Guy proposed the toast to the captains of the other teams (the Yellows, Blues and Reds) at a celebratory afternoon tea following the victory, and also, it was reported, 'contributed a song'.

Dr Gramshaw's sporting occupations were a variety of country activities. He was known for his skill with a gun and his success at bringing down game birds was reported in the local paper. He owned horses, not just for his carriage or personal use, but also to race. In 1881 he bought a horse called Welbeck for 14 guineas. The best result reported was that of his horse Tit Willow, entered in the annual Stillington races and sports day in 1887, coming in third in the Bay Horse stakes. Gramshaw also acted as field steward for point-to-point events and was a regular rider with the York and Ainsty Hunt. On several occasions, the hunt had cause to be grateful that they had a doctor riding with them. One such occasion was in the 1887-88 season when, on Monday 6 February, the hunt started from Gramshaw's home village of Stillington. The action that day is described in breathless detail by the Hunt's historian, William Garth Dixon, drawing on diaries kept by the huntsmen themselves.

'Monday, February 6th. Stillington. Found [a fox] at Stillington Carr, and ran fast for three fields towards Huby Old Whin; came to a long check; got on the line at length and ran to Sutton village; turning to the left, showed a line towards Farlington, and lost. Found at Haxby Whin and ran fast within a field of the York and Sutton road; turned short to the left and ran back to Haxby lane, over it, and pointed as if for Strensall; going through the small covert next the Oak plantation, and leaving Strensall village on our right, ran through the old fox covert; here hounds came to a slight check. Sportsman [one of the hounds] and Seaman hit off the line, and the body of the pack joining them, they swung to the right over the Farlington Beck and crossed the railway (Scarborough line) on to Strensall Common. Hunted him very well over it, and pointed for the Averhams. Turning short to the left, and leaving Smith's Whin three fields to our right, he ran up the road as if for Flaxton; turning again off the road, ran him over the railway near Flaxton station, passed Lilling Hall on our left, pointed as if for Stittenham; turning to the right, ran down the hill and up to within a field of Foston covert, and ran into him in the open – a field to the left and within half an mile of Bulmer Hagg. One hour and fifteen minutes; ten-mile point; really good hunting, fast at times and slow at others.'

While Dixon's account faithfully records the path of the fox and the names of some of the hounds, he omits to mention the accident that brought Dr Gramshaw off his horse to give medical help to a fellow huntsman. William Burbage was stud groom to the Master of Foxhounds, Edward Lycett Green. He was thrown from his horse near the village of Strensall and suffered a double fracture of his right leg and a severe sprain to his left knee. Gramshaw had him carried to the Ship Inn at Strensall, where he set his leg.

In the same year but in the next hunting season, 1888-89, Gramshaw was again called on when Lieutenant Kavanagh of the 10th Hussars was seriously injured when he fell from his horse during a hunt on 26 November. The horse came down after jumping a drain and attempting a fence, and then rolled over his rider. The horse died; and Lieutenant Kavanagh was taken by Mr Lycett Green himself to a nearby farm. Gramshaw and a Dr Halland treated the officer for broken ribs, an injury to his sternum and lacerations of the lungs. The outcome of this very serious set of injuries is not recorded.

It was not just hunting accidents that Dr Gramshaw was called to attend. Alongside his more routine practice, he was frequently called out to accidents and incidents in the area. When the driver of the bus from York to Stillington, Johnson Leckenby, arrived feeling unwell one Thursday night, he complained to his friends of pain in his shoulder. The friends said later that they heard he might have had a fall whilst loading his coach in York. Leckenby went home, tended to his horses then lay down on the sofa. There he lapsed into unconsciousness and Dr Gramshaw was sent for. He diagnosed concussion and a fractured collarbone, amongst other injuries. Despite his presence, the man died the following day. In another case, the cause of the injury was much more obvious: two men who had been out drinking together returned to the home of one of them, Thomas Lofthouse, after which Lofthouse 'seized a coal rake and inflicted twelve serious gashes' on the other man's head, fracturing his skull. The cause of this was apparently that Lofthouse had woken up to find the other man, John Wilson, talking to his, Lofthouse's, wife. Dr Gramshaw thought that Wilson's injuries were so serious that a 'deposition' should be taken from him. Such a 'dying declaration' was intended to gather the victim's evidence for a possible court case, in case he died before Lofthouse could be prosecuted. However, Wilson recovered from his injuries and this was not needed. Unfortunately, Thomas Lofthouse had 'decamped', according to the local paper, and was never prosecuted for the 'murderous assault'.

A much more tragic accident resulted in doctors from both Stillington and Easingwold being called to help a fourteen-year-old boy whose leg was crushed by farm machinery. Thomas Shepherd was a farmer's son, who was driving two horses pulling a thrashing machine. He was heard to shout, and the horses stopped: Thomas was found with his leg 'fearfully crushed and mangled.' Dr Still from Easingwold and Dr Gramshaw from Stillington were sent for. Between them they had to amputate the boy's leg above the knee. The boy died four hours later. It was thought that he had been getting down from the machine before the horses stopped, and his leg had become caught up in the still-moving threshing apparatus.

At the other end of the social scale, Gramshaw was called to tend to the high-profile victims of a traffic accident, when a car carrying Sir Francis and Lady Winnington plunged over some railings and fell into the mill race at Stillington:

'Sir Francis and Lady Winnington of Stanford Court, Worcestershire, accompanied by a valet and driver, were travelling by motor car from Northallerton to the residence of Lord Listowel at Settrington.

They were travelling through Stillington at seven that evening: it was a dark, wet and rather windy night and a powerful acetylene lamp had been placed at the front of the motor to help light the way. But it just wouldn't work properly so the driver, Frank Noble (27) was obliged to put it out.

He now had to rely on two small side lights for illumination, so really couldn't see properly and as he approached Stillington Mill followed some railings going to the right, when he should have taken the left hand turn. Suddenly the car plunged down a steep incline into the mill race.

Sir Francis and his valet, who were riding in the back of the car, were thrown clear into the water: they were relatively unhurt. However Lady Winnington and Noble were less fortunate – they were trapped in over a metre of water under the heavy car, a 20 horse power Wolsey, which despite the combined efforts of Sir Francis and the valet wouldn't move enough to free them. The two men shouted for help and were heard by the miller, William Gibson. With his men from the mill they managed to lift the car releasing Noble and Lady Winnington.

They were rushed into the mill house and medical aid summoned. When Dr Caister from Stillington arrived he found both Lady Winnington and Noble unconscious and in a serious condition. Immediately he ordered that Dr Gramshaw, who was in York, be telegraphed. Both Doctors stayed with their patients all night and Mr Gibson did all he could.

Her ladyship had sustained three cracked ribs and concussion. She regained consciousness after seven hours. The chauffeur was less lucky. He had also sustained a concussion, but he had a fractured jaw. He remained comatose. His condition was described as 'dangerous'.

By Tuesday evening, though, things were looking up. Both patients were fully conscious. It was reported that Lady Winnington was well pleased with the care she had received at the mill house, though moves were afoot to take her to Stillington Hall as soon as she was more recovered.

Sir Francis took it upon himself to praise their driver, to whom no blame was attributed. Noble was described as a steady man who had just returned from the Boer War.'

Two other notable events took place during the Gramshaw family's time at Stillington. On 3 January, 1884, Gramshaw's mother Jane died at the family home, Blenheim House in Kew. She was 55 years old and had borne 'much suffering.' Six months later, on 31 July 1884, the widower Henry Gramshaw made a second marriage, to Agnes Robinson; and his son Farbrace Sidney Gramshaw was one of the witnesses to the happy event.

A few years later, Gramshaw and his son had a brush with death themselves. It was Cecil, the eldest son, who was with his father in their carriage one Tuesday afternoon, driving home from Sutton Forest. They had reached Dight's Cottage when the horse shied, spun round and overturned the trap. Both the men were thrown violently out of carriage onto the ground. The horse bolted down Moxby Lane for about 250 yards, still dragging the vehicle on its side. Some local labourers, seeing the accident, came to the Gramshaws' assistance. Both men were severely bruised but were thought to have escaped lightly. The horse was badly injured and the carriage had to be sent to York for repairs.

Hunting and shooting, arranging concerts and the occasional accident call-out could not make Dr Gramshaw a living. He had arrived in Stillington as a doctor's assistant and only qualified as a general practitioner whilst living there in 1873. He needed to build a professional career and reputation to generate the kind of income he needed to support his growing family. He started by designating his house a 'maison de santé'.

Chapter 4

THE 'VILLAGE DOCTOR'

The house known as The Villa, where the Gramshaws lived, was part of a row of houses on the main street of the village. The Bay Horse Inn stood on one side, run by eighteen-year-old Clara Backhouse, and a master blacksmith lived on the other. It was not a particularly large house; but in his entry in the Medical Directory for 1875, the year after he joined the Medical Register, Gramshaw listed it as a 'maison de santé', and himself as the proprietor.

A 'maison de santé' is literally a 'house of health', a kind of nursing home where a sick person could be looked after for a fee. Given that Gramshaw was very newly qualified, he had no nursing help and only very limited space available, it was unlikely that this venture was going to bring him much income. He seems to have dropped that idea quite soon: just a few years later, the occupants of the house are listed as the Gramshaw couple, a medical assistant, four children and three servants. These ten residents of The Villa ensured that there was no room to admit patients. Instead, Gramshaw had acquired a handful of medical posts to supplement his income from patients who could afford to pay for his services. He was the medical officer for the Oddfellows, and 'various other Friendly Societies'; and a medical referee for the General Insurance Company. These Friendly Societies were a form of medical insurance for working people, allowing them to pay a small regular sum for access to a doctor when needed.

But the big job for a local general practitioner – more high-profile, with a regular income and the potential for a long term of office – was being appointed Medical Officer of Health for a district. The Public Health Act of 1848 had started to encourage local boroughs to take action on the conditions which bred ill health: poor drainage, refuse in houses and in streets, and contaminated drinking water. Any area where the death rate was above 23 per 1000 had to set up a local Board of Health. The next Public Health Act, in 1875, brought together all these measures and gave local authorities new powers to control water supplies, regulate living conditions and create sewers. They were also required to appoint a medical officer and a sanitary inspector (who could be the same person) to advise on matters of public health. Appointments were by election by the local Board of Guardians; and the Medical Officer of Health had some interesting statutory duties to perform alongside his traditional medical practice. Section 116 of the Act says:

'Any medical officer of health or inspector of nuisances may at all reasonable times inspect and examine any animal carcase meat poultry game flesh fruit vegetables corn break flour or milk exposed for sale or deposited in any place for the purpose of sale, or of preparation for sale, and intended for the food of man, the proof that the same was not exposed or deposited for any such purpose or was not intended for the food of man, resting with the party charged; and if any such animal carcase meat poultry game flesh fish fruit vegetables corn bread flour or milk appears to such medical officer or inspector to be diseased or unsound or unwholesome or unfit for the food of man, he may seize and carry away the same himself or by an assistant, in order to have the same dealt with by a justice.'

The Act also specified that the Medical Officer of Health had to be a qualified medical practitioner, with the exact qualification, appointment and duties, salary and tenure in office to be decided by the Local Government Board.

The prospect of inspecting local meat and vegetables put up for sale and confiscating spoiled goods did not apparently trouble Dr Gramshaw. The London Evening Standard of 6 October 1874 reported that Farbrace Sidney Gramshaw had been appointed medical officer for the Stillington sub-district of the Easingwold Rural Sanitary District for a fee of seventeen pounds a year. He was re-appointed in the following year – but only for a further twelve months. After several renewals, he applied again in 1878 with the aim of achieving a permanent position. But this time the position was not uncontested and the outcome was not a foregone conclusion. The York Herald in September 1878 reported on the meeting held to elect a candidate to the post:

'The fortnightly meeting of this Board [of Guardians] was held yesterday, when Mr Thomas Woodwood, chairman, presided. There was an unusual number of Guardians present owing to this being the meeting for electing medical officers for the Alne and Stillington districts. The present officers for these districts only possessing one qualification, they were only appointed for one year at a time, which year expires on the 29th inst. Mr B E de Lautour for the Alne district was re-elected for another year, there being no opposition. For the Stillington district there were two applications, viz. Mr F S Gramshaw, the present officer, and Mr J F Witz, of Easingwold, who is duly qualified. Mr Gramshaw now produced two diplomas, he having obtained an additional one since the last meeting of the Guardians, and was therefore duly qualified to hold the office permanently. Both gentlemen were proposed, and the result of the voting was Mr Gramshaw, 16; Mr Witz, 6.'

Having succeeded in securing Stillington against his rival from Easingwold, Gramshaw did not limit his ambition to the local village. Just over two years later, in February 1881, he set his sights on the larger Easingwold district as well. Once again there was competition for the position. The Yorkshire Post and Leeds Intelligencer reported:

'Easingwold Rural Sanitary Authority – Appointment of Medical Officer of Health. There was a large attendance at the meeting of this authority yesterday, the principal business being the election of a medical officer of health for the ensuing year. Mr Hicks, of Easingwold (the present officer), and Mr Gramshaw, of Stillington, having been proposed and seconded, the result of the voting was as follows: For Mr Hicks, 15; for Mr Gramshaw, 4. Mr Hicks was therefore declared elected.'

Gramshaw had failed on this occasion; but he did not give up. A year later, in February 1882, the same two doctors applied again for the Easingwold position. The papers reported:

'Easingwold Rural Sanitary Authority. Yesterday this authority proceeded to the election of a medical officer of health for the ensuing year, at a salary of £50 per annum. Mr Hicks, of Easingwold, and Mr Gramshaw, of Stillington, surgeon, were both proposed. The voting was as follows: Mr Hicks, 7, Mr Gramshaw, 15.'

So with the voting almost exactly reversed, Gramshaw became Medical Officer of Health for Easingwold, as well as for Stillington. Easingwold was 'a parish, market and union town, head of a County Court district, polling place for the North Riding'. The Easingwold Union covered twenty nine parishes and townships, including Stillington, with a population by this time of more than 10,000 and an area of 80 square miles. Gramshaw was rapidly enlarging the medical territory on which he could build his career.

Another key role which Gramshaw had taken on at the very start of his medical practice, in September 1874, was that of 'public vaccinator'. This meant that he was responsible for vaccinating children in his district against smallpox. Although the principles of vaccination had been known and practised in China and other countries for hundreds of years, it was an 18th century English country doctor from Gloucestershire, Edward Jenner, who is credited with introducing smallpox vaccination in a systematic way to the British public. Like many very important discoveries, it started with an observation based on real-life practice. Both Dr Jenner and local farmers and milkmaids had noticed that women with that occupation, who were often exposed to the much milder disease of cowpox, seemed to be protected against smallpox. Smallpox was a very much more dangerous and highly infectious disease. It caused pus-filled lesions to break out all over the body and was fatal in up to 60% cases, with even higher mortality in babies and young children. Those who survived the disease often had extensive scarring of the skin, and some were left blind. Jenner was supposed to have heard a Bristol milkmaid boast that 'I shall never have smallpox for I have had cowpox. I shall never have an ugly pockmarked face.'

Jenner's observation led him to try out 'inoculation': taking some of the pus from the lesions of a cowpox sufferer, and inserting it under the skin of a healthy person. The idea was that their body would react to this mild dose of the cowpox virus contained in the pus and produce antibodies to protect the person against the related virus that caused smallpox. In Turkey, earlier in the same century as Jenner's experiment, they were already using a similar technique which they called 'ingrafting'. This technique used smallpox material – pus from lesions of the disease – rather than cowpox material to set up a milder infection to protect the patient. One of the champions of this practice was Lady Mary Wortley Montagu, wife of the British Ambassador to the Turkish Court. She had survived smallpox herself, leaving her scarred from the pocks; and her brother had died from the disease. So when she observed a method of preventing children catching the disease, she was immediately interested. She wrote about it:

'Small-pox so fatal and so general amongst us is here entirely harmless by the invention of ingrafting (which is the term they give it). There is a set of old women who make it their business to perform the operation. Every autumn in the month of September, when the great heat is abated, people send to one another to know if any of their family has a mind to have the small-pox. They make parties for this purpose, and when they are met (commonly fifteen or sixteen together) the old woman comes with a nutshell full of the best sort of small-pox and asks what veins you please to have opened. She immediately rips open that you offer to her with a large needle (which gives you no more pain than a common scratch) and puts into the vein as much venom as can lye [sic] upon the head of her needle, and after binds up the little wound with a hollow bit of shell, and in this manner opens four or five veins … The children or young patients play together all the rest of the day and are in perfect health till the eighth. Then the fever begins to seize them and they keep their beds two days, very seldom three. They have very rarely above twenty or thirty [pocks] in their faces, which never mark, and in eight days' time they are as well as before the illness.'

In China, according to medical writings, the technique was different, and involved crushing smallpox scabs to a powder, then blowing this powder up the nose of the person to be protected. The intended effect was exactly the same: inducing a mild disease to convey immunity.

Lady Mary had her own children vaccinated by variolation, one in Turkey and one in London; and the Royal Family followed her lead – though only after a successful trial had been carried out on prisoners in Newgate gaol. Lady Mary was keen to promote the idea more widely but had serious doubts about whether this would get the support of the medical profession. She wrote:

'I should not fail to write to some of our doctors very particularly about it if I knew any one of them that I thought had virtue enough to destroy such a considerable branch of their revenue for the good of mankind, but that distemper [smallpox] is too beneficial to them not to expose to all their resentment the hardy wight [sic] that should undertake to put an end to it. Perhaps if I live to return I may, however, have courage to war with them.'

Lady Mary clearly did have an impact on this practice on her return to Britain, and she is credited with introducing the process to Britain. Variolation became widespread for a while but faith in it was undermined when epidemics continued to occur.

Dr Jenner was also clearly one of the doctors who did put the 'good of mankind' above the income to be made from treating smallpox, and he inoculated his first patient, eight-year-old James Phipps (the son of his gardener) in 1796. He used material from the cowpox lesions of a local milkmaid, Sarah Nelmes, for the purpose. James developed a mild illness but recovered. He was later shown to be immune to smallpox, when Jenner put material from a case of smallpox into both of the boy's arms, and he failed to catch the disease.

In spite of Jenner's scientific papers on the subject, and the example of high-class and Royal families, there was still deep suspicion of the practice of inoculation against smallpox amongst the public at large. A famous 1802 cartoon by James Gillray caricatures this concern. It shows a doctor inoculating a worried-looking woman, surrounded by previously-inoculated patients who all have cow's heads sprouting from different parts of their bodies. The picture is called 'The Cow-Pock – or the Wonderful Effects of the New Inoculation!' By midway through the 19th century, however, the efficacy of vaccination was sufficiently accepted for the Government to make it compulsory. The Vaccination Act 1853 made it mandatory for all children born after 1 August that year to be vaccinated against smallpox before they were three months old. Local Boards of Guardians were responsible for ensuring implementation and parents could be fined for failure to comply with the law. Soon, two thirds of babies were vaccinated and death rates from the disease fell; but there were still epidemics, and resistance emerged in organised form in local anti-vaccination leagues.

By the 1870s, when Gramshaw started in practice, the anti-vaccine lobby had two main objections: they did not believe the vaccine was safe or effective; and they did not believe that vaccination should be compulsory. They wanted the compulsory element of the legislation repealed, but instead the law was tightened in 1871. Local doctors like Gramshaw were employed to implement the vaccination regime and paid between £1 and £3 per child, depending on the distance the doctor travelled to treat them. Meanwhile, the controversy continued around them. The Graphic paper set out its position – accepting the need for vaccination but sympathetic to the concerns of parents – in an editorial in 1876, which said in part:

'Among the vast majority of educated people the advantages of vaccination are held to be as firmly established as the doctrine of the spheroidal figure of the earth. They are regarded as facts which have passed out of the region of argument. But just as there are [those] who deny that the earth is an oblate spheroid, and declare it rather resembles a dinner-plate in shape, so there are persons – and we fancy that their number is increasing – who hold either that vaccination is altogether bad, or that the advantages are over-balanced by the undoubted evils which it brings in its wake … In the first place it must be remembered that there is a traditional hatred of vaccination handed down from the grandfathers of the present generation. When the practice first began people were shocked at the idea of transferring the substance of a beast into a human being … this objection has less weight nowadays partly because we are more rationalistic than our forefathers were but still more because the cow has very little to do with modern vaccination…

It must also be borne in mind that vaccination is not quite the same process for the poor as it is for the rich. In the case of the well-to-do mother

her little darling's arm is punctured by the family medical adviser, in whom without doubt she has every confidence, and who of course looks in a few days after to see how his small patient is getting on; whereas in the case of the poor, mothers and their babies are often kept hanging about in draughty passages... and the mysterious rite is performed rapidly and unsympathetically (on account of the number of cases) by a total stranger who is sometimes, as recent disclosures at Belper show, an unqualified person. Should the child afterwards catch cold, or should an eruption break out, the blame is apt to be laid on the lymph [vaccine], and sometimes, if serious consequences ensue, both father and mother are converted into a pair of anti-vaccine martyrs.'

An example of 'anti-vaccine martyrs' were the Miller family. G W Miller wrote to the newspapers to say that all five of his children had died following vaccination: 'One fine little fellow died quite rotten ... I would not, if I had five children again, ever have one vaccinated.'

Many parents felt sufficiently seriously about their concerns that they tested the law and felt its consequences. Amongst many such cases, Charles Gillett, a banker from Banbury who was also President of the National Anti-Vaccination League, was fined £1 and expenses for not having his child vaccinated. Ten 'respectable working men' appeared in Gainsborough Police Court charged with neglecting to have their children vaccinated, on the grounds that they were conscientious objectors. They were all fined the maximum £1 plus expenses, with 14 days' imprisonment if they defaulted. Another Gainsborough man, George Airthorpe, was jailed for refusing to vaccinate his child. On his release, somewhere between three and four thousand people attended a mass meeting in the market-place, with Airthorpe presiding, which demanded the repeal of the Vaccination Laws.

Meanwhile, doctors tried hard to counteract the effects of the anti-vaccine movement by publishing statistics which showed the dramatic drop in deaths from smallpox following the introduction of compulsory vaccination. The Medical Officer of Health for Birmingham, Dr Alfred Hill, went to the trouble of publishing tables showing deaths from smallpox per thousand deaths from all causes, with figures from 150 years of public record keeping. These showed that in 1761-70, there were 102.7 deaths from smallpox amongst every 1000 deaths; by 1861-70, after compulsory vaccination, this had fallen more than 90% to 10.4. In spite of this, the Government eventually succumbed to the pressure from anti-vaccine campaigners. Following a Royal Commission, the compulsory element of the vaccination programme was abolished and exemptions were allowed on the grounds of conscience.

Gramshaw was employed as Public Vaccinator for Stillington by the Board of Guardians for Easingwold. At one of their meetings in 1875, the Board was invited to support the anti-vaccine actions of a neighbouring Board:

'The fortnightly meeting of this board was held yesterday; when Mr E S Strangwayes, JP, presided. The Clerk produced a letter from the guardians of the Keighley Union, enclosing a copy of a memorial respecting compulsory vaccination asking the board to assist them (the Keighley guardians) "to set free the entire country from the cruel despotism of compulsory vaccination". There was also enclosed a list of disasters from vaccination deposed to before the Keighley guardians.'

The Guardians for the Easingwold Union, however, were not interested. 'The Clerk, on asking if he should read the communication, was asked not to do so, the Board expressing its opinion that vaccination worked well in that union.'

Gramshaw went on to be a prime mover in the success of the local smallpox vaccination programme. Ten years later, in 1885, it was reported that:

'Dr F Sidney Gramshaw, of Stillington, has received the first class Government award for efficient vaccination, this being the fifth occasion of his so obtaining it.'

Building his medical reputation, Gramshaw also published papers in the leading medical journals: 'Carbolic Acid in the Successful Treatment of Enteric Fever' and 'Ovariotomy in Country Practice' both appeared in *The Lancet*. '30 years in midwifery practice' was published in the *British Medical Journal* (with ten other authors). He also encouraged the next generation of first-aiders by handing out the certificates to successful graduates of the St John Ambulance Association. He had prepared them with a course of lectures 'without fee or reward'; and his generosity was recognised with the presentation of a silver-mounted riding whip, paid for by members of the Association.

The members of the Easingwold Board of Guardians were probably very pleased with their appointment of the efficient Dr Gramshaw as Medical Officer of Health and award-winning Public Vaccinator for Stillington and the Easingwold Union. If they had looked more closely at his qualifications when they made him their permanent appointee, however, they might have been a lot less impressed.

Chapter 5

A FLEXIBLE APPROACH
TO THE TRUTH

When Dr F. Sidney Gramshaw first appeared in the
Medical Directory, he listed his qualifications as
Licentiate of Apothecaries Hall, Dublin, 1873 and
'MD Pennsylv 1871'. A degree in medicine from
the University of Pennsylvania would have been an
impressive achievement. The University had created the
first medical school in the United States and employed
the leading medical faculty in the nineteenth century.
Obtaining a degree in medicine from the University
required students to be at least 21 years old, and to
undertake a medical course lasting nineteen weeks.
The course started in October each year and ended the
following March.

The prospectuses of the University list all students who 'matriculated' – that is, were accepted onto courses – in each year in the medical school, and in all of the other schools. However, the prospectus for 1871 does not list Farbrace Sidney Gramshaw amongst the students in its medical class for the session 1870-71. Nor does he appear in the 1870 or 1872 prospectus. The only international students in either class were from Cuba or Nova Scotia.

If Gramshaw did not attend the University and obtain a medical degree there, it may well have been because he was not eligible to do so. The Regulations of the Medical Department of the University required a candidate to be aged 21, and to have:

'... applied himself to the study of Medicine for three years, and been, during that time, the private pupil for two years, at least, of a respectable practitioner of Medicine. The candidate must also have attended two complete courses of the following Lectures in this Institution: Theory and Practice of Medicine, Anatomy, Materia Medica and Pharmacy, Chemistry, Surgery, Obstetrics and the Diseases of Women and Children, Institutes of Medicine, Clinical and Demonstrative Surgery.'

On applying to the Dean for admission to the medical school, the candidate had to provide tickets proving his attendance at these courses, as well as providing a thesis on 'some medical subject' and being examined on it by one of the school's professors.

Gramshaw could not have fulfilled these requirements. In late 1869, he was in England, employed as a medical assistant in Nottingham. In 1871, he was in Somerton in April, still working as an unqualified medical assistant; and he was there in December that year, though his address was in Easingwold, when he married Mary Poole. He simply did not have time to spend three years studying medicine and attending two courses of lectures in Pennsylvania.

He was also ineligible on the grounds of age. When he first worked for Dr Huthwaite in Nottingham as his unqualified medical assistant, he was 15 years old, having been born in October 1853. In March 1871, when he supposedly finished his medical course and gained his degree in the United States, he was still only 17. Although he claimed to be 20 in the 1871 Census, when he was in Somerton and still working as a medical assistant, he was actually 17. And he had not long turned 18, at the end of October 1871, when he married Mary Poole on Boxing Day that year. He claimed on the marriage certificate to be 'of full age' – meaning 21 years old. He also gave his 'rank or profession' as 'surgeon', even though he had no medical qualifications at all at this time. Interestingly, the two witnesses to the marriage were both from the bride's family: William and Isabelle Poole. Perhaps the groom's family were unaware of his early marriage, as the banns were read in the parish church in Somerton, many miles from any other member of the family; or perhaps they knew but did not approve of it. By the 1881 Census, his first in Stillington, Gramshaw was claiming to be 33, though his actual age in April that year was 27.

His lack of years would not have mattered if he never actually applied to the University of Pennsylvania. But he did apply to Apothecaries Hall in Dublin, and he did obtain his Licentiate from them. It is difficult to see how he managed this, since he does not seem to meet their eligibility requirements either.

Apothecaries Hall required candidates to show a certificate proving that they were over the age of 21 and of 'good moral character'. When Gramshaw was entered onto the Apothecaries Roll, on 11 September 1873, he was still only 19 years old, his twentieth birthday falling in the following month. He should also have been able to prove that he had 'passed an Examination in the Arts' prior to entering on the 'four years of professional study' and 'three years' apprenticeship to a qualified apothecary' as well as 'two winter and two summer sessions of lectures in medicine' and 'one summer and one winter session of lectures in surgery', all required before sitting the Hall's exams. Unlike the University, the Hall did not provide the necessary courses itself; it just administered the final examination, which took place over a week, and would have required Gramshaw to travel to Dublin. How he provided documentary evidence to convince the Hall that he met the pre-exam requirements is a mystery. He certainly had some considerable experience, having been working as a medical assistant since at least the age of 15. So maybe he had also picked up the necessary knowledge during this time, even if he could not prove it. Although in later entries in the medical directory he implied that he had been educated in London, by adding 'Univ. Coll' after reference to his Licentiate, there is no evidence that he attended medical lectures at University College in London. (Although there is now a University College in Dublin too, this had a different name at the time.) There is also very little time for him to have fitted this in between his time as a medical assistant in Nottingham until at least the end of 1869, and his taking up the assistant post in Easingwold in 1871 that led him directly to Stillington. Because while he was in Nottingham, he claimed in his medical directory entry, he had also been Resident Medical Officer at the Nottingham General Dispensary.

The Dispensary in Nottingham had been set up in May 1831 to treat outpatients and patients at home. It was part of a movement which started in London in the late 17th century, and which was initially opposed by many physicians and apothecaries who thought that it represented competition to their services. The 'anti-dispensarians' protested against the opening of these new organisations, which mostly offered free services to the 'sick poor', and they were particularly incensed when the Royal College of Physicians itself proposed building one. But the numbers continued to grow, and by the 19th century, they were widespread. Dispensaries were mainly funded by subscribers, who paid an annual fee, and could then recommend people to receive services. In 'provident' dispensaries, people could pay a small regular subscription themselves and then receive free care when they needed it. It would take a few hundred of these 'club' members paying their regular subscriptions for the dispensary to afford to pay for a doctor.

One reason for the growth of dispensaries was that they often treated patients who were excluded from inpatient hospital services, such as children, pregnant women, 'incurables', and patients with fevers or contagious diseases. So, interestingly, the dispensaries were often treating as out-patients people who were more, not less, sick than those in hospitals. In 1868, just before Gramshaw came to Nottingham, the dispensary there treated well over 10,000 patients as outpatients, and 1,000 patients who were too sick to travel were treated at home. The conditions treated were not necessarily minor; they included fractures, burns, abscesses, infectious diseases, poisoning and haemorrhage.

Another reason suggested for the growth in the dispensary movement was that they advanced the interests of a group of physicians who were 'outsiders' – that is, they could not get a post in a hospital. Perhaps that was why Gramshaw worked at the Nottingham General Dispensary: he was not qualified to be on the staff of a hospital, but he could do useful work at the dispensary.

Unfortunately, there is no evidence that he was ever employed, as he claimed, as Resident Medical Officer at the dispensary. In December 1869, Gramshaw was still an unqualified medical assistant for Dr Huthwaite. In February 1869, the then Resident Medical Officers of the dispensary, Benjamin Lamb Powne and Allan Waring, had resigned, having completed their three years of service. In their place, the dispensary board elected Mr J L Thomas as Resident Surgeon, Mr T D Atkin as Assistant Surgeon and Dr Brookhouse as Honorary Surgeon. In April 1871, the staff was Dr Robertson, Mr Stanger and Mr Hind. Neither the Annual Reports nor the minutes of meetings of the dispensary during the period that Gramshaw was in Nottingham make any reference to a Dr (or Mr) Gramshaw, nor to his employer Dr Huthwaite. If they had an association with the dispensary, it was a purely informal one. And this would not be surprising in the case of Gramshaw, as he did not gain his first qualification as a doctor until 1873, by which time he was settled in Stillington.

It seems extraordinary that none of Gramshaw's subsequent examiners or employers appears to have required documentary evidence of his 'medical degree' from Pennsylvania, or his employment as 'Resident Medical Officer' at the Nottingham Dispensary, and so uncovered his misrepresentations. Maybe they took the word of a medical man – or student – without actually requiring evidence: but this seems unlikely in the case of either the Dean of the Medical School at the University of Pennsylvania, or the examiners at Apothecaries Hall, Dublin. Or maybe they did ask for documentation and were provided with something that convinced them that Gramshaw met their requirements with respect to age, 'good moral character', a previous Examination in the Arts, and attendance at the necessary lectures and courses. Gramshaw's great-grandfather, grandfather, father and uncle were all doctors: perhaps they could open doors for him that would otherwise be firmly shut to a man of his young age and inexperience.

The claim to have a medical degree from the University of Pennsylvania was the most audacious of his CV embellishments. Gramshaw was possibly inspired to this by the coincidence that while he was in Nottingham, working alongside, if not at, the Nottingham Dispensary, there was also an American Dispensary in the town. The physicians here were Dr Kirk, advertising himself as a 'legally qualified Medical Practitioner, University of Philadelphia, Licentiate of Midwifery, Dublin, Andersonian University, Glasgow'; and Dr Wilson, 'University of Philadelphia, Medical College, New York.' Maybe he saw the respect paid to these American-educated doctors by local people, and thought that claiming an American medical degree, along with adding a few years to his age, would be a shortcut to respectability and recognition in his own medical career.

Gramshaw continued to add genuine qualifications to his directory entry as his career developed. In 1878, he became a Licentiate of the Royal College of Surgeons of Edinburgh. This was awarded following an examination, and it licensed the successful candidate as competent to practise surgery. It was a highly respected and officially recognised medical qualification, often used as an alternative to a university medical degree. In 1885, 12 years after his initial registrable qualification of Licentiate of Apothecaries Hall (LAH), Dr Gramshaw became a Licentiate of the Royal College of Physicians of Ireland – known at the time as the King and Queen's College of Physicians of Ireland. This had onerous requirements for training and experience. But if the candidate already had a recognised qualification, such as LAH, he need only provide his registration certificate, and certificates confirming his six months' training in Practical Midwifery at a maternity hospital, and his three months' attendance at a fever hospital, as well as certificates of character from two Fellows of the College (or two registered physicians or surgeons), and sit one of the two final examinations. One way or another, Gramshaw provided this evidence, in spite of the fact that he had been working as a local GP in Stillington for all of the preceding 12 years. He travelled to Dublin by steamer in June 1885 to sit the exam, and his name was duly entered on the records of the Royal College that year.

In 1896, Gramshaw was awarded a medical degree from the University of St Andrews in Scotland, like his father. The Scotsman newspaper reported: 'The following registered medical practitioners, having passed the required examinations, had the degree of Doctor of Medicine conferred upon them: ... Farbrace Sidney Gramshaw, Stillington ...' It is interesting that Gramshaw set out to obtain this degree. He did not need two medical degrees, so maybe this was a tacit acknowledgment, later in his career, that he never did have one from Pennsylvania. He went on claiming the 'MD Pennsylv' in the commercial medical directory for thirty years: but he never included that qualification in the formal Medical Register, run by the General Medical Council. Apart from regularising his professional position with a genuine medical degree, maybe the St Andrews medical degree was also something of a personal vanity project. It enabled him to enjoy academic respectability and also to wear the imposing insignia of academic achievement. Years after being awarded the degree, Gramshaw hosted a soirée for the York and District Field Naturalists' Society. The local paper's write up was headed 'Exhibition and Conversazione', and described the event in gratifying detail:

'A most successful social and exhibition was held in the Galleries of the Museum [home of the York Philosophical Society]. The society's new president, Mr F. S. Gramshaw, MD, FRCS (who wore his resplendent doctor's robes of St. Andrews University), did the honours of the evening in full style. After receiving his guests at the portal of the Yorkshire Philosophical Society's Museum, Dr and Mrs Gramshaw and Miss Gramshaw [the Gramshaw's elder daughter, Amy] served light refreshments in the Library, and at the close of the soirée they again dispensed their hospitality.'

The Easingwold Board of Guardians had appointed Gramshaw to the permanent position of Medical Officer of Health for Stillington on the basis that he had obtained an additional qualification. That was in September 1878, so it may have been the Licentiate from the Royal College of Surgeons of Edinburgh that tipped the balance. Had they realised that he did not have a medical degree from America, and had not worked for the Nottingham General Dispensary, but had started out in Stillington with only a simple LAH from Dublin (obtained when he was below age and had probably not completed the prerequisite training courses), they might have felt that his rival for the position, Mr Witz from Easingwold, was the better man for the job.

Chapter 6

PROBLEMS IN STILLINGTON

In June 1883, the Yorkshire Gazette reported a case heard at the Petty Sessions – equivalent to a magistrate's court – at Easingwold:

> 'On Wednesday, before the Hon. P. Dawney, Mr Strangways, Mr Edwards and Mr Croft, Mr Farbrace Sidney Gramshaw, of Stillington, surgeon, was charged by Thomas Smiddy, of Helperby, excise officer, with wearing armorial bearings without a licence. Mr Wilkinson appeared for the Crown, and Mr Cass, of Thirsk, for the defendant.
>
> Mr Smiddy stated that he had warned the defendant about wearing a certain ring with a motto and crest on it. Fined £1 1s and costs.'

So Gramshaw had been found guilty and fined a guinea for wearing a signet ring. His crime was not, however, displaying a crest and motto to which he was not entitled. The Gramshaw family had long had its own crest, listed and described in 'Fairbairn's Book of Crests of the Families of Great Britain and Ireland'. The entry reads: 'Family – Gramshaw. Motto – amicitia (Friendship). Blazon – a demi-griffin segreant.' A griffin was a mythical beast with the head of an eagle and the body of a lion. 'Segreant' meant that it was shown in a rearing posture, which would be called 'rampant' for other animals. So Gramshaw was entitled to the crest and motto. His problem was that displaying 'armorial bearings' such as these was subject to a tax – and he had not paid it.

Personal coats of arms had been used by individuals as a symbol of their identity and social status since the twelfth century. A tax on displaying arms was introduced in 1798 and repealed only in 1944. To be taxable, a device had to include a motto, wreath or other recognisably heraldic element – in Gramshaw's case, the ring had the crest and motto on it, making it fall firmly into the category of items on which the tax needed to be paid. But it was not only jewellery that counted: if armorial bearings were displayed on a coach, on furniture or buildings, or on clothing or household goods, they would all be taxable. Theoretically, the tax was applicable even if an individual owned a second-hand item displaying armorial bearings relating to someone else altogether. Since 1870, the tax had been an excise licence and enforced locally, with collection delegated to locally appointed officials. Hence the case against Gramshaw was brought by Mr Priddy, the local excise officer, and the accusation was not having the requisite licence. The rate of tax was two guineas for arms on a carriage, and one guinea for any other form of display, payable either through a post office, or directly to the excise officer. The usual fine for not having a licence was £20.

Priddy must have been kept busy on this front. It was well known that many people who should pay the tax for displaying armorial bearings did not do so. 'Not one in fifty who ought to pay it actually does so', wrote a columnist in 1800.

The incident with the signet ring – for which Gramshaw was lucky to have been fined only one guinea and costs – was not his first run-in with the excise authorities. Five years earlier, in 1877, he had been charged with employing two male servants while only holding a licence for one. The excise officer this time was William Harris of Easingwold. He gave evidence that he had visited the Gramshaw house some time before and found two servants in the doctor's employment. He spoke to him about this and reminded him several times of the need for a proper licence, without any effect. What Gramshaw should have done was to complete a schedule at the start of the year, applying for a licence for both the armorial bearings on his signet ring and his two male servants, and then paid the tax on each of them. Gramshaw's defence was that he did not believe he was liable to take out a licence for the 'surgery boy'. Once again, Gramshaw was lucky in the outcome: he was fined what the newspaper described as 'the minimum fine of £5' rather than the maximum £20.

The year after the signet ring charge, Gramshaw was taken to court again – but this time the County Court – on a different matter. Mr Townshend, headmaster of Easingwold Grammar School, was seeking to recover school fees owed to him by Gramshaw for his second son William's education. William had been enrolled at the school 18 months before, in October 1882, on terms set out in the school's prospectus. Mr Townshend claimed that he was owed £10 17s 6d – worth over £1,000 today – after Gramshaw removed the boy from the school without notice. The judge ruled that, although the prospectus containing the terms and fees had been sent to Gramshaw, it had not been stamped 'as it should have been'. On these grounds, he gave the verdict for the defendant, without costs, leaving the headmaster unable to recover the fees owed to his school and out-of-pocket to the tune of the court costs.

So Gramshaw had won that case, if only on the technicality: but his luck in the courts was about to run out. A few years later, he was again pursued for fees due, this time for his eldest son, Cecil, who was apprenticed to an electrical engineer. This was a more serious case: it was heard in London, in front of Mr Justice Lawrance and a jury in the Queen's Bench Division of the High Court of Justice, with barristers representing both sides.

Mr Manville was a Consulting Electrical Engineer, practising in London. He was a respected professional, the electrical engineer to the Corporations of Dublin, Salford, Portsmouth, Kilkenny and various London vestries. In 1889, whilst connected with the Electrical Engineering

Corporation, Manville was carrying out an electrical installation at a mansion in Yorkshire. During this time, Gramshaw met him and negotiated for his eldest son Cecil to become a pupil with the Corporation. Manville used his influence with the Corporation to reduce the premium paid for this apprenticeship from 300 guineas to 200 guineas (around £20,000 in today's terms), and young Gramshaw was taken on at the Corporation's works at West Drayton in London. The newspapers covering the court case reported what happened next:

'On January 6 1891, as fire occurred at the plaintiff's works, which destroyed much property and placed the Corporation into considerable difficulties. When the company went into liquidation, the defendant's son was transferred as pupil from the company to the plaintiff, and the latter sent him over to Dublin where a large central installation centre was being erected. After being there some time, young Gramshaw left and took a situation at a small salary. Evidence was given by electricians that young Gramshaw would have gained valuable experience if he had stayed with the plaintiff in Dublin.

For the defence, Dr Gramshaw and his son gave evidence. The former said that he never agreed to transfer his son as a pupil from the company to the plaintiff, and the latter's testimony was to the effect that the working of the apparatus was not properly explained to him and he left because he learned nothing.'

This time, the court did not show leniency to the Gramshaws. Upholding the primacy of the financial and professional relationship between apprentice and master, the jury found for Mr Manville for the full amount claimed.

The Gramshaws were not always on the defensive in court. In 1892, when Cecil and William Gramshaw were 19 and 17 years old, they were the aggrieved parties in a case against some local youths, heard at the Easingwold Petty Sessions. A group of labourers, Agar Scaife and Walter Lane of Stillington, George Hart from York and George Boast from Dringhouses – a village south of York – were accused of assaulting Cecil and William Gramshaw. The court heard that it had become the custom for young men from Stillington to gather in the evenings in Dr Gramshaw's saddle room. Then the doctor put up a notice in the saddle room saying that 'persons going there in future, except on business, would have to take the consequences.' The four young men charged had apparently taken exception to this, and, on meeting the Gramshaw sons in the village one evening, began to 'ill use and assault them.' The young men headed for home, where the pursuing youths tried to force their way into the house.

In a 'cross-summons', Agar Scaife claimed that William Gramshaw had started the fight, and tried to have him accused of assault. According to the local paper's report, 'the case occupied the court for a long time.' Eventually, the defendants were all found guilty and fined £1 7s each, including costs; and the cross-summons was dismissed.

Dr Gramshaw meanwhile suffered some setbacks in realising his local ambitions. In 1895, he stood as a candidate in the County Council elections. The results were disappointing for him. Mr S Frank, a farmer, received 348 votes; Mr R Souter, a merchant, had 327 votes; and Dr Gramshaw trailed them both with just 47 votes.

An application to be appointed Registrar of Births and Deaths for the Stillingfleet area was also unsuccessful. In spite of the fact that he had been deputy Registrar, when the Registrar post became vacant due to the death of the incumbent, Gramshaw was not appointed. The position went instead to Mr William Gibson, son-in-law of the late Registrar, who was elected unanimously.

However, while he had also failed to be elected to the local parish council, he did spend many years involved in the 'vestry meetings' at St Nicholas's church in the village, so he clearly belonged to some local parish committee. His first meeting was in 1874, when the new vicar, the Reverend Jamieson, took charge of the parish; and he continued to be involved until he left the village in 1903. In November 1902 he was at the meeting that agreed that the church pinnacles needed to be taken down, following a report from the York architect and builder Walter Brierley that said they were 'in a very shaky condition and require immediate attention.' Gramshaw retained his connection with St Nicholas's even after he left Stillington: three years later, the vestry minutes record that he, together with the Lord of the Manor and the Vicar, were paying the premium for the church's fire insurance through their own voluntary contributions.

Village history, based on the recollections of older residents passed down over the years, says that Gramshaw was considered 'a bit of a bully, and very difficult'; and that his sons were accused in one newspaper account of 'acting like little lords'. If true, and combined with his family's various brushes with the law, it may not be a coincidence that the Gramshaws seemed to have trouble keeping their domestic servants. Between 1887 and 1896, they were constantly advertising for new servants in the local papers. In September 1887, they were seeking a general servant. Four months later, they were advertising for a housemaid/ nurse. Then, less than a year after the last advertisement for a general servant, they were in need of another one. Six months later, they needed a housemaid. And three months after that, a new general servant was sought. That advertisement was repeated three months later: whether because of a lack of response to the first, or because a servant had come and gone in the meantime, is not clear. Less than a year after that, there was another advertisement. This time, unlike the others, it was Dr Gramshaw, not Mrs Gramshaw, whose name was on the advertisement. Maybe they thought it would attract more interest if the potential applicants knew they would be working for the local doctor. If so, it didn't work: they were advertising again, in two different newspapers the following month. In total, there were 10 different advertisements in a period of nine years – eight for a general servant and two for a housemaid – which suggests a rather high rate of turnover amongst their employees.

Finally, in the summer of 1903 and after thirty years in the village, the Gramshaws left Stillington. Perhaps their motivation was simply to enhance Dr Gramshaw's medical career by moving from the small village to the nearby City of York, where he was already a 'country member' of the York Medical Society. Or perhaps village life and the scrutiny of neighbours had ultimately become insupportable. Village history suggests a possible additional reason for the move:

'It is said that the Gramshaws moved away from Stillington because Farbrace had an affair with an unmarried lady who lived in the village. She was an accomplished musician who suffered with her nerves and he would visit her, quite often, to give her medication. His wife found out and it was the last straw. It has been said that he conducted a few affairs with local married ladies, indeed there was an elderly gentleman in Stillington … who was rumoured to be the product of a liaison his mother had with Gramshaw and was passed off as her husband's child. It was said that no one else in his family was the least bit musical, but he was like his supposed father!'

Whatever the reason, the Gramshaws left Stillington in 1903 for what should have been a fresh start in York. Just before he left, in the summer of that year, 'the village doctor' was publicly thanked for his efforts in raising money for repairs to the clock of St Nicholas's church. Just five years later, Gramshaw would be back in Stillington, buried in the churchyard of St Nicholas's, while his widow and children fled York for good.

Chapter 7

TROUBLE IN YORK

In exchanging the small rural village of Stillington for a life in the City of York, the Gramshaws were making a huge change to their lives. Stillington had a population of 600; York had nearly 80,000 residents. Instead of the parish church of St Nicholas, they had the Cathedral and Metro Political Church of St Peter in York – better known as York Minster and one of the largest cathedrals in northern Europe – on their doorstep. Amateur dramatics in the school hall were replaced by the professional offerings of York's Theatre Royal. It had opened in 1744 on the site of the former St Leonard's hospital, and boasted a Victorian Gothic façade, a stage 30 feet deep with a proscenium arch 21 feet high, and seating for 1,400 patrons. In the September after they arrived, they could have seen the

'Les Cloches De Cornville' company perform in the 21st year of their tour. In October, Mr George Edwardes's London Company were performing 'The Toreador' at the Theatre Royal; they were followed by the Carl Ross Opera Company.

The Gramshaws – Dr and Mrs Gramshaw, and their unmarried daughters Amy and Hilda – settled themselves into a house at number 9 St Leonard's Place. St Leonard's was a sweeping Regency terrace directly opposite the Theatre Royal and the De Grey Rooms. Theirs was the end house of the terrace, built side-on to the rest, facing Exhibition Square and the city walls, and just around the corner from the Minster. St Leonard's Place was part of the medical district of York, which included the adjacent road of Bootham. Number 9 St Leonard's Place had previously been occupied by Henry Hopton, dental surgeon: numbers 2, 3, 6, 8 and 10 also housed doctors, while Glaisby, Walter and Leonard, dental surgeons, occupied number 4.

One of the biggest changes for Gramshaw, arriving to practise in York, was his place in the medical community. In Stillington he had been the only doctor, and the public vaccinator, and the Medical Officer of Health for that district as well as for Easingwold Union. In York, he was just one of many doctors in a medical community that included surgeons and physicians from the local hospitals and the York Dispensary, and the City Council-appointed Medical Officers, in addition to general practitioners.

As a major city, York had a significant and well-developed health service infrastructure. The County Hospital had been in place since 1742 and had become a 100-bedded training hospital in 1851. The York Dispensary had been one of the earlier ones, founded in 1788 and working initially from the York Merchant Adventurer's Hall. When the Gramshaws arrived in York, the Dispensary was situated in Duncombe Place, very close to St Leonard's Place, and offering medical, dental and maternity services on a charitable basis to more than 7,000 people a year. Another local institution, the York Home for Nurses, provided both private nursing in their own homes to paying patients and nursing home care on its own premises. It used the funds generated from these private patients to provide free district nursing services to the 'sick poor' of the city. In this busy and well-established health service, the newly-arrived Dr Gramshaw needed to find his own place in the medical community.

He was not entirely unknown in York. He had been elected a 'country member' of the York Medical Society in September 1890, together with 16 other doctors who practised in Yorkshire, but outside of the City of York. And he had many social connections with the city. He had attended Medical Society dinners at the De Grey rooms in York; and he sent his daughter Amy to art school in the city, while his youngest son Guy attended St Martin's School in York. But his strongest connection with the city was through his membership of the York Lodge of Freemasons, into which he had been initiated in 1885. In May 1887, his completion of the Three Degrees of Freemasonry was reported in *The Freemason*, the Craft's own journal:

'York. Zetland Chapter (No. 236). The usual quarterly meeting of this chapter was held on the 27th ult. [i.e. in April] when Comp. J. Sykes Rymer was duly installed as M.E.Z...There were four candidates for exaltation, viz., Bros. Wm. Page, Farbrace Sidney Gramshaw, Herbert Leeds Swift, and Wm. Ward, who were all duly exalted to the Supreme Degree and the lecture given to them by the M.E.Z. The ceremony was throughout performed by all concerned in a very creditable and impressive manner... Several minor matters were then disposed of, and the chapter closed, after which the companions dined together in the banqueting hall of the lodge, when the usual toasts were given and acknowledged, and the rest of the evening spent in harmony.'

York had an interesting history in relation to freemasonry in England. According to tradition, Prince Edwin was supposed to have presided over a meeting of masons in York in 926, considered to be the first masonic meeting in England. References to 'speculative' freemasonry in York – that is, concerned with moral work rather than actual building work – go back to the 1660s. When four of the ancient London freemason lodges set up the Premier Grand Lodge (the 'Moderns') in 1717, and installed the first Grand Master, York was one of the cities that objected. York declared itself separate and created a rival 'Antients' Grand Lodge of its own. Its members were local gentlemen and tradesmen, often related and often involved in local politics, together with local landowners and leaders of the community. After its spirited start, the Lodge became dormant through the 1740s and 50s, before a revival led to the foundation of the Union Lodge in the city in 1777, with both 'Moderns' and 'Antients' as members. In 1813, the rest of the movement followed suit, formally integrating both arms of the craft and beginning to heal with divisions between them. The United Lodge set the pattern of organisation, regalia and ceremonies for the 19th century, and these would have been in place when Gramshaw was initiated into the York Lodge in 1885.

The Union Lodge in York (its original name – it became York Lodge in 1870) did not initially have its own premises. When it was created in 1777, it met in Lockwood's Coffee House on Micklegate. It moved between coffee houses, hotels and merchants' halls until in 1863 it settled in the Masonic Hall in Duncombe Place, where it still meets today. It was here that Gramshaw undertook his roles in the Lodge. In December 1891, he was appointed 'Inner Guard' with responsibility for monitoring entry to Lodge meetings and ceremonies from inside the door (the Tyler guards the outside of the door). This position is usually that of a fairly junior member, giving them the chance to meet members and observe ceremonies. It is at the beginning of the 'progressive offices' leading to the Chair; and over the following years Gramshaw duly moved through these. He was elected Junior Warden of the York Lodge in 1895; then Senior Warden in 1896, and Master of the Lodge in 1897. His name is engraved on the Honours Board in the Masonic Hall recording his period in this highest office in the Lodge. Amongst six Masters who were Reverends, and two who have an academic suffix after their name, Gramshaw is the only Master listed as a Doctor of Medicine.

Gramshaw also fulfilled another role connected to the Lodge. He was a member of the Zetland Chapter of the Lodge, which had been consecrated in 1848. In the Chapter, he held the office of Principal Sojourner in both 1895 and 1896. This is the highest rank a member can hold before going into one of the Three Ruling Chairs: 3rd, 2nd and 1st Principal. His job in this office was to guide new recruits from a Lodge to become Companions of the Holy Royal Arch Chapter. Royal Arch Masonry, which started out as an addition to the 'Three Degrees' of Freemasonry, became, after the union in 1813, the completion of the Master Mason's Third Degree.

So Gramshaw was well-connected in York even before he and his family moved into St Leonard's Place. Amongst his brother Freemasons in the York Lodge were the Archbishop of York, Arthur Purey Cust, and Henry Hopton, the dental surgeon who had previously occupied number 9 St Leonard's Place. Other members included Dr James Ramsay, the Honorary Medical Officer of the York Home for Nurses, and Dr George Auden, who succeeded Dr Ramsay in that position, together with Dr Henry Foster. These last two medical men would be closely involved in the tragic events at the end of Dr Gramshaw's life.

From his arrival in York in 1903, Gramshaw continued to build his medical career. He switched from being a 'country member' of the York Medical Society to a full member and became more active in the Society. In October 1903, he donated £50 towards the Society's renovation of a memorial tablet in Holy Trinity Church, commemorating the work of Dr John Burton, who had been involved in the foundation of the York County Hospital. He also attended the Society's annual banquet. In December he attended a clinical meeting of the Society, held at the County Hospital. His expertise as a surgeon was recognised in the same year by the *British Medical Journal* which noted that he had been awarded an extra fee of £5 'for successful performance of a surgical operation not included in the schedule.' Perhaps his proudest achievement of the year was securing Fellowship of the Royal College of Surgeons of Edinburgh, by examination, on 21 October 1903. He was 49 years old and by any measure, a very successful proponent of his profession. He was making an impact on York society too. He joined the York Philosophical Society, and in 1905 he was elected President of the York and District Field Naturalists' Society. He must have felt he had truly 'arrived' in York when he hosted the 'exhibition and conversatzione' in the galleries of the Yorkshire Museum, 'wearing his resplendent doctor's robes of St Andrews University', with his wife and daughter Amy alongside him.

As with his life in Stillington, however, his appearances in the local papers were not all positive. In August 1904, the Sheffield Daily Telegraph carried a very strange story concerning Dr Gramshaw and an elderly lady residing in his house, headlined 'Singular case at York'.

Mrs Jane Walpole was over 80 years old, the widow of Samuel Walpole of Goodramgate, York. For a year or so after her husband's death, Mrs Walpole had lived with her niece. But 'the latter finding her too much trouble', she had asked Mrs Walpole's sister, Susannah Kirk, to take her away. Mrs Kirk planned to take her sister to live with her in a farmhouse just outside Selby, south of York. Poignantly, she reported that Mrs Walpole had asked her 'Will you look after me?' and Susannah had promised to do so. The newspaper story continues:

'When Mrs Kirk went to York to take her sister away she found that she had been taken to the house of Dr Gramshaw. She visited her there once or twice, but was afterwards positively refused admission to the house, and denied an interview with her. Two or three applications had been made to Dr Gramshaw to allow Mrs Kirk to see her sister, and he (Mr Turner) [Mrs Kirk's solicitor] had also been denied an interview. Mrs Walpole was out about a fortnight ago, and she assured a witness whom he had in court that her wrists were black and blue caused by some ill-usage during the time she had been in Dr Gramshaw's house. She also stated most definitely that she was being detained against her will, and that she wished to be out of Dr Gramshaw's house. They were told that the old lady was not insane, and therefore he [the solicitor] could not take proceedings under the Lunacy Acts but he asked the magistrates to grant him an order for an interview between the two sisters, or for an order against Dr Gramshaw to bring the old lady before them. Failing that, he should apply for a summons for assault against the nurse who attended her.'

Richard Wood, a plumber, was called as a witness to the proceedings. He testified that he had seen Mrs Walpole recently and she had complained that she wanted to be away from Dr Gramshaw's house, and that she was kept there against her will. She also said that the nurse had 'had her down, and bruised her'; though Wood had not seen the bruises himself.

The solicitor, Mr Turner, suggested that the magistrates might want to adjourn the case while the name of the nurse involved was established. But instead they granted a summons for assault against the nurse, to be actioned as soon as her name was known. No action was taken against the doctor who seemed to be keeping the woman in his house against her will, and away from her sister; and who had not himself taken any action to prevent her being abused by a nurse under his roof.

Around 1906 or 1907, the Gramshaws moved house within York, taking up residence at a house called 'Dunholme', at number 78 Bootham. This was a four storey, red brick house, just a little further out from the centre of the city on the road from Bootham Bar, but still in an area occupied by many medical men. It sits opposite the grounds of Bootham Park Hospital, which was then an institution for the mentally ill, known as – and infamous as – the York Lunatic Asylum. The asylum building, designed by John Carr and completed in 1777, was grand and elegant; so much so that the Precentor at York Minster said that it should be advertised as 'a lunatic hotel'. However, for all its grandeur, it was later found to be housing inmates in very squalid conditions. When an inquiry was opened, a convenient fire destroyed many records, and the institution was found to be keeping two sets of accounts. The poor care given at the asylum was said to be the stimulus for the foundation of The Retreat in 1796. This new, private institution for the care of the mentally ill was started by William Tuke and the Society of Friends, following the death in the York Asylum of a Quaker from Leeds called Hannah Mills. The Retreat aimed to introduce humane, 'moral' treatment of the mentally ill, based on the Quaker principles of self-control, compassion and respect; and it became a world-leading institution in its field.

The house on Bootham near the asylum was to be Sidney Gramshaw's last place of residence. And ironically, The Retreat hospital would also feature at the inquest on Margaret Eleanor Brown, at which Gramshaw was a witness in April and May 1908.

Chapter 8

THE INQUEST WITNESS

Dr Gramshaw was no stranger to inquests. He had been called as a medical expert to many such investigations during his career and was accustomed to being regarded as an authority by the presiding Coroner. The Coroner's was an ancient office, dating back to 1194. His role was to inquire into deaths that were accidental, suspicious, violent or otherwise unnatural, and to come to a conclusion, with the help of a jury of local people, about the events leading to the death. For this, his 'inquisition' required the help of an expert medical witness. The doctor, paid one guinea for testimony alone or two guineas for a post mortem, was selected mainly on the basis of proximity to the deceased. So the doctor who last attended the person, or the doctor called in around the time of death, would be the most likely medical witness at an inquest. Whether this local general practitioner was qualified or expert enough to undertake this role was hotly debated through the latter half of the 19th century. Courses in 'medical jurisprudence' – forensic medicine – proliferated to try to teach the necessary knowledge and skills for this work, alongside everything else the GP needed to know. Meanwhile Gramshaw, as the local GP for Stillington, was earning his guineas giving evidence on a wide variety of local deaths.

One of his first inquest appearances was in November 1874, just a year after he qualified as a doctor. The inquest was held in Witherholme, a village north east of Stillington, at the home of Mr C Dresser, whose housekeeper of 25 years, Hannah Leonard, was the deceased. It was not unusual for the inquest to take place in a house – or, often, a public house – for two reasons. Firstly, the Coroner did not, at that time, have an actual courtroom, so had to use any available venue. Secondly, a key duty of the jury was to view the body of the deceased: so they convened where, or close to where, the body was and a local pub was sometimes a convenient place to take a body. As late as 1902, the Licensing Act only forbade pub inquests 'if any reasonable alternative existed.' And a Home Office survey in the early 1930s found that pub inquests in parts of Britain continued well into the 20th century.

Gramshaw had not seen Hannah Leonard immediately before her death. Although he had been called, he arrived too late. Her employer, Mr Dresser told the Coroner and jury what had happened:

'Lately she had been much addicted to drinking, and on Sunday night Mr Dresser was using some linament [sic] for his back, and the deceased asked for the keys of the spirit closet. She was under the influence of liquor at the time, and Mr Dresser refused the keys. Deceased then said her back was bad also, and poured some of the linament into a tumbler, and on Mr Dresser refusing a second time to give her the keys she said she would take some of the linament. She swallowed a portion of it and died in about three quarters of an hour before Dr Gramshaw could attend.'

The 'linament' contained aconite (from the buttercup family, but alarmingly known as 'queen of poisons') and belladonna (deadly nightshade), two potentially fatal poisons. The jury decided that Hannah Leonard had taken the linament not knowing that it was poisonous, in an attempt to get the keys to the liquor cabinet. This was a fairly self-evident case; as were others where Gramshaw gave his medical take on the deaths of a drunken man who fell off his horse and fractured his skull; a man who fell off a hayrick and broke his back; and a man burnt to death when he accidentally knocked over a benzaline lamp.

Cases that involved illness rather than accident presented more of a challenge to a doctor called on to explain the cause of death. Here a post-mortem would probably be required, and an interpretation that combined known medical history with the findings in the body after death.

Thomas Arrowsmith had been a farm labourer, living in Sutton on the Forest, a village between Stillington and York. He was 63 years old and lived with his wife. On the night of his death, he had gone to bed shortly after nine o'clock. A little later, his wife took hold of his shoulder, saying 'I think you are falling out of bed.' In fact, Arrowsmith was dead. He was said to have been a delicate man but he had not complained of any illness that day. Gramshaw gave his opinion that the death was due to 'syncope'; and the jury returned a verdict to that effect.

'Syncope' is not really a cause of death. It simply means a temporary loss of consciousness and muscle control caused by low blood flow to the brain, and it is more generally known as 'fainting'. But it was accepted as a reasonable cause of death in this case and in several other cases in which Gramshaw gave evidence. An inquest was held at the Boot and Shoe Inn in Stillington into the death of John Bradley, an agricultural labourer. He was 68 years old and said to be suffering severely from rheumatism. After he was found dead in bed by a neighbour on Sunday morning, Gramshaw was called to examine the body. Again his evidence to the inquest was that the man had died of syncope; and this was the verdict recorded. Syncope also carried off John Stanton, of Huby, in what the papers called a 'strangely sudden death near York.' Stanton collapsed and died while drinking a pint of beer at the New Inn. Gramshaw explained to the inquest that the man had suffered from heart disease, and a mouthful of cold beer could have caused the syncope from which he died.

There were times when Gramshaw's inquest evidence was pertinent not only to the determination of cause of death, but also to criminal proceedings. He was unequivocal in his evidence about the death of Mary Hedley, an elderly spinster from Marton-cum-Moxby, another village near Stillington. The woman was paralysed down one side of her body and lived with a labourer called William Gileson. She died suddenly one Saturday afternoon, after having been found earlier in the day to have a broken leg. Dr Gramshaw was attending her, but she died in spite of his care. At the inquest, Gramshaw gave evidence that 'the leg had been broken by violence, probably by bending the leg.' The jury's verdict was that Hedley had died 'from paralysis, possibly exacerbated by the fracture of the leg.' There was a clear case for the police to investigate this death and probably interview William Gileson, the only other person in the household with the helpless woman. But there is no record that this happened.

There is a similar blank in another case at which Dr Gramshaw was a witness. This was the inquest into the death of Sophia Turner, the 21-year-old daughter of a local gamekeeper living at Creyke, near Easingwold. Finding herself pregnant, and having already had one stillborn child, the young woman, according to her employer's wife, 'sent for some medicine she had seen advertised in a local paper.' If this medicine had been intended to end the unwanted pregnancy, this would have been crime, on the part of both Sophia Turner and the person selling the product. Procuring an abortion had been explicitly outlawed since the beginning of the 18th century, and the Offences against the Person Act 1861 forbade either the woman herself or anyone else to do anything, or promote any means, to end a pregnancy:

'Section 58 – offence of using drugs or instruments to procure abortion, replaced section 6 of the Offences against the Person Act 1837, and provides:

58. Every woman, being with child, who, with intent to procure her own miscarriage, shall unlawfully administer to herself any poison or other noxious thing, or shall unlawfully use any instrument or other means whatsoever with the like intent, and whosoever, with intent to procure the miscarriage of any woman whether she be or be not with child, shall unlawfully administer to her or cause to be taken by her any poison or other noxious thing, or unlawfully use any instrument or other means whatsoever with the like intent, shall be guilty of felony, and being convicted thereof shall be liable ... to be kept in penal servitude for life ...

Section 59 – offence of supplying or procuring poison or instruments for the purpose of criminal abortion, and provides:

59. Whosoever shall unlawfully supply or procure any poison or other noxious thing, or any instrument or thing whatsoever, knowing that the same is intended to be unlawfully used or employed with intent to procure the miscarriage of any woman, whether she

be or be not with child, shall be guilty of a
misdemeanor, and being convicted thereof
shall be liable ... to be kept in penal servitude...'

Regardless of the law, women with an unwanted
pregnancy resorted to all kinds of desperate measures
and subterfuge to end it. The use of purgatives was
one method, with pennyroyal, aloes and turpentine
all thought to be capable of bringing on a miscarriage.
Mechanical methods to induce miscarriage included
very hot baths and gin, extreme exertion, a deliberate
fall down stairs, or veterinary medicines. There were
always 'backstreet' abortionists available, though this
was a risky business. Or there were pills and potions that
were advertised – discreetly – in local papers, as Sophia
Turner discovered. Advertisements offered medicine for
women who were 'temporarily indisposed', or claimed to
treat 'female complaints', to 'restore female regularity' or
to treat 'irregularity', 'obstruction', 'menstrual suppression'
or 'delayed periods'. The content of these medicines were
often clearly substances that could cause a miscarriage,
and included pennyroyal, tansy and savin.

In Sophia Turner's case, the medicine was in a bottle
labelled 'Zanthoria', advertised and sold by A. Dasmail
through two local papers. The name may be a reference
to Zanthorea or xanthorrhoea, a genus of grass tree found
only in Australia. The plant (which is neither a grass nor
a tree, but related to the lily family) produces resins, for
which there were well-established uses as a polishing
material and in the manufacture of illuminating gas. It

had been exported from Australia for these purposes. An article in the American Journal of Pharmacy in 1881 discussed the medical uses of the resins:

'Their medicinal properties appear to be likewise not well marked. As early as 1795 acaroid resin was said by Kite to neither vomit, purge nor bind the belly, nor to act materially as a diuretic or diaphoretic. Dr. Fish ("Boston Journal," x, p. 94) employed it in the form of tincture with opium in fluxus hepaticus and the colliquative [profuse] diarrhoea of phthisis [TB], and it has been recommended in chronic catarrhs.'

So there could have been legitimate medical uses of the substance in the bottle labelled Zanthoria, though there was no claim that Sophia was suffering from any of the conditions it might have treated. The inquest into Sophia's death was adjourned while the substance in the bottle was sent for analysis. Gramshaw, who had been called to attend Sophia, had confronted her with the accusation that she had taken something to procure an abortion. However, when the analyst's report was returned, it cleared the medicine of containing any poisonous substance. Sophia's death was attributed to 'peritonitis and inflammation, following inflammation of the bowels, following on a miscarriage.' Whether the contents of the medicine had any bearing on Sophia's death, and whether A. Dasmail was ever held to account in a court for supplying a substance with intent to cause a miscarriage, is not known.

On several occasions, Gramshaw acted as a witness in criminal proceedings rather than at an inquest. In one, he commented on the injuries of a man who had been subjected to an attempted drowning. He said that there was no evidence that the cuts and bruises sustained by the complainant were caused by the ducking in the horse pond; and the charge of attempted murder in that case was dismissed. In another court case, he gave evidence about the injuries received by a drunken cart driver who had been taken home by two policemen. He then accused the policemen of assaulting him. Gramshaw corroborated the witness statement of another doctor about the severe bruising sustained by the driver, and the injury to his arm which, it was said, could not have been caused by falling off the cart whilst drunk. The case was dismissed when the judges decided that the police had not used any more than necessary force. The Bench did, however, 'take the opportunity of intimating to the police the desirability of using as little force as possible in all cases.'

The Coroners who appointed Gramshaw as medical witness at their inquests all came from the Wood family. The earliest inquests he attended were convened by John Prescod Wood, a local solicitor. He was followed as Coroner for York District by Henry Wood, before whom Gramshaw gave evidence in at least seven inquests in and around Stillington. Aside from his coronial duties in Yorkshire, Henry Wood was for some time a member of the Council of the Coroners' Society of England and Wales, so would have been familiar with the debates at national level about the pros and cons of using local GPs as medical witnesses and practitioners of post-mortems. The Coroner for York City, which was a separate jurisdiction, was John Richardson Wood, son of John Prescod Wood. He had attended the same York Medical Society dinner as Gramshaw in 1900, and it is quite possible that they knew each other, or at least had met – though there is no listing of J R Wood as a member of the Lodge in York, so they were not brother Freemasons. It was John Richardson Wood – at that time Coroner for both York City and York District – who was the Coroner in charge of the inquest into the death of Margaret Eleanor Brown, Gramshaw's young patient at the Glynn Hotel.

Chapter 9

THE INQUEST:
DAY ONE – 28 APRIL 1908

Nothing in Dr Gramshaw's experience of inquests could have prepared him for the scale of this one. Instead of the usual setting of a public house or local room, this inquest was conducted in the Law Courts in York, housed in an imposing neo-classical building next to York Prison. Two flights of stone steps led up to a grand columned entrance, and inside there was a huge central entrance hall with the court rooms at each end of the building.

Instead of Gramshaw being the only medical expert present, there were five medical witnesses at Margaret Brown's inquest. In addition to Gramshaw, Dr George Watson from Leeds, Dr Harry Reynolds, the police surgeon, and Drs C W Gostling and Henry Foster, who had also attended the post-mortem, were all present in court. Also in attendance were Henry Craven, the Town Clerk (also a Freemason in the York Lodge); the Chief Constable of York, James Burrow (who at 42 was more than ten years younger than Gramshaw); Norman Crombie, Gramshaw's solicitor; and nine other witnesses. Margaret's parents, William and Helen Brown, and her sister Alison were there: they had not yet been able to bury Margaret. Conducting proceedings was the Coroner for the City of York, John Richardson Wood, who was also a solicitor in the city. He was almost exactly the same age as Gramshaw.

Then there was the jury. A minimum of 12 (and possibly as many as 24) men had been sworn in as jurors: no women could sit on a jury until after the 1919 Sex Disqualification (Removal) Act. To quality for jury service, they each had to own land worth at least 10 pounds per year. They and Mr Wood the Coroner had together viewed the body of Margaret Brown, a procedure which had to be carried out before any testimony was heard. Originally, the 'view' had been part of the process of deciding how a person had died, when evidence of bodily violence, for example, might be obvious even to the laymen. Latterly, people had begun to object to it as an affront to the deceased and their grieving family – especially when the body was still at home, and the jury visited it there. There were also concerns about the sanitary aspects of viewing a dead body, with jurors concerned both about the assault on their senses and also the risk to their health. Engineering firms spotted an opportunity and devised 'body preserving apparatus' to contain the corpse, while allowing it to remain visible to the visiting jury and Coroner. One advertisement for such apparatus said:

> 'We desire to call the attention of Coroners and Public Health Authorities to an invention which is capable of rendering incalculable service to all those whose duties bring them in contact with dead bodies. The apparatus ... consists of a box in the form of a rectangular prism which is divided into two parts by metallic shutters. One is a disinfecting chamber in which the dead body rests on a metal litter of wide meshed gauze. The top and sides are furnished with double glass windows which render the whole of the interior readily accessible to view ... At present the practice of viewing the body is liable to be not only a particularly trying discipline but in some cases a very dangerous one. Emanations from decomposing corpses are not only revolting to the senses; they are often exceedingly dangerous to health. [Using the apparatus] putrefaction is not only arrested; it is absolutely and finally abolished.'

Less technical solutions included viewing the body in a glass-topped coffin, or behind a glass screen: though it was regularly pointed out that there was little to be learned from such a limited sight. The other practical change to address the problem of the 'view' was the introduction, in the latter half of the 19th century, of purpose-built mortuaries intended to be discreet, hygienic, convenient for the doctors and the Coroner, and most importantly, away from the home of the bereaved family. Not that families were necessarily grateful for this: some objected so strongly to their loved one being taken away that Coroners had to use the local police to help them remove bodies to the mortuary. Whether the Brown inquest jury viewed the body in the Glynn Hotel or elsewhere is not known; but having done so, they were ready to start hearing the testimony of the witnesses in the case.

When the proceedings began on the morning of Tuesday 28 April, during a week when 'winter had returned in April' according to the papers, the very first witness called was Margaret's eldest sister, Alison Brown. At 27 years old, she was seven years her senior, but still probably young and inexperienced enough to be thoroughly unnerved at being the first witness at this intimidating occasion. Questioned by the Coroner, Alison confirmed that she was a governess working in Hurstpierpoint in West Sussex. Her sister Margaret was aged 19 and unmarried. They had arranged that they should both take a holiday in York for Easter. But before the date that she was due to arrive in York, she had had a note from Dr Gramshaw saying that her sister was very ill. She did not, she said, attach very much importance to it, as she had seen her sister very recently, when she seemed alright. Later, she received a telegram from Dr Gramshaw, summoning her to the place her sister was staying. When she arrived, on Thursday 23 April, she found her sister confined to bed. She did not know, she said, that her sister was 'in trouble'. She stayed with her until she died on the

Sunday. With that, Alison's formal part in the proceedings was over; she and her parents could only wait to hear what had happened to bring about the death of a young and healthy woman so suddenly.

The next witness was Mrs Elizabeth Dennison. She told the inquest that she had only taken over the management of the Glynn Hotel on Micklegate, with her husband Luke, on 4 April. She was also reported to have said that 'she had known Dr Gramshaw all his life but he had nothing to do with their taking the Glynn hotel', which is a strange statement as she was only 28 years old, and he was 54. Perhaps the reporters made a mistake, and she had said that *he* had known *her* all her life. On 6 April, she went on, Dr Gramshaw called and engaged rooms for two young ladies; but afterwards he said that he had had a letter to say that one of them was not coming. He ordered a front room for the girl who was coming, and asked Mrs Dennison 'to be a mother to her' during her stay. Margaret arrived nine days later, on Wednesday 15 April with, Mrs Dennison recalled, her luggage in a Japanese basket. She seemed very well.

From then on, matters moved quickly. Dr Gramshaw called on Margaret on the Wednesday evening of her arrival, and again the next day. When Mrs Dennison took Margaret her breakfast in bed on the Friday morning – Good Friday at the start of the Easter weekend – the young woman said that she should 'see what the doctor said before she got up.' The doctor called again that day and went out briefly to a fruit shop before returning to Margaret's bedroom. At midday, a young man arrived, asking if Dr

Gramshaw was there and saying 'There is a case here.' He was admitted to Margaret's bedroom. At about two o'clock, Mrs Dennison said, a nurse had come and had also been taken by the doctor into Margaret's room. When the nurse came into the kitchen at about four o'clock, Mrs Dennison had asked her what was taking place. The nurse said that 'Miss Brown had had a miscarriage and seemed surprised that the witness did not know anything about it.'

If that was a shock to Mrs Dennison, the nurse's next actions would only have increased her concern about what was happening in her hotel. The nurse told her, at about seven thirty that evening, that she was leaving and would not be returning. She said that 'There was nothing prepared, and she didn't like the looks of things.' True to her word, she left and never came back. Dr Gramshaw was not in the hotel at the time. When he returned, between eight and nine o'clock that evening, Mrs Dennison confronted him with the nurse's actions, and her reasons for them. She asked the doctor what was the matter with Margaret Brown and he told her that she had had a miscarriage. Mrs Dennison replied, she told the inquest, that he had deceived her and ought to have told her. Gramshaw had apologised, saying he did not know what was the matter with the girl; he suspected it on Thursday but had not been sure: 'if he had known, he would not have brought a case like it [to the hotel]'. Mrs Dennison then confronted the doctor with a very serious accusation: 'I had read about these illegal operations in the papers' she reported saying, 'and I didn't like these cases.' Asked about Gramshaw's reply to this, Elizabeth Dennison reported, 'He said he was surprised at me, knowing him as I did, having thoughts of such a thing.'

Perhaps chastened by the doctor's response, Mrs Dennison did not insist that the girl was removed from her hotel. She did say that she would not act as a nurse to the girl but that she would take her food upstairs to her. She also told Margaret what she thought: she said she was annoyed and told the girl, 'You have deceived me.' Margaret's response, Mrs Dennison reported, was to say that she didn't know what she was talking about and what she meant. Three different nurses from the York Home for Nurses had attended during the following week. On Easter Sunday, Dr Gramshaw had called in another doctor; but Margaret Brown died a week later.

Following on from this evidence, the Chief Constable, James Burrow, had some questions for Mrs Dennison. 'At the time you were letting the rooms, did Dr Gramshaw say in what relationship he stood to those two young ladies?' he enquired. The hotel proprietor replied, 'I understood he was their guardian.' The Chief Constable asked, 'When did you first find out he was not?' The reply was 'On the Sunday after Good Friday, when he said he would telegraph for her father and mother.'

At this point the Coroner said that 'he thought they had better call Dr Gramshaw, if he desired to give evidence.' Dr Gramshaw said that 'he certainly desired to do so' and he was duly sworn in. His first statement was that he knew the deceased and her sisters very well and had 'attended them all'. About a month before, he said, he had had a letter from Margaret Brown saying that she was obliged to take a holiday and would like to come to York, as she could not afford the long journey to Brighton and back to see her family. The Coroner interrupted to ask if Gramshaw still had the letter from Margaret – the answer was that he had not. Margaret also asked in the letter, he said, to consult him about her health, and asked about cheap respectable rooms in York. 'I wrote back,' he continued, 'and said I would be very pleased to see her, but I thought it would be better if she had her elder sister with her.' A few days later he had another letter saying that Margaret was 'delighted with the suggestion', and that her sister also had to take a holiday at Easter. Gramshaw said he then wrote to Alison Brown with the idea but had a letter back from her 'regretting that she was unable to accept the invitation.' Evidently undeterred, he made the arrangements for the room with Mrs Dennison, and called on Margaret on the evening of her arrival. He said that 'she did not look very well and was particularly depressed'. In the course of the conversation she expressed her fear that she was pregnant, but 'he very much doubted if she were.' He asked her if she had been taking anything, but she said 'no'.

On Good Friday, according to Gramshaw's account, things started to go wrong. When he called on Margaret, he found she was about to miscarry. He sent a boy to his house to fetch his nephew, a fifth year medical student at Newcastle who was spending Easter with him, and who came to the hotel with a medical bag and a small bottle of chloroform. This was the 'young man' Mrs Dennison had reported as arriving at midday on the Friday. Gramshaw administered some chloroform to the girl, then, 'not liking to be there with only a young student in a case of that sort', Gramshaw left briefly to send for a nurse.

At this point in his evidence, Gramshaw interrupted himself to say that he had forgotten to mention that 'Miss Brown had told him that about a month previously she had had a fall.' On visiting the house on Good Friday evening, he continued, he found 'to his extreme surprise' that the nurse had gone.

Here the Coroner interrupted him. 'Before we get away from this point', he said, 'let me ask you: did you use any instruments?' 'Not of any sort', was Gramshaw's unequivocal reply. He had remained with Miss Brown from 10 o'clock to three fifteen, he said, and she was under chloroform intermittently. He also talked about the nurse's visit and departure. He said that Mrs Dennison gave him to understand that Nurse Cook, who was first called, said that 'She didn't like waiting on unmarried girls' and 'she did not like people who came in motor cars.' Gramshaw described the efforts he had made to obtain a nurse for Margaret, because 'on Sunday morning the girl's temperature had risen to 104° and he felt the responsibility was very great, the girl being so young and so far from home.' He had asked her permission, he said, to send for her mother and sister; but this she had 'absolutely refused.' On that Sunday – Easter Sunday – he had gone to Dr Fell and asked his advice. Dr Fell had visited and advised about other remedies.

So far, the inquest had heard nothing that was not already public knowledge. Margaret had come to York, had lost her baby, become very ill and been attended by

Dr Gramshaw and some nurses before, sadly, she died. But the jury, press and interested public were about to make the first of several unexpected discoveries in the course of day one of the inquest.

Dr Gramshaw asked the Coroner: 'Shall I tell you of the visit the Chief Constable paid me or shall I confine myself to the case?' Mr Wood replied: 'Perhaps you had better say all about it.'

Then Gramshaw recounted an extraordinary turn of events. 'The Chief Constable called on me on Tuesday 21st April and told me an anonymous letter had been sent to the police concerning the deceased and my treatment of her; and he advised me to lose no time in communicating with her friends.' Following this advice, Gramshaw had telegraphed to Margaret's parents and her sister, and her mother and sister had come to York, arriving on the Thursday. On the same day, the Chief Constable had called on Gramshaw again. This time his advice to the doctor was that 'it would be better to take the girl's depositions.'

A deathbed deposition – or 'dying declaration' – was, in 1908, admissible in the English courts if what was said had any bearing on the cause of the individual's death. It depended on the common law principle of *nemo moriturus praesumitur mentiri* – no-one on the point of death should be presumed to be lying. So a deposition would be Margaret's chance to tell the truth about what had happened to her, knowing that it could be used after her death, if necessary, in criminal proceedings.

Gramshaw had baulked at this advice. At first, he flatly refused to allow a deposition to be taken. As he explained, this was 'solely in his patient's interest, because he was under the impression that a person had to be told they had no possible chance of life, and he had been encouraging her to live.' In this, he was correct. For a deposition to be admissible in court, the individual making it had to have a 'settled hopeless expectation of death'. Ultimately, he must have conceded on this point and made it clear to Margaret that she was indeed going to die. A magistrate came to the hotel on the Thursday and took her dying declaration. Afterwards, Margaret appeared to 'rally' several times, before she died on the Sunday after Easter. The cause of death, Gramshaw testified, was 'puerperal persepsis' – childbed fever.

The Coroner returned to the question of when and why the doctor had – or had not – admitted the seriousness of Margaret's condition and sent for her family.

'Why did you not communicate with her father and mother in the first instance?' he asked.

'She was my patient and implored me not to do so,' Gramshaw responded, 'and I didn't want to give her away if I could help it.'

Mr Wood pressed him: 'But wasn't she sufficiently serious before you saw the Chief Constable to communicate with her parents?' Gramshaw conceded that her condition was 'alarming' on the Sunday – 'or I should not have sent for another medical man.'

'But she was ill and could not judge for herself', insisted the Coroner.

Stubbornly, Gramshaw stuck to his defence: 'I did not want to betray the girl's confidence if I could help it.'

Then the court heard a second revelation.

'Has she been under your charge before?' the Coroner asked Dr Gramshaw.

'Yes, on several occasions', he replied.

'You know to what I refer?'

'I attended her in her confinement previously on February 2nd 1907', confirmed the doctor.

'Is that child alive?'

'It is.'

'Do you know the father of these two children?' enquired the Coroner

'I know the father of the first', said Gramshaw, then clarified: 'I know what she told me. I do not know the father of the last.'

'But if, as you say, "you did not want to give her away to her parents", did you not think it was your duty to find out the young man who was responsible and communicate to him the serious condition she was in?'

Dr Gramshaw replied weakly: 'It never occurred to me. I did not even know she was pregnant at first.' This was a strange admission from a doctor of 35 years' experience, who knew this young woman had been pregnant before, and had heard her say that she thought she was pregnant again.

The Coroner did not pursue the question of who was responsible for Margaret's condition. Instead he turned back to the events of Good Friday, when the medical problems began.

'Are you quite sure that on Good Friday you didn't take your bag?' he asked.

'I had a bag,' Gramshaw defended himself, 'but not an operating bag.'

'You remember telling me you took a bag and a little chloroform but it was not sufficient?'

'I took a little emergency bag.'

'You know she had no friends in York but yourself, why did you not begin to look after [for] a nurse?'

Again Gramshaw's answer was feeble: 'But it might have gone on for days.' Whether he was concerned about the costs of hiring a nurse for an unspecified period, or he knew the attitude of some nurses to 'waiting on unmarried women', he did not explain. In a final to-and-fro of questions and answers, Gramshaw confirmed that he had looked for the letter Margaret had sent him, but could not find it; that he was positive no instruments were used during his attendance on her; and that it was true that the nurse had heard Margaret ask for more chloroform, as he had promised it to her on the Friday: she had had chloroform in her previous confinement. Then his testimony was over, and he could only sit and listen while the inquest heard from other witnesses and formed its conclusion about what had caused Margaret's death.

At this point, the Clerk of the Peace, Mr Henry Craven, produced the depositions sworn by Margaret Brown in the presence of a magistrate three days before she died. Knowing their potential importance if criminal charges were to be brought, the jury must have been particularly keen to hear this evidence. After all, they knew that there was an absolute presumption that what was said in a dying declaration was true. What Margaret had said in her declaration was that she had come to York for a holiday and asked Dr Gramshaw to find her some rooms. She thought her sister was coming too. He found the rooms and came to see that she was settled all right. In response to further questions, she said that she was not sure that she was 'in a particular condition'. Dr Gramshaw came and stayed with her all Good Friday until she was confined. The child was dead when born. She believed the premature birth was due to a bad fall which she had had some weeks before.

While the jury absorbed the implications of that, the next witness was called. This was the nurse, Janet Cook, whose actions and opinions Elizabeth Dennison had already commented on earlier in the proceedings. Mrs Cook was a 'certificated trained nurse of 15 years' experience'. She told the Coroner that, when she entered the hotel bedroom on Good Friday, she had noticed a very strong smell of chloroform. The doctor, she said, used a pair of long, scissor-like instruments – contradicting Gramshaw's assertion that he had not used any instruments in the course of his attendance on Margaret. She had seen the same things used in hospitals for the throat. Norman Crombie, Gramshaw's solicitor, intervened at this point to say that 'long forceps were recognised instruments, but the word "scissors" would create a false impression'. Nurse Cook finished her evidence by saying that she had stayed until seven thirty that evening, then left saying she should not return.

'What was your reason?' asked the Coroner.

'Because I did not think it was a straightforward case,' replied the nurse. Questioned by the Chief Constable, Nurse Cook denied having said that she was leaving because she did not like attending on unmarried women. She also denied that she was afraid she would not get her fee: 'she never gave the fee a thought, though the doctor told her the money was alright.' Interestingly, there was another nurse involved in the case, who was not called on to give evidence. The Chief Constable asked if the inquest could hear about a conversation that took place between the hotel proprietor, Elizabeth Dennison, and a Nurse Enoch from the York Home for Nurses. But, the papers reported, both the Coroner and Gramshaw's solicitor Mr Crombie said 'No! No!'

The final witness on day one was Dr George Watson, from Park Square, Leeds. He was attending at the request of the Coroner, and he gave the results of the post-mortem examination he had carried out on Margaret Brown's body. Responding to a specific question from the Coroner, Dr Watson said that there was no evidence that 'any undue violence had been employed'. He also said that 'there was not the slightest indication of any instruments having been employed.'

'Is there anything in the evidence today to cause you to modify your opinion?' the Coroner enquired.

'Of course I have heard that instruments were used,' the doctor replied, 'but there is no evidence of it.' He gave his view that death was due to peritonitis, resulting from infection.

By this time, the jury had been sitting continuously for seven hours. It was time to adjourn the proceedings.

The Coroner did so, setting the date for resumption of the inquest as the following Monday, 4 May.

In the intervening six days, there was much for the jury and the witnesses to puzzle over. There was confusion over Margaret's sister Alison's visit to York. Alison had said that 'they' had arranged to have a holiday together in York; but it was Dr Gramshaw who had written to invite her, and she had immediately declined. Margaret had said in her dying declaration that she thought her sister *was* coming to York. Had Alison ever planned to go to York? Had Margaret known when she set off for the city that she would be alone in York? And was this visit an Easter holiday – or did the missing letter from Margaret to Gramshaw say, as he testified, that she wanted to consult him about 'her health'? She had sworn in her deposition that she did not know she was pregnant; but she had told Dr Gramshaw on her first day in York that she feared she was. Having been pregnant before, she would have known the signs; and surely this must have been what she wanted to consult him about.

Another question in the minds of the jury – and one Gramshaw must have pondered as well for the past week – was the identity of the anonymous informant who had urged the police to look into his treatment of Margaret Brown. Had Elizabeth Dennison made the complaint, concerned about what was happening in her hotel? Or had Nurse Cook alerted the police because of her concerns about the case? Someone was sufficiently aware of an irregular situation to want to ensure some official inquiries would take place.

They might also have wondered what Nurse Enoch could have told the court, had her conversation with Mrs Dennison been allowed as evidence. Had she seen or heard something in Margaret's room that the jury should have known? Did she have some insight into the case or the people involved that she had shared with the hotel proprietor, and wanted to share with the inquest? Whatever it was, the legal men in the room were united in their decision that her evidence should not be heard.

Finally, the jury might well have been confused about what actually took place in the hotel bedroom. Mrs Dennison, informed by stories in the newspapers, thought an illegal operation might have been performed, though Dr Gramshaw seemed shocked at the suggestion. Nurse Cook thought that instruments had been used on the young woman, and a significant quantity of chloroform; but Dr Gramshaw was adamant that he had used no instruments and Dr Watson from Leeds saw no evidence of instruments having been employed when he undertook the post-mortem. Yet undoubtedly the young woman had lost a child, acquired an overwhelming infection and died as a result.

Day two of the inquest would hear from nine more witnesses, including the medical men; and a new series of revelations would enthral the national press, and give the jury even more to think about.

Chapter 10

THE INQUEST:
DAY TWO – 4 MAY 1908

When the inquest resumed at nine thirty on the second day, it returned immediately to the question of what had happened in Margaret Brown's hotel bedroom. The new witness on this subject was Kenneth Allan, Gramshaw's medical student nephew. Allan's father, Thomas Allan, had worked as a medical assistant to Dr Gramshaw in Stillington in the 1880s. He had qualified as a doctor, and married Gramshaw's sister Frances. Kenneth Allan was their eldest son; by studying medicine, he became the fifth generation of the family to go into the medical profession.

Allan was only 22, just three years older than the patient he was called to help. He told the inquest that he had recently come to stay with his uncle in York, arriving on 14 April. On Good Friday, 17 April, he had received a note from his uncle at about ten thirty in the morning. Although he had since destroyed the note, he recalled its contents as being something like: 'Come at once to 18, Micklegate, and bring midwifery bag and chloroform.' 18 Micklegate was the address of the Glynn Hotel.

'What was in the bag?' the Coroner enquired.

'I did not examine it but I think there were some instruments', was the response.

Allan went to the hotel, where he was met by his uncle. Gramshaw told his nephew that 'he had a case of miscarriage on and he required his services to administer chloroform as the patient bore the pain very badly.' Allan gave her a little chloroform and found that she had had some already.

At this point the reporting of the inquest was sanitised for public consumption. 'Having described the processes employed by Dr Gramshaw', the papers reported euphemistically, 'witness said that about half past one the doctor asked if he would mind being left alone as he wanted to get a nurse.' Dr Gramshaw left the house and half an hour later the nurse arrived. Then Allan gave some crucial testimony. He said, 'After the arrival of the nurse, Dr Gramshaw attempted to use a pair of forceps.' This matched the evidence of the nurse, Janet Cook, given on day one of the inquest; and directly contradicted Dr Gramshaw's evidence in which he emphatically denied using any instruments at all.

At two thirty, Allan continued, Gramshaw sent him out to fetch some ergot – a drug used to contract the uterus and reduce bleeding – and when he returned an hour later the doctor informed him that 'the case was over.'

Questioned by the Coroner, Allan said that he had attended other confinements and had used chloroform before. In fact, he had completed a hospital-based midwifery course, and since the previous March he had administered more than 200 anaesthetics. In this case, he said, he was in the room with the patient continuously for about four hours. The Coroner then turned again to the disputed question of the use of instruments on Margaret Brown.

'During that time you say the only instrument used was the forceps produced?' he asked.

'Yes.'

'And they were used only once?'

'Yes.'

'You are quite sure of that?'

'Yes.'

'Then, if Nurse Cook has told us in evidence that the instrument was used several times by the doctor, what do you say about that?'

'It was only used once while I was there,' was the medical student's response. Then, with commendable but potentially damaging honesty, he added: 'I do not know if it was used after I left.'

Henry Craven, the Town Clerk, who was representing the Chief Constable James Burrow at this session, had his own questions for the medical student. He asked several questions 'related to the medical aspects of the case', which again were not included in the press reporting. Then he focused on the key question: the use of instruments.

'Can you,' he asked, 'express any opinion why it was necessary to interfere with the natural course of events at all?'

'No, I cannot,' replied Kenneth Allan. Crucially, the Town Clerk did not follow up to discover whether the young man meant that he could not express an opinion, either because he was not sufficiently qualified, or because he chose not to do so in the presence of his uncle – or that, with his midwifery qualification and experience, he could not think of any reason 'to interfere with the natural course of events' by using instruments. Allan must have been relieved that his evidence was over, as the inquest turned away from the details of Margaret Brown's death to hear from those who knew her in life.

The Reverend George Talbot Whitehead, Rector of Thornton Watlass in North Yorkshire, was called as Margaret's employer. He was 38 years old and had arrived in Thornton Watlass with a degree in Divinity from Cambridge University, in 1900. In 1908, he and his wife, also called Margaret and herself the daughter of a London vicar, already had four young children. He said that Margaret had come to them on 8 February that year in response to their advertisement for a governess. She came with a recommendation from Dr Gramshaw – although unfortunately he had destroyed that letter. To the best of his recollection, he said, he understood that Gramshaw was Miss Brown's trustee. He acknowledged that his letter did not say that she had any previous experience as a governess.

Relating the short history of her employment at the Rectory, the Reverend Whitehead said that Margaret had started her employment on 8 February; had visited York for a weekend around 7 March; and had left for her holiday in York on 15 April. She was, he also pointed out, 'going to leave for good in May as they didn't think her suitable.' He was at pains to dissociate his family and his position from the young woman who, he now knew, had twice become pregnant whilst unmarried: 'He wished it to be made quite clear that she was only with them for two months at the outside, but reports in the papers last week said nothing definite, and it might appear that she was there for a year or more.'

Following Margaret's departure for York in time for Easter, Mrs Whitehead had received a letter from Dr Gramshaw. It was dated 20 April – Easter Monday – and told the Rector's wife about the course of Margaret's illness. The letter said that 'On the girl's arrival in York she had sent for him [Dr Gramshaw], but he had not found much wrong with her, and had advised her to keep quiet. He could not receive her this Easter as his boys and nephews were spending their holidays with him. On the Thursday she was not quite so well, and later had a severe attack of blood poisoning. On Saturday morning, her temperature was 105 and her condition so alarming that he had had to get the services of three nurses. She was at the time of writing weak and unable to get up.'

The letter concluded by saying that Dr Gramshaw 'trusted she would be quite well in a few days.'

'Did you receive a further letter from Dr Gramshaw?' the Coroner asked the Reverend. He said that he had and handed this letter to the Coroner to read. In it, Gramshaw acknowledged receipt of a cheque for Miss Brown, and 'regretted that he had been rather too sanguine' in his previous letter. 'She has had a relapse and been very ill, but there is a change for the better today', he wrote now. He also asked that Margaret's box, containing her belongings, might be sent to the care of Mrs Dennison at 18, Micklegate. Then the Coroner asked what seemed a strange question:

'Have you seen any letters to Miss Brown in the same handwriting?' he enquired.

'I could not say,' the Reverend answered. 'I never see the letters. They are brought by the postman and the servant would take them to Miss Brown.' He went on to confirm that Margaret's health was normal when she left for York – 'but she was very inert and did not seem to care to exert herself in the way of outdoor exercise.'

The Coroner knew where he was going with the enquiry about letters to the Rectory. The next witness was the servant who handled the post at the Rectory: Annie Wilson, the housemaid. Her evidence was detailed and devastating: it would fundamentally change the jury's understanding of the events surrounding Margaret Brown's death.

The first piece of information Annie Wilson gave was confirmation that Margaret had had a fall at the Rectory before coming to York, on 1 April. At least, Annie said rather dismissively, 'she had fallen on one of her knees.' Then she moved on to talk about her duties in relation to letters arriving at the Rectory. She often took letters to Miss Brown, she testified, in what she understood was

Dr Gramshaw's writing. She knew this because a letter had arrived for Margaret the day after she arrived at the Rectory, and it was taken to the dining room by mistake. Mrs Whitehead, the Rector's wife, had told Annie to take it to Margaret and said it was from Dr Gramshaw. After that, according to Annie's testimony, Margaret received a letter from Dr Gramshaw almost every day: 'six days out of seven.'

The Coroner asked her what had happened to these letters. 'She always burnt them', Annie told him. 'I saw her burn a good many that I supposed had come from Dr Gramshaw as soon as she had read them.' Annie also took parcels to the governess, addressed in the same handwriting as the letters from Dr Gramshaw. They contained gifts: sweets, a pair of gloves and a veil. Letters also went in the other direction: Annie posted letters from Margaret to Dr Gramshaw at the York Medical Society, Low Ousegate, York, 'almost every day'. During April, Annie said, Margaret had told Annie several times that she was going to Northallerton to meet a 'gentleman friend from York.' One Thursday morning when she was due to go to Northallerton, she received a letter from Dr Gramshaw and after reading it, the housemaid reported, she 'waved her arms about' and said to Annie, 'Hooray, he is coming to meet me!'

While the jury absorbed this astonishing turn of events – was this 19-year-old governess really having an affair with the respectable, married, father-of-five York doctor, 35 years her senior? – the Coroner returned to medical questions. He asked Annie if she knew whether

Margaret had taken any medicines or drugs while she was at the Rectory; and she said, 'Not to my knowledge.'

The inquest moved on to Margaret's former employer. This was Charlotte Thompson, Matron of The Friends' Retreat, the Quaker mental health institution in York. She said that Margaret Brown had been in service there as a probationer nurse from 30 September to 6 December the previous year, 1907. She came with a recommendation from Dr Gramshaw. She left because she was found to be 'unsuitable for the post of a nurse'.

Then it was the turn of Mrs Mary Taylor, aged 82, who told the inquest that Margaret had lodged with her in Huntington Road, York, from the end of August to the end of September 1907 – just before going to The Retreat for nurse training. It was, Mrs Taylor said, Dr Gramshaw who had replied to the advertisement about the room, saying he wanted somewhere for 'a young lady who was staying in York until she got a situation as a governess, or went to The Retreat as a nurse.' The doctor arrived in a carriage with Margaret and her luggage. The young woman was perfectly well whilst staying in the lodgings at Huntingdon Road. The witness went on: 'Dr Gramshaw visited her every other day during the time she was at the house and stayed half an hour to an hour. They were alone in the sitting room on those occasions. He said he came as her guardian.' In response to a question from a juror about who paid for the room, Mrs Taylor said that Margaret had paid herself, regularly, every week.

The inquest paused after this long morning's evidence, and the jury had a few minutes to consider the implications of what they had just heard. Annie Wilson seemed to have established that Dr Gramshaw was Margaret's 'gentleman friend', writing to her from a club address, sending presents and arranging clandestine meetings out of town. But could his actions have been just those of a very conscientious guardian or trustee: finding her accommodation, recommending her for jobs, visiting her regularly and giving her trivial gifts? What about the two pregnancies? Surely, as the Coroner had pointed out, if he was her guardian, he should have been making strenuous efforts to find out who was responsible for her condition and holding him to account? That, Dr Gramshaw said, 'had never occurred to him.' If they were having an affair, and he was responsible for the pregnancy, then the question of what happened in the hotel bedroom became even more dangerous. Was the doctor simply looking after his young lover when she miscarried – or did he carry out one of the 'illegal operations' Mrs Dennison had read about, to deliberately end the life of his own child?

In the afternoon of day two of the inquest, the jury heard the final medical evidence. And to make their task harder, the doctors did not agree with each other. Dr Watson from Leeds, who had carried out the post-mortem, was recalled to answer more questions. He told the Coroner that there was no evidence in the post-mortem of any disease that might have lead to the death of the child.

The Coroner reminded him: 'You have heard the evidence today of the fall which she had on April 1st, and to which Dr Gramshaw spoke, would that cause it?' Dr

Watson responded that, from what he had heard about the fall, it was too trivial to have had any effect on the pregnancy.

'Could it have been killed by drugs?' suggested the Coroner.

'It might be killed by drugs without killing the mother, but it would be a very rare occurrence. I have never met with such a case. I have only read of one.'

'What was the drug used in that case?'

'Ergot.'

'Would you find any trace of that in the post-mortem?'

'Not so long afterwards as in this case.' Dr Watson was referring to the fact that Margaret had been given ergot on the afternoon of Good Friday, 17 April, and as she did not die until 26 April, there was no chance of the drug still being in her system.

The next doctor to give evidence was Dr Harry Reynolds, the police surgeon. He had been present at the post-mortem examination. He agreed with Dr Watson's findings, and said that the cause of death was acute peritonitis – an inflammation of the inner wall of the abdomen – set up by septic infection. He thought the infection was set up about Good Friday, the day of the miscarriage. In reply to a question from one of the jurymen, Dr Reynolds said that the stomach had been examined and did not show any evidence of drugs having been taken. The contents were not analysed, but were, he said, 'entirely natural.' Any ergot taken about the time of the miscarriage could not be detected so long after; and the same applied to any other drug. Dr Gostling, a house surgeon at the County Hospital, agreed with his colleagues about the post-mortem and about the cause of death.

At this point Dr Gramshaw's solicitor, Norman Crombie, stepped in. He asked the Coroner to call Dr Henry Foster, who had also been present at the post-mortem, and had 'carefully followed every detail.' Mr Wood, the Coroner, duly called Dr Foster. Dr Foster agreed with the other doctors – except, he said, 'in regard to one or two important points.'

Firstly, he could not agree that a sufficient period of time had elapsed between the delivery of the child and the death of the mother for the various changes in tissue found at the post-mortem to have taken place. He thought the changes had started before she came to York; and said that evidence of this was that she had had a 'shivering fit' in the train. In other words, he thought she already had an infection before the miscarriage. He thought the starting point for the miscarriage was the fall Margaret had had at the Thornton Watlass Rectory, and it was the fall that had caused the death of the child she was carrying.

Mr Craven, acting for the Chief Constable, questioned this scenario. 'Can you tell me how the infection was introduced, if not through the laceration?' 'The laceration' is presumably a reference to the medical evidence heard by the jury but not reported in the press: the post-mortem must have found an internal laceration or cut in Margaret's body.

'I cannot say how,' Dr Foster admitted. 'But I have known it be introduced, when a medical man has once been infected, to as many as eight cases.' What he was referring to was by then a well-understood phenomenon: that without careful attention to hand-washing and clothing, a doctor could spread infection amongst vulnerable patients such as new mothers, increasing the rate of puerperal or 'childbed' fever, which was often fatal. This evidence put Gramshaw in a difficult position. Dr Foster's implied defence against the charge that an instrument used by Gramshaw caused a laceration and introduced a fatal infection, was that the very experienced general practitioner has been so lax in his basic hygiene technique that he had introduced a fatal infection just by touching the patient. It also implicitly accepted that it was Gramshaw who had infected Margaret, which contradicted Dr Foster's own earlier assertion that she already had the infection before she arrived in York. There was no suggestion that she had seen a different doctor, who might be blamed for the infection, before she left Thornton Watlass.

Mr Craven must have been processing these issues about the infection for himself. 'Well, how it was introduced?' he pressed.

'Oh, I cannot say', Dr Foster said again. 'Microbes can penetrate almost anywhere.'

'We will leave it at the microbes, then, if I cannot get a better answer,' was the Town Clerk's somewhat acerbic response. It was met by possibly the only outburst of laughter to be heard during the proceedings. 'But was it introduced,' the Clerk continued, 'by the air, the hands or an instrument?'

'Nobody can tell you', said Dr Foster. Pressed further, during 'further medical evidence of a technical character', he continued to insist that he did not believe that 'the track from the laceration was caused by the instrument.'

Then day two was over. The Coroner adjourned the inquest until the following day and the jury went away to think about what they had heard.

The biggest revelation of the day was that Margaret Brown had been having a relationship with the doctor who treated her, in spite of the 35-year difference in their ages and the fact that he had a grown-up family of his own. Was he then responsible for her pregnancy? And had he also been the father of her first child, born 18 months previously? His answers on this had been, perhaps deliberately, opaque: 'I know the father of the first: I know what she told me. I do not know the father of the last.'

Turning to the matter on which they had to adjudicate, the jury must have felt that the facts of what took place in the bedroom at the Glynn Hotel on Good Friday were still not entirely clear. The nurse and the medical student both said that Dr Gramshaw had used an instrument – forceps – on Margaret Brown, at least once, and possibly more than once. But he denied it and the doctor who carried out the post-mortem saw no evidence of the use of instruments, albeit the examination was carried out 14 days after the events of Good Friday and five days after the woman's death.

The doctors agreed that Margaret had died from an infection but disagreed about when and how she had acquired the infection. Dr Foster, called by Dr Gramshaw's solicitor and a brother Freemason to Gramshaw at the York Lodge, seemed to believe that she had already been ill when she arrived in York; but no-one else, including Margaret herself, thought so. Although admitting the presence of an internal laceration, Dr Foster would not say that this was the entry point for the infection, preferring to think that the GP could have passed it to her, or she could have acquired it 'through the air'.

He also believed that the fall at the Rectory could have led to the death of the child – but Dr Watson from Leeds felt that the fall was too trivial, and the housemaid at the Rectory described it only as Margaret having 'fallen on one of her knees.' Margaret herself, in her dying declaration, said that she thought it was the fall that had caused her to give birth prematurely. Dr Watson also ruled out any disease in the mother, or drugs taken by the mother, as the cause of the death of the child.

At the end of the second day of evidence, Gramshaw must have felt that the jurymen were at least considering that he was guilty of gross medical negligence in his treatment of Margaret Brown; and they could even be contemplating something much worse. But maybe his position was not hopeless. After all, he had been involved in a case with quite startling similarities at the very start of his career, which had ended with a criminal prosecution at the Assizes. That case, against all the odds, had ended well for the practitioner involved.

Chapter 11

THE AFFAIR AT NOTTINGHAM

One Sunday evening in October 1869, a farmer's cart made its slow way along the road from Nottingham to Mansfield. On the cart were two brothers from the Brown family, and their brother-in-law, William Dodd. They had made the five hour journey in the other direction earlier in the day; now they were returning to Mansfield. Although dark, it was not cold: there had been an unseasonal warm spell of weather, with temperatures in the north of England reaching more than 23 degrees. The men had reason to regret the mildness that night: because in the back of the cart, there was an uncovered coffin carrying the body of their sister.

Harriet Brown had died at the house of a friend, Mary Limb, in Broad Marsh in Nottingham. When her father had learned of her death in a letter received that morning, he had dispatched the brothers to bring her body home. There had been a delay in Nottingham, waiting for the doctor to be available to provide a death certificate. The men had bought a coffin in the town and they put the young woman's body in it, half-dressed as they found her, together with a quantity of sawdust to soak up the blood. Then they put the coffin in the cart, without any additional covering, and set off on the long journey home.

On Monday morning, George Brown, one of Harriet's brothers, went to see John Parks, the Superintendent of the Mansfield Cemetery, at his lodge in the cemetery grounds, to make arrangements for the burial of his sister. Samuel Brown, Harriet's father, found she had some money saved in her box at home; enough to pay for the funeral. Harriet Brown was buried in Mansfield Cemetery on Monday 11 October. She was 26 years old.

Rumours and gossip about the young woman's death were immediately rife in the neighbourhood. Within days, the County Coroner for South Nottinghamshire, Mr Heath, had cause to discuss the case with the Mansfield Superintendent of Police, whose officers were already questioning a local man. The Coroner heard enough to make him issue an exhumation order; and at six o'clock in the morning on Friday 15 October, the fresh grave was re-opened, and Harriet's coffin was lifted out. Knowing that there would need to be an inquest into this death, the Coroner summoned 14 jurymen to the cemetery and they were all duly sworn in, in the chapel in the cemetery grounds. Mr W Jackson, a chemist, was the Foreman of the jury. His fellow jurors were two grocers, three printers, a shoemaker, an iron founder, a plumber, a bootmaker, a druggist, a victualler, a corn factor and a clerk. Together they viewed the body of Harriet Brown, clad only in blood-stained petticoats, a chemise and a nightgown. The body was handed over to Mr Worth, a surgeon from Nottingham, and his colleagues Mr Cooper and Mr Godfrey, for a full post-mortem examination. Then the jury moved on to the Plough Inn, where the inquest was to take place, to hear about the last days of Harriet's life.

On the Monday afternoon five days before her death, the young woman left the house she shared with her father to catch the train to Nottingham. It was Goose Fair week and for the last two years she had been to the town in the same week to enjoy the traditional travelling fair. Already over 500 years old, the fair brought in merchants selling animals, dairy products and poultry, including geese ready for the Michaelmas celebrations. It also featured sideshows and attractions calculated to draw in people from far afield even if they did not have livestock to buy or sell. These including Bostock and Wombwell's Menagerie, freak shows and waxworks. Harriet arrived at the house of Mary Limb at 20 Broad Marsh on Monday evening, saying she would stay until Wednesday. Harriet had her little girl with her. Mrs Limb, Harriet and some others went to the fair on Monday night, staying out until about 11pm. On Tuesday, Harriet told her friend that she didn't feel well and she didn't know, but thought she might be pregnant. Mrs Limb suggested going to see a Mrs Emily Jennings, a midwife, whom she thought 'a clever woman' who would be able to tell Harriet one way or the other. Mrs Jennings examined Harriet for about ten minutes, then told her she was pregnant and she should go home as soon as possible. She asked her if she had 'taken anything' – Harriet said she had not. Mrs Limb noticed that Mrs Jennings' hands were bloodied after the examination, and she had to wash them.

From that point, just as with Margaret Brown, the situation rapidly grew worse. On Wednesday morning between eight and nine o'clock, Harriet, who was still at Mrs Limb's house, was feeling very unwell. At about 11 o'clock, she told her friend that she had 'been confined.' Mrs Limb saw the stillborn child, which was darkly discoloured. The next day, Mrs Jennings visited the house and noticed black marks on Harriet's back, which the young woman said were caused by a fall she had had in Mrs Limb's house on Tuesday. She had fallen down 10 or 11 steps after feeling faint. Mrs Jennings asked to see the body of the child: when she saw it, she gave her opinion that the baby had been dead for a month. She disposed of it down the water closet.

By Friday evening, Harriet was very ill. Mrs Jennings was called again, and she recommended that a doctor be summoned, although she thought one would not come out that night. She told Mrs Limb to give Harriet some castor oil and laudanum, and to let her know in the morning if she was no better. Harriet insisted that she did not want a doctor.

In the morning, however, she was worse. Mrs Limb reported to Mrs Jennings at nine o'clock, and at shortly after 10 o'clock they went together to the premises of Dr

Charles Huthwaite in Alfred Street to ask for an urgent visit. Dr Huthwaite was not in; his assistant, Mr Farbrace Sidney Gramshaw, did not know where Dr Huthwaite was, but said he would come to see the patient himself. He was not yet qualified as a doctor; and – possibly unknown to his employer – he was still only 15 years old. The two women told him that the younger woman had had a miscarriage and 'was very bad, the uterus having fallen'. By this, they meant that Harriet had suffered a prolapse of her womb, a condition in which the womb drops down into, or even protrudes out of, the vagina.

Gramshaw accompanied Mrs Limb back to her house – Emily Jennings did not go with them – and was shown up to the back bedroom where Harriet was in bed. He found her vomiting dark matter, barely conscious, with very pale skin and dark marks under her eyes. Her pulse was 140 compared the normal rate of around 80 beats per minute. Her abdomen was swollen, and the skin over it was tense. The 15-year-old medical assistant replaced the uterus, noting that there were no visible lacerations on it, and no marks of violence or of pressure having been applied to the abdomen. He told Mrs Limb that the girl was dying – though not in earshot of the patient – and urged her to communicate with the girl's family or friends. Back at the surgery, he said the same to Mrs Jennings. He also saw his employer Dr Huthwaite on his return and asked him to visit Harriet Brown as soon as possible.

Mrs Limb wrote a first letter to Samuel Brown, Harriet's father, saying: 'Dear Friend – I write to inform you the reason that she did not come home. Harriet was taken with pain in the bowels. Mrs Limb, 20, Broad Marsh, Nottingham'. It was Mrs Jennings who had told her that this was the cause of Harriet's illness.

On Saturday afternoon, at 2 o'clock, Dr Huthwaite also visited the patient at 20 Broad Marsh. He found her in intense agony, her legs drawn up and her pulse now 160. She was no longer even barely conscious. Like his assistant, Dr Huthwaite did not notice any signs of violence. He did ask Mrs Jennings if Harriet had taken anything, or whether anything had been done, to procure a miscarriage. Mrs Jennings said no to both questions. She told the doctor that Harriet had had two falls: one before coming to Nottingham and one on Tuesday. There was nothing the doctor could do and Harriet died at 11.30 that night. Mrs Limb sent a second letter to Samuel Brown: 'Harriet died at half past eleven. Come over. She wants putting in the coffin. Mrs Limb.' She dispatched this one to Mansfield on the mail cart: it arrived on Sunday morning, less than half an hour after her first letter.

Dr Huthwaite was out on Sunday. When he returned home in the evening, he was visited by Harriet's brothers and brother-in-law, who asked for a death certificate so that they could take the woman home for burial. The doctor initially said that he could not issue a certificate as he had not attended the woman: an odd assertion, as he had visited her, though only once and he had not actually 'treated' her. The men returned to Mrs Limb's house and told her this. She sent for Mrs Jennings, who had attended on Harriet for several days; and the two women accompanied the three men back to Dr Huthwaite's house.

On the way, Mrs Limb told the brothers that Harriet had died from 'inflammation of the bowels and the womb.' Back at the doctor's house, Harriet's brother and Mrs Jennings together asked again for a death certificate so that they could take Harriet home. Dr Huthwaite was about to comply, when Harriet's brother-in-law, William Dodd, commented: 'It's a curious thing; she was right and well when she went out of my house on Monday.'

At this, Dr Huthwaite put down his pen and responded, 'You had better then have an inquest and not a certificate.' This was not what the men wanted: they reiterated that they wanted to be able to take the girl's body home. Then Dr Huthwaite left them, stepping into another room with Mrs Jennings, the midwife. After an absence of only a few minutes, he returned and wrote out a death certificate giving the cause of death as miscarriage, followed by acute peritonitis. The men paid two shillings and sixpence for the certificate. With this, they were able to take Harriet's body home and arrange the burial.

The results of the post-mortem, however, told a different story. Thomas Godfrey, the Mansfield surgeon, gave evidence at the inquest about the findings of the examination he had carried out on Harriet Brown's exhumed body with the assistance of Mr Worth, a surgeon from Nottingham. They noted the swollen abdomen bearing the marks of a previous pregnancy. They also saw that there was a wound in the uterus, which they believed to be the cause of the inflammation and acute peritonitis. The wound would have been caused by 'violence with a blunt instrument.' In answer to a question from the

Foreman of the jury, Mr Godfrey said it was very unlikely that the wound could have been caused by the woman herself. Mr Worth agreed. He thought that a wooden instrument had been used and that it was 'the extremest of impossibilities for the wound to have been caused by the young woman herself.'

At the inquest, the Coroner questioned Dr Huthwaite closely about the private conversation he had had with Mrs Jennings before issuing the death certificate. The doctor recounted his recollection of the visit from the Brown brothers and Mrs Jennings:

'I was going out so the friends of the deceased and Mrs Jennings came to me again in the evening for a certificate. I sat down to write it out, and whilst doing so, an old man who was present said "It was a curious thing for a person to die so suddenly in that way." I at once put down my pen and said "I will not give you a certificate if you think anything is wrong." A young man then got up and said from the conversation with Mrs Jennings he thought there was nothing wrong at all. I then thought it wise to question Mrs Jennings and asked her to go with me into another room. I said to her "Do you think everything is straightforward in this case?" Her answer was "Upon my word it is." I then dictated the certificate to a friend of mine who was in the room (Mr Lille, a surgeon) and afterwards signed it. The certificate produced was the one I gave.'

The Coroner then read out the certificate to the court with the cause of death entered as 'first, miscarriage; secondly, acute peritonitis.' Dr Huthwaite continued his account:

'I asked Mrs Jennings into another room in order to investigate the matter. I had no particular reason for not asking the questions in front of the others.'

The Coroner probed further: 'But one of them having expressed surprise at such a death, why did you take Mrs Jennings into another room?'

'I wished to get the facts from her,' the doctor explained. 'I have not seen her since.'

'Why did you certify that it was a miscarriage?' continued the Coroner.

'Because Mrs Jennings, who is a properly certified practitioner, told me so.'

'You certified it on hearsay?'

'I certified it from what Mrs Jennings told me.'

'Why did you certify acute peritonitis?'

'Because from my own opinion, and from what was told me, I thought peritonitis had been brought on by miscarriage.'

'Then the second opinion was also on hearsay?'

'No. If I had not been told there was a miscarriage, I should still have said that death resulted from peritonitis. My opinion was partly formed on what we call "the history of the case".'

The Coroner seemed to be growing increasingly exasperated. 'Did you tell Mrs Jennings or Mrs Limb,' he asked, 'that death was caused by inflammation of the bowels?'

'I said there was inflammation but did not say of what part. I have known death to be as quick in cases of miscarriage or abortion.'

At this point, Mr Belk, one of the solicitors in court, sought clarification; and the embattled doctor confirmed that 'peritonitis was the immediate cause of death, which might have been induced by miscarriage.'

The Coroner then dismissed Dr Huthwaite with some stern words. He said he hoped that the case had been 'a caution to him':

'Dr Huthwaite would see upon reflection that if he had an inquiry to make in a case like this, he should have had it made by proper parties. It was hardly the proper thing to make private enquiries of persons on whose information he had relied for a history of the case, together with slight observations of his own. Dr Huthwaite held a good position, and possessed a high character in Nottingham, and he (the Coroner) regretted that he acted hastily and rather indiscreetly as he had done in this case.'

Dr Huthwaite, the press reported, thanked the Coroner for his observations. His assistant, F. Sidney Gramshaw – who had given his own evidence to the inquest in the absence of his employer – was present to hear this caution from the Coroner.

In addition to the crucial medical evidence, the inquest focused closely on the actions of two people. One was Mrs Jennings, the midwife; the other was a local Mansfield man, Richard Hibbert. Hibbert was a 40-year-old publican, landlord of the Brown Cow at Ratcliffe Gate. He had known Harriet Brown for many years and he said that he had heard about her death on either the Sunday or the Monday after it happened. He was questioned repeatedly about how he heard about the death, and when, but he could not be specific. It may have been talk in the tap room, or he might have been told by a neighbour of the Brown's, Mary Massey, or he could have heard it from his lodger, Thomas Hant. Mrs Massey's prevarications on the subject saw her detained by the constable while the Coroner 'considered what he would do with her.'

Hibbert said that he had not seen Harriet since the Monday she left Mansfield to go to the Goose Fair. He admitted that he had been to Nottingham himself for the day two days later, on Wednesday, possibly because he had met various other local people on the train who could have testified to his trip. But he denied seeing Harriet in Nottingham. He also denied going to Nottingham twelve months before with Harriet and knowing that she had been 'ill' on that occasion. He denied having paid anything towards Harriet's coffin or her interment.

Samuel Brown, the dead woman's father, knew Hibbert. He said that Hibbert used to come to the house in the last three or four months, and he had told him to keep away, 'as I did not want my house disgraced by him. Reports were getting about.'

Mary Ann Hibbert, Richard's wife, tried to support her husband's position by denying everything – including that he had travelled to Nottingham on Wednesday, which he himself had already admitted. She said that he had not been to Nottingham; they had had no post delivered all week so he could not have had any communication about Harriet Brown's condition; there had never been any difference between her and her husband about the deceased; and 'he has never told me he loved the ground she walked on.'

The gossipy neighbour, Mrs Massey, added to the denials. She did not know of any intimacy between Harriet Brown and Richard Hibbert. Nor did she know anything about a quarrel between Hibbert and his wife on the day of Harriet's funeral. She denied that Mrs Hibbert had then gone away for two days.

The net effect of all their denials was to cement the view that Richard Hibbert was having an affair with Harriet Brown and was therefore likely to be the father of her most recent child. If they had been together in Nottingham the previous year, and Harriet had been ill whilst there, perhaps this was another 'miscarriage' resulting from their relationship. Mrs Limb, from Nottingham, testified that Hibbert had in fact visited Harriet at Mrs Limb's house during his visit to the city this time, on the Wednesday of Goose Fair week. She thought he was the girl's cousin, as Harriet had told Mrs Limb that she was expecting a visit from her cousin. He stayed with Harriet for 45 minutes in her bedroom. With this view of Hibbert's relationship with Harriet Brown in mind, the inquest set out to uncover Hibbert's role in a bizarre episode which had taken place in Mansfield on the afternoon of Saturday 9 October – more than six hours before Harriet's death in Nottingham.

Mary Parks, wife of John Parks, the Superintendent of Mansfield Cemetery, described the events of that afternoon. At five o'clock, a man had come to the Lodge at the cemetery where the Parks lived. She remembered that he looked a little dishevelled, with his coat and waistcoat both unbuttoned. He asked if it was too late to make preparations for a funeral to be held the next day,

Sunday. Mrs Parks said it was. The man's response was: 'She should be buried tomorrow by all means.' Mrs Parks asked if the deceased was a child or an old person and the man replied that it was a woman of about 30 years of age. Mrs Parks reiterated that it was too late and asked when the woman had died. 'On Thursday,' the man replied. When Mrs Parks asked why he had not made arrangements before now, he said that the woman had a brother in Sheffield who was seeing to it all. She told the man that he could make arrangements at the office on Monday morning, and get an order for the grave to be dug. On Monday, Harriet Brown's body was brought to the cemetery, and duly interred. Asked at the inquest to look at Richard Hibbert, Mrs Parks said she thought that he was the man who had come to the Lodge hoping to arrange a hasty Sunday funeral, though he was now dressed differently.

Hibbert himself strenuously denied going to the Lodge or asking about a funeral. He said he had not helped to pay for the coffin or the interment. But the implication left in front of the jury was that he had known, either from visiting Harriet in Nottingham on Wednesday or from some subsequent communication, that she was very ill, and he had taken steps to ensure the fastest possible burial of her body after death to avoid an investigation. Or as the papers put it, he had undertaken 'A concerted attempt to defeat the ends of justice.' The Coroner was sufficiently suspicious that he bound over Hibbert in his own recognizance of £50 to appear at the second day of the inquest.

It was on the second day of the inquest, which took place a week later on Friday 22 October, that the crux of the case was addressed, as the inquiry focused on the actions of Mrs Jennings the midwife.

Chapter 12

THE 'CLEVER WOMAN'
MRS JENNINGS

There was a good reason why Emily Jennings did not appear at the Plough Inn in Mansfield for the first day of the inquest: she was at home in Nottingham, being arrested on suspicion of having wilfully murdered or caused the death of Harriet Brown.

Emily Jennings had lived in Nottingham all her life. She was 49 years old in 1869, and married to Richard Jennings, a policeman with the Nottingham Borough police force. They had no children and shared their house with a boarder, another young policeman. Mrs Jennings was a certified midwife, an experienced practitioner with a large practice. This was over forty years before the Central Midwives Board was established, so there was no national standard of training and competence for midwives: but the local doctors knew her as a 'certificated' fellow professional.

Superintendent Bexon of the Nottingham police had gone to her home at Kent Street, together with Superintendent Palethorpe. When questioned by the policemen, Mrs Jennings had admitted having examined Harriet Brown one evening, when she was brought to her by Mrs Limb. She said, 'I never did anything at [sic] her only examine her. At first I had no light, but having got one, I found her in a state unfit to be out and recommended her to go home.' The officers proceeded to search the Jennings house and they sent for her husband. Although they had said they would search the ground floor rooms first, Mrs Jennings immediately went upstairs. The policemen followed and found her standing in front of a chest of drawers. A search of the drawers produced a leather case containing some suspicious instruments. After this, they arrested the midwife for causing the death of the young woman she had examined on the Tuesday evening 10 days before. From then on, the inquest into Harriet's death and the criminal investigation into Jennings' conduct continued in parallel.

At the second day of the inquest, Mrs Jennings was present, in the custody of Superintendent Bexon. She was represented by Mr Belk, a Nottingham solicitor. She heard the evidence of the Brown family and the medical witnesses, Dr Huthwaite and his assistant Mr Gramshaw, including the former's explanation of the conversation he had had with her in a separate room before signing the death certificate. Mary Limb gave her evidence about taking Harriet to see Mrs Jennings, and the young woman's subsequent illness and death in the house at Broad Marsh. Then the doctors who had carried out the post-mortem gave their evidence, highlighting the laceration of the womb which they believed to have been caused by a wooden instrument, and which had led to the fatal bout of peritonitis. Superintendent Bexon himself was called as a witness and described Jennings' arrest.

Just before the Coroner summed up for the jury, Mr Belk, Mrs Jennings' solicitor, got permission from the Coroner to ask a question of one of the witnesses, and then to address the jury. He asked Mrs Limb about the examination of Harriet Brown by Mrs Jennings. He asked her where she was during the examination; and she responded that she was 'within a yard of the parties and saw all that took place.' Pressed to be more specific on the key question, she said, 'I noticed all that took place and if she [Mrs Jennings] had had anything in her hand, I must have seen it.'

Turning to the jury, Mr Belk said that this showed that Harriet's internal injuries must have been acquired before she came to Nottingham – and so before the midwife ever saw her – because if they had happened during the examination by the midwife, Mrs Limb would have seen the instrument used. He also drew attention to the 'excellent character' of Mrs Jennings. With that, both he and his client must have hoped that the matter would be settled in their favour. The Coroner summed up the case, the room was cleared, and the jury deliberated.

Shortly afterwards, they returned to deliver a verdict of wilful murder against Emily Jennings. Bail was refused, she was to be committed for trial at the next Nottingham Assizes, and she was taken to the Mansfield lock-up.

On the following day, Saturday, Superintendent Bexon took his prisoner to be remanded in front of Sir Edward Walker. He later recounted a conversation he had with Mrs Jennings during this journey.

'How do you think I shall go on?' she asked him.

'I cannot tell you that', was his reply.

'The worst thing against me is you finding those things in my house,' she admitted, referring to the leather case of instruments the police had found in her chest of drawers. 'I found them, just as you found them, in Parliament Street, on the day of the nomination.' This was stretching the Superintendent's credulity to the limit. She also added that Mrs Limb was wrong in saying that she, Mrs Jennings, had been to her house on Wednesday. At this point the Magistrates' Clerk intervened to caution her that anything she said would be taken down and might be used against her at her trial.

Mrs Jennings' next appearance was at Mansfield Town Hall on the Tuesday. She was brought in front of the magistrate, Mr W Need, in a hearing attended only by officials and witnesses – the general public was not admitted, and there were no solicitors present. Richard Jennings, her policeman husband, was however allowed to sit in in the magistrate's court. His appearance was said to indicate that the position of his wife had been a source of trouble and anxiety to him; perhaps unsurprisingly.

By contrast, the reporter wrote that Mrs Jennings was '… masculine in appearance, and the proceedings, neither at this court nor at the inquest, seemed to give her much concern.' The court heard again from all the witnesses who had been at the inquest at the Plough Inn, including the Brown family, the doctors and Mrs Mary Limb, in whose house Harriet had stayed. Although Mrs Limb told the court that she had only known Mrs Jennings 'by reputation' before she took Harriet Brown to see her, her evidence was crucial to the case. When Mrs Jennings was asked if she wanted to question any of the witnesses, she took the opportunity to clarify the version of events given by Mrs Limb.

'Did I not say', she asked the woman, 'when you came to my house with the deceased that she had much better have gone for a doctor than have come to me?'

'Yes, you said so,' Mrs Limb confirmed.

'Did I ask her whether she was suffering from disease?'

'Yes; and you also said she must have been taking or doing something.'

This attempt to implicate the dead woman in her own misfortune was immediately contradicted by the two surgeons from Mansfield and Nottingham who had carried out the post-mortem examination. They both agreed that the wound in the uterus had caused the woman's death; that it could not have been caused by a fall; and there was only an extreme possibility of the woman herself causing it.

At the end of the hearing, Mrs Jennings was committed to Nottingham gaol to await trial at the next Nottingham

Assizes. She asked if it was any use her applying for bail and was told that it was not. She was then taken by train to Nottingham, and the local papers reported on the scenes accompanying her journey:

'A large number of women of the lower class assembled in the station to witness the departure of the prisoner, who was in the custody of Mr Superintendent Bexon. As she stepped into the carriage, Mrs Jennings turned to the women who had assembled, remarking that they seemed to have had a good look at her and would probably know her when they met again. One woman replied (when out of the prisoner's hearing) that she might think herself well off that she did not get well-hissed. Arrived at Nottingham station, the prisoner met several females who seemed much distressed. The prisoner herself however showed no such signs, but shook hands with a policeman on the platform with an appearance of cheerfulness. She was then conveyed in a cab to the County Gaol, her husband following in a vehicle of the same character.'

The case came up at the Winter Assizes in Nottingham just less than two months later. In fact, it was the very last case of the session, heard on Saturday 18 December in front of Mr Justice Blackburn. Mrs Jennings was said to look as if 'she had suffered from her confinement in gaol' in the interim; and her husband, Richard Jennings, was described this time as an 'ex-policeman'. Mrs Jennings was placed at the bar and the charge was read to her. She replied confidently, 'Not guilty.'

Two Queen's Counsels conducted the case. Mr Bristowe appeared for the prosecution, instructed by the Clerk to the Magistrates and the Coroner; and Mr Mellor, instructed by Mr Belk, the Nottingham solicitor who had represented Mrs Jennings at the inquest, stood for the defence. Mr Bristowe opened proceedings with a speech 'of considerable length'. Then the various witnesses repeated the evidence they had given at the inquest and in front of the magistrates. This time the two surgeons who had conducted the post-mortem were more definite: the wound to the uterus *could not* have been caused by the woman herself.

And Dr Huthwaite, recalled following the policemen's evidence about the search of the midwife's house which had found 'instruments for procuring an abortion', also had damning evidence to contribute. He testified that 'none of the instruments found in the prisoner's house were legitimate instruments of midwifery'. The instruments were produced in court and Dr Worth, one of the surgeons, gave his opinion that either of them could have caused the fatal wound but the wooden one was most likely. 'Such instruments', he said, 'would not be required by any midwife.'

Mr Mellor's defence was that there was no evidence to connect his client Mrs Jennings with the death of the unfortunate Harriet Brown and that 'the deceased was far more likely to have procured her own abortion from which death ensued.' Accepting this defence would require the jury to disregard the two doctors' evidence that this would have been physically impossible.

In his summing up, Mr Justice Blackburn set out clearly the decisions the jury had to make:

'The jury had to consider first whether it was made out that the prisoner did this act, inflicted this wound which caused the death of Harriet Brown. If they were not satisfied of this, then they would acquit the prisoner.

Second, if they did think that it was satisfactorily made out that the prisoner did the act, then came the question of whether they thought the amount of injury inflicted on Harriet Brown was so great as to amount to malice and thus make her guilty of murder.

Thirdly, if they did not find her guilty of murder, they would find her guilty of manslaughter, but still they would have to say whether the prisoner used this violence with the intention to produce an abortion. If they did find her guilty of having done the act with this intention, he would submit a case to a higher court, whether he was bound by the law to import the "constructive malice" into the act, which would make it amount to murder.'

The jury's decision was literally a matter of life and death. Although in 1861, just eight years earlier, the death penalty had been abolished for lots of less serious crimes which had previously seen thousands of people executed, there were exceptions. The death penalty still applied in cases of murder, as well as high treason, piracy with violence, and arson in the royal dockyards.

After the judge's summing up, the jury retired to consider their verdict at a quarter to six in the evening.

They were out for just over 30 minutes. When they returned, they gave their verdict: not guilty. There was applause in court 'which was taken up outside with vigour'. In the dock, Emily Jennings burst into tears. She left the court with her husband. Although her name remains in the Criminal Register for England and Wales, with the charge of murder against it, the final column in this final entry for 1869 reads: 'Acquitted'.

The reporting of the trial stops there. There is no record of Mr Justice Blackburn, or the County Coroner Mr Heath, making any remarks about the verdict. Yet they must have been taken by surprise by it. The jury had been told very clearly that the internal wound Harriet had suffered had been the cause of her death and that she could not have inflicted it on herself. Mrs Jennings had been found in possession of instruments to procure an abortion, hidden in her home: instruments which were not needed by any midwife and which she claimed to have stumbled upon by accident. She was the only person to have touched Harriet before she lost the baby and became so ill. And the inquest jury, hearing the same evidence, had been certain that Mrs Jennings was guilty of wilful murder. But the trial jury set all of that aside and decided that the prosecution had not shown that it was Emily Jennings who had inflicted the fatal wound on the dead woman. They did not of course have to come up with an alternative explanation for the young woman's death: they simply had to pronounce on the case in front of them.

Were they perhaps reluctant to pass a verdict that could have led to the death penalty? Before the abolition of the death penalty, juries were known to underestimate the value of stolen goods in order to be able to convict a felon without committing them to execution. But the jury in this case had been instructed that they could bring an alternative verdict of manslaughter, which would have avoided the death penalty unless a higher court intervened.

Could they have been influenced by what the papers called the 'frightful state of immorality' disclosed by the case, in which some of the evidence was deemed 'unfit for publication'? Did they choose to believe that an unmarried woman who already had an illegitimate child and had got herself pregnant again would go to any lengths to end that pregnancy, and so convince themselves that it was something Harriet had done that led to the wound and infection that killed her? Perhaps they just saw in front of them a well-known, long-serving and certificated professional midwife, who swore she had done nothing but examine her patient and was backed in this by the only eye-witness to events, Mrs Limb; and they believed her.

Whatever their reasoning, the jurors' decision was made and their role was over; they could return to their everyday lives. Richard Hibbert, the local publican thought to be having an affair with Harriet, did not get away so lightly: he was charged with perjury for his witness statements. He died suddenly in a pub 14 years later, falling off his stool with a can of ale in his hand. Samuel Brown returned to Mansfield to live out his life without the daughter who had returned home to care for him when he was widowed and was said to have been a great comfort to him.

Emily Jennings was widowed a few years later. She continued to practise as a midwife, listing that as her occupation when she was over 70 years old. Only one of the many papers covering her trial for murder had reported the words of one of Mrs Limb's neighbours, who had said to George Brown that 'she had done it too much'. He asked what she meant; but she would not say any more. Perhaps Emily Jennings was known to be helpful to women who did not want their pregnancy to continue and maybe that was why Mrs Limb took Harriet – and other women in trouble – to her.

Another case involving Emily Jennings was reported in 1884, which also cast doubt on the professionalism of her actions as a midwife. This case too began with an exhumation, this time of the body of a male child which was said to have died at birth. Once again, Mrs Jennings had been the midwife; and again, she had declared the child to be under-developed and stillborn. She had signed a burial certificate and, with the child's grandmother, had taken the body to a burial ground for interment – though she admitted that this was not her usual practice. The inquest heard that the child's grandmother had asked a friend of hers to be present at the birth, and 'when the child was born, to lay it down on its face'. The pregnant woman, Sarah Riley, was a widow who had had two other pregnancies since her husband died, both resulting in 'stillbirths'.

The doctors who carried out the post-mortem concluded, in contradiction to Mrs Jennings' account, that the child was fully developed and had breathed after being born. Death was due to suffocation, they said, and exposure might have weakened the child. Mrs Jennings had testified that after the birth the child had lain on the bed without any covering for about three quarters of an hour. When she next looked at the child, she said, it was dead. The Deputy Coroner in charge of the inquest clearly drew his own conclusions from the words of the three women: the mother, the midwife and the grandmother. He said:

'The evidence which had been given was not sufficient to justify the jury in committing any of the female witnesses concerned in the affair on a charge of manslaughter, although the evidence pointed very much that way, and he should have been very pleased to see the crime brought home.'

The jury's verdict was that the child died of suffocation, but the evidence was insufficient to show how it was suffocated.

The doctors in the first Jennings case also continued their professional lives. Dr Huthwaite continued to practise in Nottingham, becoming a Freemason and a Fellow of the Royal College of Surgeons of Edinburgh. F. Sidney Gramshaw had his 16th birthday between the inquest and the trial. He left his assistant post with Dr Huthwaite to go to Somerset, where he met and married Mary Poole, before moving to Easingwold as medical assistant to Dr Hall and later to Stillington as the village doctor.

Did he, at the end of the second day of Margaret Brown's inquest in 1908, remember his very first inquest in Mansfield nearly 40 years before, and the remarkable similarities between the two cases? Two young women named Brown, both unmarried, both with an illegitimate daughter already, both finding themselves pregnant again, seeking medical help, and blaming a fall for their subsequent 'miscarriage'. Both of them dying of peritonitis afterwards and the practitioner in each case coming under intense scrutiny for their actions in the case.

In the face of a great deal of incriminating evidence, and the damning inquest verdict, the Nottingham midwife had walked away from the situation without any official stain on her character. Surely, however uncomfortable the questioning he had faced, and however embarrassing the revelations, the respected York doctor would do so too?

Chapter 13

INQUEST INTERRUPTED

Eleanor Camplin, the Gramshaw's housemaid at Dunholme, had only been in post for six weeks: but her tenure was about to come to an abrupt end. The house on Bootham had been full over Easter. In addition to Dr and Mrs Gramshaw and their two unmarried daughters, Amy and Hilda, the Gramshaw sons were home for Easter and they were still in residence two weeks later when the inquest on Margaret Brown was held. In addition, the boys' uncle Thomas Allan, their aunt Frances and their cousin Kenneth Allan, the medical student, were staying at the house. The two servants, Eleanor and the cook, were kept frantically busy attending to the household and its guests for most of April and May.

On the morning of Tuesday 5 May, both Dr Gramshaw and Kenneth Allan were due back at the Law Courts for the final day of the Brown inquest, due to start with the Coroner's summing up. Eleanor Camplin went upstairs to wake Gramshaw at seven thirty in the morning. She had seen the master of the house the previous evening, when he had seemed in his usual state of health. She knocked at the bedroom door and awaited his summons. When there was no response, she continued to bang on the door. Although it was not unusual for the doctor to lock his bedroom door – she had known it happen a few times in her short time at the house – something concerned her on this occasion. Having tried three times to rouse the doctor by knocking, she went back downstairs to ask the cook for help. The two women ventured to try to open the door to the master bedroom; but they found that it was locked. The only thing they could do was go to Mrs Gramshaw and tell her what they had found.

Mrs Gramshaw called on her eldest son Cecil, and her nephew, Kenneth Allan, for help. Allan had already been woken by the banging on the door and had come out to see what was happening. When he realised the problem, he sent the maid to fetch Dr Henry Foster, who was staying locally to attend the inquest at the request of Gramshaw's solicitor, and a constable. With Dr Foster and the police officer in attendance, Cecil Gramshaw and Kenneth Allan tackled the door and succeeded in breaking it open at around eight o'clock. They burst into the bedroom, anxious to see why there was no response to the housemaid's knock.

They had arrived at a critical moment. Allan saw immediately that his uncle was lying in bed and that he was not breathing. He was 'very blue' and his pupils were contracted. Although in respiratory arrest, his heart was still beating – a few minutes more and he would have been in full cardiac arrest: they would have been too late to try to save him. Dr Foster and Kenneth Allan immediately began artificial respiration, trying to ensure that Gramshaw had sufficient oxygen to keep his brain and vital organs alive until he could breathe for himself again. Their efforts at resuscitation lasted for the next four hours. Meanwhile, they sent out for Dr George Auden, Honorary Medical Officer to the York Home for Nurses and (like Dr Foster) a brother Freemason of Gramshaw's, and he came straight to the house to help attend to the unconscious man. Dr Thomas Allan, Gramshaw's brother-in-law and father to Kenneth, joined the other doctors in the fight for his brother-in-law's life.

At the Law Courts, the Coroner was informed of the illness of a key witness at the Margaret Brown inquest. He immediately adjourned the proceedings for two weeks, telling the jury that it would not be appropriate to continue. The jurymen were sent away to await developments. Meanwhile, the national press, which had been following every twist and turn of the Brown case, also became aware of this unscheduled interruption to the inquest. 'Sensational affair at York – Doctor found unconscious', read one headline. 'Dramatic sequel to death of a governess', said another. In the hours that followed they seized on each report of the condition of 'the well-known York doctor', waiting – as were the Coroner and the jury – to see what would happen next.

'Dr Gramshaw better', read a headline in one Scottish paper on Thursday morning, 48 hours after the discovery of his illness. 'Condition improved after time of anxiety.' Another reported: 'The York Sensation. Dr Gramshaw recovering':

> 'The latest reports concerning the condition of Dr Gramshaw, whose sensational illness has caused the adjournment of the inquest at York on the body of the young governess, Margaret Eleanor Brown, are reassuring, and it is regarded as almost certain that he will recover ... Late on Tuesday night the symptoms of the patient were so serious that his life was despaired of, but under the watchful care and skilful ministrations of the medical attendants the danger was averted ... Yesterday Dr Gramshaw was restored to partial consciousness, and throughout the day was making slow and steady progress.'
>
> 'His condition during the night had been very precarious,' [ran a different article], 'and he had not regained consciousness at noon yesterday, but was gradually recovering. Later in the day consciousness returned. He is however still very ill, and it will be some days before he can be removed.'

Dr Foster and Dr Auden, in 'professional attendance', and Gramshaw's brother-in-law Dr Thomas Allan, had had a very difficult time. For most of the first day, Tuesday, after the successful restoration of Gramshaw's breathing, his condition remained 'very precarious' and they still did not know if he would pull through. By later on Wednesday, things were improving. Having remained unconscious all morning, he began to rouse. He was only semi-conscious but beginning to try to speak. He seemed confused, but occasionally answered questions; and he was able to recognise those at his bedside.

The papers had, however, been too optimistic. At midnight on Wednesday, another bulletin was issued and picked up by the local papers. It said that Dr Gramshaw had 'taken a turn for the worse. Pulmonary complications had set in, and his condition was precarious.' He deteriorated rapidly, his pulse weakening and his heart gradually failing. The Scottish paper, publishing its hopeful report on Thursday, was behind the breaking news. At half past four on Thursday morning, Dr Gramshaw had died.

As this was an unexpected death, an inquest was required to discover the circumstances leading to it. John Richardson Wood, the Coroner for York who was already conducting the inquest into Margaret Brown's death, now had to set up a new enquiry into the death of Farbrace Sidney Gramshaw. He did so with commendable speed: the proceedings began at four o'clock in the afternoon on the following day, Friday 8 May. This time, the jury convened in much humbler premises: the parish hall of St Mary's church in York. Although St Mary's could claim some points of interest – it was an old medieval church, with some stonework dating back to Saxon times and the tallest steeple in York at 47 metres high – its parish hall could not compete for gravity with the York Law Courts, where Margaret Brown's inquest was being held. Perhaps the venue reflected the Coroner's view that this inquest was likely to be a more straightforward affair, with no potential criminal charges resulting from it. His timing – starting at four o'clock on a Friday – suggests that he did not think the proceedings would detain the jury for long.

Many of the same witnesses attended this second inquest, including Mr Crombie, the solicitor now representing the Gramshaw family instead of Dr Gramshaw, the Chief Constable, James Burrow, and Dr Henry Foster, who was involved in Margaret Brown's inquest at the request of Mr Crombie. The process of the inquisition was also the same. Evidence of identification of the deceased was given; in this case, by Gramshaw's eldest son, Cecil. Then witnesses were called to say what they had observed about the unexpected death.

Kenneth Allan, Gramshaw's nephew and the medical student who had given evidence at the inquest in the Law Courts, was now a witness at his uncle's inquest. He said that he had been with his uncle on Monday evening, from 10.45 until midnight. His uncle seemed more cheerful than he had been earlier in the day and had talked about 'a few trivial things about his work.' Next, Allan reported, 'He then got up and said he thought he had better go to bed. He remarked: "I am going to take a third of a grain of morphia tonight. I haven't had any sleep for a week and must have some tonight".'

Allan left his uncle locking the front door and did not see him again until the morning, when he was woken by the maid banging on Gramshaw's bedroom door. He described the breaking down of the door, and how they had found Gramshaw on the bed, 'very blue' and not breathing. He did not know, he said, whether his uncle was in the habit of 'taking anything.' The housemaid, Eleanor Camplin, gave more details of her attempts to rouse her master, and how she had called for help when she found the door locked. She estimated that half an hour had passed between her first knock on the door and when it was broken down by the men in the house.

Kenneth Allan had said that he had not at first known the cause of his uncle's sudden collapse. Another witness, Dr Henry Foster, who had entered the bedroom with Allan, was also initially unaware of the circumstances. He said that when he first went into the bedroom 'he saw nothing which might have been likely to have brought about the deceased's condition.' But at some point he was shown a two-ounce graduated measure which contained a few drops of some fluid. He also noticed several 'pocket instruments' which included a hypodermic syringe. He described the 'methods taken to restore the patient', including the administration of antidotes, and the hope on Wednesday that the patient was beginning to recover, before his relapse and death in the early hours of Thursday morning. Dr Foster concluded '... that the deceased had taken three or four grains [of morphia] hypodermically [under the skin].' The evidence of this, he said, was that 'on the outside of the left thigh there was a smear of blood surrounding a very minute puncture such as might have been made by a hypodermic needle.'

'Is it possible or probable,' the Coroner asked, 'that a medical man would inject three or four grains accidentally?'

'No, I think not,' was the doctor's reply. Then he tried to mitigate this by adding 'It would depend on the state of his mind. A mistake might be made.' He also told the Coroner that the syringe he had found in the bedroom 'had been put away tidily. If it was used, it was not used in a state of excitement.'

Dr Auden, the local doctor called in to help treat Gramshaw, gave similar evidence. He had concluded that Gramshaw was suffering from 'the effects of poison in the shape of some morphia compound.' The primary cause of death, in his opinion, was morphia, with heart failure and congestion of the lungs as secondary consequences. Dr Foster however had slightly different take on it, trying hard to separate the taking of the morphia from the cause of death. The Coroner, perhaps a little exasperated by these medical manoeuvrings, had to press him to clarify the issue:

'That [the cause of death] is a little complicated,' Foster said, 'because, so far as I can judge, although it is evident that he was suffering from morphia, the antidotes and the treatment adopted had apparently neutralised or modified the effects of the morphia, and death, therefore, did not result from morphia poisoning pure and simple. I conclude that the actual cause of death was pulmonary congestion, bringing on cardiac failure.'

'Was that the result of the opium?' asked the Coroner.

'Yes,' Foster conceded. 'I think morphia, by acting on the respiratory nerve centre, contributed to his death.'

'Was it not the primary cause of death?' the Coroner insisted.

'I am bound to consider that morphia was the primary cause of death', admitted the doctor.

'Did you form any idea of the quantity taken?'

'He must have taken considerably more than a medicinal dose. Possibly three or more grains, taken hypodermically.'

'I am bound to say,' remarked the Coroner, clarifying his own view pointedly for the jury, 'that I cannot see that it is possible for a doctor to have taken the quantity of morphia sufficient to cause the symptoms he [Dr Foster] had observed inadvertently.'

Mr Crombie, the family's solicitor, however, sought to introduce the suggestion that it was not unusual for Gramshaw to take morphia or other substances for medicinal purposes. Perhaps he was hoping to give the impression that this was a routine practice that had simply gone tragically wrong on one, fatal, occasion. Questioning Cecil Gramshaw, the eldest son of the family who was now practising as an engineer in London, he asked about his father's drug habits. The young Gramshaw confirmed that his father had been 'in the habit of taking hypodermics on very rare occasions when he was not very well, or when he was very worried. At times also he smoked opium when he had a bad cold.' Cecil Gramshaw was probably aware of the solicitor's strategy on the subject of routine drug-taking, because according to one newspaper report he then produced some of his father's drugs in court, saying 'I have some of the opium here.'

If Dr Gramshaw took morphia or opium regularly, he was not unusual amongst medical men. Both drugs derive from the same source, the opium poppy, and they could be used either as a stimulant or as a sedative. The beneficial effect on people's mood was known from ancient times, when locals in Mesopotamia (now Iraq and Kuwait), where the plant was grown in abundance, called it 'the joy plant.' Opium derivatives, including morphine, were widely used to relieve pain in the 1800s. They were also used for a variety of personal reasons. John Haller Jr. wrote of opium: 'Used and abused by layman, charlatan, and practitioner alike, opium represents one of the most significant and confusing episodes in the history of medicine.'

Doctors of course had ready access to the drugs. For some of them, addiction to morphine – or 'morphinism' – came to dominate their lives. In a paper called 'Opium addiction in medical men', published 25 years before Gramshaw's time, J B Mattison described how he tried to cure members of his profession of this condition. He observed that:

'... the majority of his patients have been, are, and probably will be, members of the profession ... physicians form a large proportion of opium habitués in general, and the great majority of any professional class ...

As to why so many opium habitués are recruited from the ranks of our profession, it may be said that the physician's calling involving, as it often does, especial inroads on his mental and physical well-being, exposes him more than any other to the various influences which stand as factors in the aetiology of this disease.

Then, again, addiction, hypodermically, is likely to prevail largely in medical circles, inasmuch as the very nature of this method requires a more or less intimate knowledge of morphia and the hypodermic syringe, which the average layman does not possess.

Then, too, may not this very knowledge and the frequent employment of this potent agent for evil as well as good which the modern practice of medicine involves, disarm fear of its ill-effects, and make easy the occasional taking, which so easily and so soon forges the fetters of confirmed addiction?'

In speculating why doctors should want to give themselves the benefits of morphine or opium, Mattison puts his finger on the exact reason that Cecil Gramshaw gave for his father's use of the drug:

'Another special factor is the peculiar power that opium possesses to give strength, bring sleep, and relieve portendings incident to the anxious hours, the weary days, and wakeful nights, such as the experience of every busy practitioner so often involves.'

Gramshaw may not have been addicted – his son spoke of 'very occasional' use – but he had clearly stated his intention of taking one third of a grain of morphine to help him sleep on the night of Monday 4 May. And the Coroner had clearly stated his view, corroborated by the doctors present, that taking three or four grains of the drug was far more than was needed for this purpose, and that a doctor must know that.

The Coroner asked Dr Foster about Gramshaw's state of mind. 'You saw a good deal of Dr Gramshaw in the few days before his death. Did you see any signs of mental aberration?'

'I did not see anything of him from the time of the adjourned inquest until next morning,' was Foster's rather evasive reply. He had been in the inquest court with Gramshaw for two full days and must have had some idea how his friend was feeling at the end of the second day.

The Coroner was not going to let him get away with that. 'That was the day', he said. 'Did you see any signs?'

'No', Foster finally admitted. Then he added, 'I saw nothing beyond a good deal of sighing and depression.' This would fit with the description given by reporters at the inquest who described Gramshaw as appearing 'distracted and listless' on the second day of proceedings. Whether this amounted to significant mental illness or was simply a reasonable response to the stress of the inquest into the death of his patient – who was also his mistress – the jurymen would have to decide. The issue of Gramshaw's intention in taking the dose was now at the heart of the inquisition. Mr Crombie, the family's solicitor, again pressed the suggestion that the overdose could have been a mistake. He asked Dr Foster if a measured dose would be used – in other words, could Gramshaw have estimated the dose and got it tragically and fatally wrong? Foster offered some support for this theory: he said that 'it was customary to use small tablets of morphia, dissolved in water, for hypodermic injection. It was possible, but not probable, to mistake one third of a grain for three grains.'

The Foreman of the jury then spoke up, seeking clarification of this complicated dance around the amount, purpose and method of administration of the drug. 'What,' he asked reasonably, 'would be a fatal dose?' Dr Foster's response was not very helpful to the struggling laymen on the jury:

'A grain is a very dangerous dose,' he said, 'although a great many people get over that. Three grains are not necessarily fatal. There is not much difference between swallowing morphia and injecting it, and people have recovered from 12 grains.'

This may have been a reference to a case written up in a medical journal 14 years before by a Dr Pope, titled 'A large quantity of morphia (twelve grains?) taken hypodermically with suicidal intent; recovery.' What was the jury to make of this information, that a dose three or four times larger than that taken by Dr Gramshaw would not necessarily have killed him?

Here the Chief Constable weighed in to help. 'What is the normal dose?' he asked.

'One eighth to one fourth of a grain,' Foster replied, then further confused the issue by adding 'People who are used to it habitually take more.' The jury already knew that Gramshaw was in the habit of taking morphia when he was ill or under stress. Was he so 'used to it' that the amount he had taken this time should not have killed him – though it clearly had?

'Did you find evidence of more than one puncture?' the Chief Constable asked.

'No. We were a little suspicious about another place but could not satisfy ourselves [that it was a second injection site].'

Finally, as Friday afternoon moved into Friday evening, Coroner Wood summed up the evidence for the jury.

'The question has been raised,' he said in his address, 'and properly raised, as to whether it was likely that Dr Gramshaw might have administered the dose inadvertently, with the intention of procuring sleep, but I fear, from the evidence which you have heard you will be driven to the conclusion that the quantity of morphia taken was so considerable as to make you think that that could hardly be the case. The only suggestion that was thrown out by Dr Foster was that it might have been taken in aberration of mind. I think you will be of the opinion that there is no evidence before you which would warrant you in coming to the conclusion that such aberration existed.'

The Coroner's statement was unequivocal. He had discounted entirely the efforts of Gramshaw's friend Dr Foster to avoid blaming the morphia for causing Gramshaw's death; the attempts by Mr Crombie to suggest that his former client's overdose was an accident; and the idea that Gramshaw might have been mentally ill, and therefore not responsible for his actions in deliberately taking a fatal overdose of morphia. The consequences of this were clear, and potentially devastating for the family: the jurymen were being invited to find that Sidney Gramshaw had committed suicide.

'If they found that the death was the result of the doctor's own action,' Mr Wood told them, 'and that he was not suffering from an aberration [of mind], of course, their verdict would be one of *felo de se*.' This was the Latin term for suicide, meaning literally 'a felon of himself'. The Coroner followed this with an expression of sympathy 'shared by all the jury' for Mrs Gramshaw and the family.

Suicide was not only a social embarrassment at this time; it was also still a crime. And while the perpetrator was beyond the reach of both the law and public opinion, his family was not.

Chapter 14

A VERDICT

One hundred years earlier, a person who committed suicide would have been buried at a crossroads with a stake through his heart. The crossroads, because in mythology this was regarded as a 'limbo' place between two worlds (and for the practical reason that it often marked a boundary between parishes); and the stake in order to pin down the restless spirit of the suicide. In addition, all the suicide's money and belongings were forfeit to the Crown, leaving his family with nothing. Arguing forcefully for a change to the law in the House of Commons in 1821, Sir J. Mackintosh poured scorn on this practice, and its unfair targeting of the less well-off in society:

'... if a foreigner were to form his estimate of the people of England from a consideration of their penal code, he would undoubtedly conclude that they were a nation of barbarians. This expression, though strong, was unquestionably true; for what other opinion could a humane foreigner form of us, when he found … that, on some occasions, we even proceeded to wreak our vengeance upon the bodies of the inanimate dead?…

The punishment inflicted in a case of suicide was rather an act of malignant and brutal folly. It was useless as regarded the dead, and only tortured the living. The honourable member for Ipswich had given notice of a bill regarding the disgusting course pursued in cases of suicide… He however should propose to abolish the forfeiture of goods and chattels in cases of suicide. It seemed to him that if there was a punishment peculiarly unjust, it was this, where in fact the innocent suffered for the guilty. The principal human offence of suicide certainly was the desertion of those for whom we were bound to provide—whom nature and society recommended to our care. What did the law of England do in this case? It stepped in to aggravate the misery, and perhaps to reduce the fatherless to beggary: it wrested from them the bread they were to eat; in short, it deprived them of their last and sole consolation under their affliction. It was to be observed, that the forfeiture only applied to personal property—it affected small savings chiefly, for large fortunes were generally laid out in land; so that it left untouched the possessions of the great…'

Less than thirty years before Gramshaw's death, a suicide could only be buried after dark – between nine o'clock and midnight – without any religious rites. This reflected the long-held view that suicide was an offence against God, nature and the community. Only after two Acts of Parliament in the 1880s was it possible for a person who died by their own hand to be buried at any of the usual times, and 'either without any religious service or with such Christian and orderly religious service at the grave as the person having charge of the body thinks fit.' And their possessions were no longer subject to seizure by the Crown. Before this, only a verdict of 'temporary insanity' – *non compos mentis* – could save the family's possessions: and this became the most common verdict in inquests concerning people who killed themselves before the law was changed.

During the time that Gramshaw was practising as a doctor, in the late nineteenth and early twentieth century, the medical profession developed a much better understanding of suicide as a result of mental illness rather than a mortal sin. Daniel Hack Tuke, an English physician and expert on mental health, and co-editor of the *Journal of Mental Science*, created a classification of suicide and its causes. 'Impulsive suicide', he suggested, could have several different causes, depending on the individual's mental state: they could be neurotic, hysterical, maniacal, alcoholic or epileptic, and their suicidal action would arise from this state. 'Deliberate suicide', by contrast, could be ascribed to egotistical feelings (the individual facing pain, worry, sleeplessness, ruin or shame); or altruistic feelings (a desire to save others from suffering, or to benefit others). Sometimes neither of these would be the driver, with the suicide instead impelled by 'voices' or delusions, or simply having 'a weak mind.'

The actions of the courts also reflected this more compassionate approach when they dealt with attempted suicide. It was still a crime, and people who tried but failed to take their own lives often found themselves in front of the magistrates. But while they could be sentenced to up to two years in prison, this punishment was rarely enacted. In the same year as Gramshaw died in York, 1908, there were numerous reports in the press of people charged with attempted suicide across Yorkshire. Their methods were often very violent: throat cutting was common, along with hanging, shooting, leaping into rivers and self-poisoning. The reasons given included poverty and the lack of means to make a living; depression and mental illness; and unhappiness following a quarrel or criticism. None of them went to prison.

Nellie Hesmondhalgh, from Burnley, threw herself in the canal after some of her fellow-weavers criticised her work and made her afraid to return to the mill. A young man called Alfred Sharples rushed out of a nearby mill and rescued her. She was remanded to the workhouse for eight weeks. Charlotte Bansby from Keighley tried to hang herself after a 'tiff' with her husband. She was 'black in the face' when he found her and he testified that she had made several previous suicide attempts. Charlotte was discharged to her husband's care. A painter and decorator from Mirfield, near Huddersfield, cut his throat after an accident left him partially disabled and unable to work. He was discharged by the court and taken home by relatives. A husband who drank poison after his wife died was sent to the workhouse to be kept under observation for 14 days.

All these would fit neatly into one or other of Tuke's categories of deliberate suicides with 'egotistical' or 'altruistic' feelings; and in each case, the court imposed care and supervision rather than a punitive sentence. One of the other Yorkshire cases that year fitted better into the 'impulsive' category. This was Benjamin Murgatroyd, a delver from Pudsey, who had cut his own throat, inflicting a deep, three-inch-long laceration with his pocket knife. He explained to Bradford West Riding Police Court that he had been 'a bit excited.' The doctor who treated him said Murgatroyd had been drunk at the time; and he was discharged with an injunction to 'leave intoxicating liquors alone.'

William Aloysius Cocker had a different excuse when he cut his throat with his razor: he blamed his mother-in-law. In court for persistent cruelty to his wife as well as attempted suicide, it became apparent that he had kept his wife 'in a state of abject terror', partly by constant threats to kill himself. He was reported to have said that 'There are more ways than blows to be rid of a woman.' His mother-in-law's contribution to his mental state was to call him 'idle' when he spent all day in bed and to help her daughter pack her belongings to leave. When the magistrate asked, 'Did you do it [cut your throat] because of your mother-in-law?' Cocker replied, 'Yes, and so would you if you had been tried like me.'

'Can you tell why this woman [his wife] has come here to tell such lies about you?' the magistrate enquired.

'She was put up to it by her mother,' was Cocker's prompt reply.

The court granted a separation order to his wife and ordered him to pay her 7/6 a week towards her maintenance: 'the charge of attempted suicide was dismissed, the magistrate believing that the attempts were made with a view of frightening the woman, and this being so, it constituted part of the 'persistent cruelty.'

For all the enlightenment and understanding shown by the medical profession and the courts in the face of suicide, the social stigma remained. And the jury at Gramshaw's inquest was well aware of this as they prepared to consider their verdict. They had heard the evidence that the doctor had injected himself with an overdose of morphia in his locked bedroom. They had heard the testimony, drawn sometimes reluctantly from the other doctors, that the morphia had been the primary cause of his death. And the Coroner had seemed to rule out any suggestion of mental illness: 'I think you will be of the opinion that there is no evidence before you which would warrant you in coming to the conclusion that such aberration existed.' The Coroner was ushering the jury towards what Tuke would have categorised as a 'deliberate' suicide, caused by 'egotistical' feelings: worry, sleeplessness, shame, the prospect of ruin ... rather than an 'impulsive' suicide caused by a mental aberration.

The jury was absent for only 12 minutes. They returned with a verdict that 'Dr Gramshaw had committed suicide by injecting morphia in a fit of temporary insanity.'

Whether the speed of their decision was influenced by the timing of the inquest – starting at 4pm on Friday, it must have been well into the evening by the time the jury retired – or because they were immediately unanimous in their desire to spare some of the family's feelings, is open to speculation. The Coroner did not comment on the jury's disregard of his advice. The inquest was over, the taint of *felo de se* had been avoided, and the Gramshaw family could now move on as best they could. Two days later, they buried Sidney Gramshaw in Stillington, where he had been the local doctor for 30 years.

Chapter 15

A VILLAGE FAREWELL

The York press and the national newspapers that had followed every twist and turn of the Brown and Gramshaw inquests, and reported each step of the doctor's illness, rally and death, showed no interest in his funeral. There was no announcement, no coverage and no images. Only the most local of local papers acknowledged the event.

The Easingwold Advertiser and Weekly News was based in the eponymous market town just four miles from Stillington. It came out weekly on Saturdays and provided a mixture of advertisements relevant to local rural industries; and local, national and international news, as well as a weekly serial (in May 1908 this was 'The Tragedy of Brampton Towers' by John Bakewell). The advertisements included insurance for in-foal mares, artificial fertilisers, chicken food, Coverdale's influenza mixture, and Driffield's pedigree stocks of mangolds, swedes and disease-resisting turnips.

On Saturday 2 May, the week before Dr Gramshaw died, the news from around the country included a man in Nottingham who was knocked down by a car, lost two fingers, and, when he recovered consciousness, walked three miles to hospital for treatment. It covered the first ever appeal under the Criminal Appeal Act, when a shoemaker convicted of breaking and entering and stealing leather appealed against 'the nature of the jury and the evidence of the police constable who arrested me.' The court at Newington Sessions noted his statement and sentenced him to three years penal servitude. Winston Churchill's defeat in elections in Manchester was reported: he was beaten by Mr W. Royston-Hicks by 426 votes. Other newsworthy events were a dog attacked by an otter in Norfolk, a naval disaster in the Solent, and the extradition of a Hampstead man in connection with a jewel robbery in New York. Perhaps the most interesting news was that a consignment of alligators from Florida had arrived at Tilbury Docks in London, and only two of them had died during the journey.

In local news, a farmer from Tholthorpe had been found drowned; the Easter vestry meeting had been held at Stillington Church; and a new secondary school was proposed for Easingwold. The following week's paper – published one day before Gramshaw's funeral – reported on the inquest into the death of a local Crayke farmer who had hanged himself in his barn. International news included the story of a stamp-collector in Budapest who had saved up 500 francs to buy a stamp, only to be told that the price had gone up to 750 francs. He went home and hung himself in his bedroom.

Death and its consequences were always newsworthy; and for a country audience, the involvement of animals added to the interest of the story. The Advertiser carried two such stories that week, the first amongst its international news:

'An eccentric maiden lady who recently died at Wilkebarr, Pennsylvania, bequeathed a sum of 40,000 dollars to her pet cat. The bequest of such a large sum for the benefit of an animal is believed to be unprecedented. The executors have, by common consent, decided to have the animal chloroformed and the money devoted to other purposes.'

Closer to home was another similar story:

'Owing to instructions in the Will of the late Mr W. W. Willson, auctioneer, Southend-on-Sea, his favourite pony followed him to the grave and was afterwards shot at Billericay.'

The issue of Saturday 16 May contained the usual array of headlines: 'Bride abducted', 'Juvenile smoking', 'Suffragettes mobbed', 'Windfall for station clerk', 'Husband and wife fight duel' and 'Bishop on clerical flirts.' It also carried on its front page the following notice:

'Dr Farbrace Sidney Gramshaw, Deceased. All persons having any CLAIMS or DEMANDS against the Estate of Farbrace Sidney Gramshaw formerly of Stillington in the County of York but lately of Denholme, Bootham, in the City of York, Doctor of Medicine deceased are requested to send particulars thereof forthwith to the undersigned and all Persons having any property in their hands belonging to the above deceased or indebted to his Estate are requested to deliver or pay the same to the undersigned immediately.

Dated 11th day of May 1908. Geo. Crombie and Sons, 46 Stonegate, York.'

On the back page of the paper was an account of Gramshaw's funeral. The headline read 'The late Dr Gramshaw. Interment at Stillington.' The report began by drawing a discrete veil over the circumstances that had led to the doctor's death:

'The interment of the remains of the late Dr Fairbrace [sic] Sidney Gramshaw, of Dunholme, Bootham, York, who died on the 7th inst, under circumstances so tragic and so well-known that it is not necessary to refer to them here, took place on Sunday afternoon in the churchyard at Stillington, where the deceased was the local medical man for a great number of years.'

With this, the Advertiser captured the local mood perfectly. To the rest of the country, Gramshaw might be just a disgraced doctor who took his own life after being caught out in an adulterous affair with a young woman who paid for the illicit liaison with her life. But in Easingwold and Stillington, he was their medical man who had attended their births, illnesses, accidents and deaths for thirty years. The strongest evidence of their loyalty, even five years after he left Stillington for York, was that a thousand people turned out for his funeral. As the paper put it:

> 'A considerable number of the friends of the deceased gentlemen, who had known him as a highly respected medical practitioner residing in their midst at Stillington, attended the solemn ceremony to pay a last mark of respect to the memory of their friend, and to signify, by their presence, their heart-felt sympathy with the widow and the family.'

The funeral cortege left York at one o'clock. Following the hearse with the coffin were three horse-drawn carriages carrying the principal mourners. As the cortege set off to make the journey to Stillington, its departure was witnessed by what the paper called 'an orderly crowd'. It passed through the villages of Wigginton and Sutton-on-the-Forest, north of York: and 'at almost every house on the wayside of the ten miles [sic] journey the blinds were drawn'. This was a traditional sign of respect for a passing funeral procession. For the last two miles, from Sutton to Stillington, the cortege slowed to a walking pace, as it passed through the countryside over which Dr Gramshaw had ridden on many occasions with the York and Ainsty Hunt.

The hearse and carriages were not alone in their journey from York. It was estimated that around 250 people cycled the ten miles from York to witness the burial in Stillington. When the cortege arrived at the village church at around three o'clock, the cyclists were joined by hundreds of people from other local villages in a huge crowd, estimated at around a thousand people. The cortege halted in front of the gate of the church at which Gramshaw had attended many vestry meetings, and to which he had contributed generously for the restoration of the clock and the maintenance of the fabric of the building.

The coffin was received at the gate by the vicar of St Nicholas's, the Reverend Matthew Smith. Smith, with his degree in divinity from Selwyn College, Cambridge, was relatively new in post, having been appointed to the vicarage in 1906. He replaced the previous vicar who had known Gramshaw very well: the Reverend William Jemison had come to the village in the same year as the young doctor, 1873. He lived in the vicarage at Stillington with his sister for the next 32 years. The Reverend Jemison was an unusual vicar: his degree from Trinity College, Dublin, was in law rather than divinity and he had been elected as a Barrington lecturer on political economy by the Dublin Statistical Society. He was ordained as a priest in Carlisle Cathedral in 1862 at the age of 32, before taking up the vicarage at Stillington. Jemison and Gramshaw had worked together for many years in vestry meetings at St Nicholas's and they were near neighbours in the village.

Jemison would have found it hard to bury his friend under the current circumstances; but he had died in October 1905 at the age of 75, knowing nothing of the tragedy to come.

Once the coffin and the mourners were inside the ancient church, the funeral service began. The service 'was simply that as prescribed by the Prayer Book of the Church of England', and was conducted by the Reverend Smith. 'An excellent mixed choir was in attendance', and led the congregation in singing 'Jesu, lover of my soul' and 'God moves in a mysterious way.' At the end of the service, Mrs Smith, the vicar's wife, played the solemn Dead March from Handel's oratorio 'Saul' as the mourning party left the church. The coffin, covered in wreaths of flowers, was carried from the church into the churchyard. Dr Farbrace Sidney Gramshaw MD was buried close to the grave of his friend, the former vicar, the Reverend Jemison LLB. Gathered round the grave were the principal mourners, with the three women in the black dresses and veils of Edwardian mourning: Mrs Mary Gramshaw, the widow; Amy, her eldest daughter; and Frances Allan, Gramshaw's sister. With them were the men of the family: Cecil, William and Guy, the Gramshaw sons; Thomas Allan, who had tried so hard to save his brother-in-law's life; and his son Kenneth Allan, the medical student who had been involved in treating Margaret Brown, and in trying to resuscitate his uncle after his overdose. Absent from the graveside – and the funeral – was Hilda Gramshaw, the second daughter of the family.

Dr Gramshaw's grave, against the wall of the churchyard, is marked with a bevel or 'pillow' marker: a stone set close to the ground at an angle, with the back edge higher than the front edge. It bears an inscription in lead letters which reads:

'Farbrace Sidney Gramshaw M.D. F.R.C.S. He practised his profession for thirty six years in this County and died 7th May 1908 Aged 54. In hope of the mercy of God.'

These words, recognising the dead man's profession and service but not his family relationships, sound as if they were chosen by medical colleagues; or possibly by people from the village; or maybe even by his solicitor, Mr Crombie, who was winding up his affairs. The final solemn words – 'in hope of the mercy of God' – imply a recognition of deeds in need of forgiveness. The extent of the doctor's transgressions would finally be recognised nine days after the funeral, when the long-delayed inquest into Margaret Brown's death resumed in York.

Chapter 16

THE END OF THE AFFAIR

There was no thousand-strong crowd at Margaret Brown's funeral. Her family had been given permission from the Coroner to bury her after the first day of the inquest into her death. So on Thursday 30 April, four days after her death and after a service at All Saints Pavement church in York, they accompanied her coffin to York Cemetery. The minister at the graveside was the Reverend Edward Smith, curate of All Saints Pavement. Margaret had been christened as a baby and received into the Church of England at St Thomas's church in Lowther Street, near her home. So the Reverend Smith would have used the same service as that used a few days later for her erstwhile lover: 'that as prescribed by the prayer book of the Church of England.' Margaret was buried in a private grave under a willow tree.

The place would have brought back unhappy memories for William and Helen Brown because this was not the first time they had buried a child in York Cemetery. Their third daughter, Ethel, had died in 1895 at the age of nine. The cause of death was recorded as 'dropsy', which would be called oedema, or fluid retention in the tissues, in modern terminology. Dropsy is a symptom rather than a disease; it usually arose from heart, kidney or lung disease. It is possible that Ethel had had a genetic condition affecting her from birth, leading to organ failure. Or she could have developed a disease during childhood which led to the fatal condition. She was buried in York Cemetery on 30 September 1895. Unlike Margaret, Ethel was buried in a public grave.

Burial in a public grave was half the price of burial in a private grave, as the cemetery retained ownership of the grave and only the interment fee and the minister's fee needed to be paid. But it meant that the grave was shared. When the company running the cemetery first offered public graves, their average occupancy settled at 11 bodies. This quickly rose to 24 bodies per public grave, and it could take two months to fill the grave, during which time the grave might be covered with planks to avoid people falling in but it was never properly closed. Complaints about the smell this produced were not uncommon, particularly from the Victorian ladies who used to promenade around the cemetery on Sunday afternoons. This efficiency of grave use was not unique to York. The Sheffield General Cemetery had a public grave with 109 bodies in it. Ethel's was the fifth body to be laid into the public grave, following those of four adults, three men and a woman of 23. All the later bodies were of children, ranging in age from one month to three years. Only three of the occupants of Ethel's grave have memorials on the grave; and they are three of the children. Ethel's memorial, on the kerb on the edge of the grave, reads: 'In Loving Memory of Ethel Agnes Brown, Died 27 September 1895, Aged 9.'

Thirteen years later, perhaps because the family was a little better off, a grey granite plaque was installed to mark Margaret's private grave. Its inscription reads: 'Margaret Eleanor Brown. Died 26th April 1908. Aged 19 years. Always remembered'.

The inquest into her death resumed for its final day on Tuesday 19 May, three weeks after it had begun. There were no more witnesses to call, and the proceedings began with a summing up by Mr Wood, the Coroner. It had been, he said, 'a very prolonged and painful case.' He said he thought the evidence would satisfy the jury that it was a case of abortion (or miscarriage – the reporters' accounts differ on the word he used) and that death was due to peritonitis following upon it. He went on:

'There was no evidence of any disease or natural cause for the miscarriage, and no evidence that any instrument had been used with that intent except a pair of forceps which the medical men agreed were the proper instruments to use if any instruments were required. Nor was there any evidence of drugs having been used. There was evidence of the deceased having had a fall at Thornton Watlass on 1 April and it was possible [some reporters heard 'probable'] that that was the cause of the miscarriage [or 'the trouble'].'

'Dr Gramshaw being dead', the Coroner finished, 'I refrain from any observations whatever upon his proceedings in this case.'

The jury, sent away to consider their verdict, had a lot to think about. They might have recalled the difference of medical opinion about the use of instruments, earlier in the proceedings. Dr Gramshaw had been adamant that he had not used any instruments. Nurse Cook thought that she had seen instruments used more than once. Kenneth Allan, the medical student, had admitted that he could think of no reason 'to interfere with the natural course of events.' So had something been done to Margaret involving medical instruments, or not? And if no instrument had been used, how had the young woman acquired the overwhelming infection that killed her? 'Microbes' one of the medical witnesses had suggested vaguely, could find their way into a body through a doctor's touch, or through the air.

There was also the question of the fall. Annie Wilson, the housemaid at the Rectory where Margaret worked, said that Margaret had 'fallen on one of her knees'. But even Dr Watson, called in by Dr Gramshaw's solicitor, felt that this was too trivial an event to have caused the miscarriage. The Coroner, however, was clearly inviting the jury to conclude that the fall could have been the cause of the 'trouble.' The jury would need to decide how much weight they should give to Margaret's dying declaration, taken by a magistrate, in which she herself said that she thought her miscarriage had been caused by the fall.

Dr Watson had also thrown in some confusion over the condition of Margaret's body at the post-mortem, saying that the changes found suggested that she had already been ill before she arrived in York: he alone seemed to know about a 'shivering fit' she had had on the train to York. Her employers at the Rectory said she had been well when she left for York.

Many of the witnesses had given their views on Margaret Brown during the course of the inquest. Elizabeth Dennison, proprietor of the hotel where Margaret died, was angry with the girl for having 'deceived' her. Nurse Cook had to deny she had ever said that she did not like 'waiting on unmarried women.' The Reverend Whitehead made a point of stressing that Margaret had only been in his employment briefly and was soon to leave because she was not suitable for the post. Matron Thompson from The Retreat hospital also said that she had terminated Margaret's employment during her probationary period because she was not suitable to be a nurse. Annie Wilson, the Rectory housemaid, had been happy to give the inquest all the details of Margaret's letters and presents from her 'gentleman friend' and to report on the girl's excitement when she learned that he was coming to meet her. The jury's job was to set aside the purely personal views, identify the practical, believable information and disentangle the sometimes contradictory medical evidence to arrive at a conclusion about what had happened to cause the death of the 19 year old governess.

The jury was absent from the courtroom for more than two hours. They returned with a verdict that could hardly have been clearer or more damning; they were not interested in protecting reputations or drawing a discrete veil over scandalous events. They concluded that death had been due to 'acute peritonitis caused by septic poisoning introduced into the system by wounds caused by an operation for abortion'.

They had not accepted the Coroner's suggestion, or Margaret's own testimony, that the fall had probably been the cause of a miscarriage. They had rejected Dr Gramshaw's claim that he had not used any instruments on Margaret Brown. They had dismissed Dr Watson's suggestion that Margaret had already had the infection when she arrived in York. Most importantly, they ignored Gramshaw's story that Margaret had miscarried spontaneously and he was only trying to help her in the aftermath. In doing so, they had concurred with Mrs Dennison, who had confronted the doctor about the illegal operations she had read about in the paper and didn't like happening in her hotel.

All the national papers which had been covering the inquest reported the damning verdict. The legal conclusion was that Gramshaw had carried out a botched operation for abortion and caused the death of the young woman. Along the way, it had become apparent that the woman was his mistress and the baby was most likely also his. His subsequent suicide had successfully evaded the prosecution that would have followed, and left his family to deal with the scandal and his disgrace.

Abortion in any form was illegal under the Offences against the Person Act 1861. Section 58 ruled that:

'... whosoever, with intent to procure the miscarriage of any woman whether she be or be not with child, shall unlawfully administer to her or cause to be taken by her any poison or other noxious thing, or unlawfully use any instrument or other means whatsoever with the like intent, shall be guilty of felony, and being convicted thereof shall be liable… to be kept in penal servitude for life …'

However, unlike so-called 'backstreet' abortionists, hardly any doctors were prosecuted for carrying out an abortion. Their patients had no reason to betray their illegal activities, as the operation was one they had solicited and the woman involved could be prosecuted too. Only if the woman died as a consequence of the operation would questions be asked of the practitioner, as had happened in the case of the midwife Emily Jennings in Nottingham. Had the jury at the Assizes come to the same conclusion as the inquest jury into the death of Harriet Brown, Jennings would have suffered the full force of the law. And these were not isolated cases. As late as the 1920s, fifteen percent of maternal deaths were due to illegal abortions. But whether or not the practitioner of a botched and fatal operation for abortion was brought to book, the woman in the case was still dead. The story of her life would always be focused on the manner of her death. But Margaret Brown had lived a life of 19 years before she succumbed to the fatal infection: so who was she, and what choices or circumstances had led her finally to the Glynn Hotel at Easter 1909?

Margaret Eleanor Brown was born in York on 6 February 1889. Her father, William Brown, was employed as a surveyor for the Ordnance Survey. Her mother was Helen Brown. At the time of Margaret's birth, the family had just moved to number 36 Vyner Street in York, a quiet street linking two of the main roads leading out of York to the north. There were already three daughters in the family when Margaret arrived, all of them born in Norwich, where the family had previously lived. The eldest, Alison, was seven years old; Annie was 4, and Ethel was 2. At some point there had been another child: but this one did not survive.

In 1902, the Browns left York to re-settle in Hurstpierpoint, a village in Sussex about 10 miles north of Brighton. Margaret was 13 years of age when the family moved so it is hard to imagine that the Browns would have left their youngest daughter alone in the city, when she still had another year of compulsory school education to complete. But by early 1906, she was certainly in York. Her first child, born in York in early February 1907, was most likely conceived in May 1906, when she was 17. It is possible however that Margaret was neither in Sussex with her parents, nor alone in York, between 1902 and 1906: she could have stayed in the city and lived with her older sister. Annie Brown, who was five years older than Margaret, got married around 1902 at the age of eighteen. Two years later, in October 1904, she had a son, Albert, who was born in York. So maybe Margaret moved in with her married sister in order to remain in the city and finish her schooling. She reached the age of 14, at which education was no longer compulsory, a year later in February 1903. Perhaps she had another motive apart from completing her education: maybe she was aware of Dr Gramshaw's interest in her, young as she was, and wanted to stay in the city for that reason rather than going with her parents and eldest sister Alison to Sussex. If so, this raises the disturbing possibility that Gramshaw was already grooming a girl of twelve, who was also his patient, for a future relationship before the family's departure in 1902.

Could the Browns have suspected Gramshaw's interest in their youngest daughter – or even the other daughters – and was this the reason they moved south? If so, they would surely have insisted on taking the youngest girl with them, and prevented her from returning.

At the inquest, Gramshaw had said that he knew the Brown girls and 'had attended all of them.' Since the Browns left York in 1902, the year before the Gramshaws moved to the city, this must have been while he was dividing his time between Stillington and York. He did not have a formal practice in the city before moving there; but maybe he offered some services and the Brown family were informal patients of his. If so, perhaps this respectable medical man, with a grown-up family of his own, would have seemed exactly the right person for Mr and Mrs Brown to ask to watch over their youngest girl, and her young married sister, in York. Certainly several witnesses – the hotel proprietor, the Rector of Thornton Watlass, the Matron of The Retreat and the landlady at Huntingdon Road – all initially believed that Gramshaw was Margaret's guardian or trustee. If this was the situation, the Brown family must have been wracked with guilt, as well as anger and betrayal, at the outcome of their well-intentioned plan.

It is also possible that they asked no such favour of the doctor, but that he deliberately cultivated the impression that he was Margaret's guardian simply in order to visit her, take her out and about, and buy things for her under a cloak of respectability.

Gramshaw had told the landlady at Huntington Road in August 1907 that the rooms were needed for 'a young lady who was staying in York until she got a situation as a governess, or went to The Retreat as a nurse.' This was six months after Margaret had her first baby: if she did ever live with her sister and brother-in-law, she was not doing so in 1907. At what point did her sister Annie become aware of Margaret's relationship with Dr Gramshaw? Was there a point at which she refused to have her sister living in her household anymore, maybe when it became apparent that she was pregnant?

Gramshaw was never formally acknowledged as the father of Margaret Brown's baby. But he did not deny it at the inquest, avoiding the question by saying that he 'knew the father of the first [child] – I know what she told me.' It is almost certain that it was Gramshaw's baby. As the Coroner pointed out in relation to the second pregnancy, he had done nothing to try to find the person responsible for the situation – Gramshaw said 'it hadn't occurred to him'. And the same logic would apply to the first pregnancy. If Gramshaw was a true guardian or friend to Margaret, he would have been doing everything possible to find out who had impregnated the 17 year old, to get the man to 'do the right thing' by her, and to let her parents know of the crisis. Instead, he delivered the baby himself.

The birth took place on 2 February 1907 at number 169 Haxby Road, just two streets away from Margaret's former family home, and the house she was born in, on Vyner Street. The Haxby Road house was at the end of a terrace on the corner of Haxby Road and Rose Street (previously called White Rose Street). The ground floor of the premises was a shop, trading as a tobacconist in 1902, then as a general shop in 1905; so Margaret's rooms must have been in the flat above. With Gramshaw in attendance, and with the aid of chloroform, Margaret gave birth to a baby girl. She was four days short of her eighteenth birthday. Four weeks later, Gramshaw himself registered the birth at the York Registry Office. The baby's name was recorded as Mary Ronayne Brown, and the mother was listed as 'of no occupation.' The space for the father's name and occupation was struck through. The informant was Dr F. Sidney Gramshaw MD, 'present at birth.' Baby Mary Brown was adopted by a local couple, George and Frances Flatt. He was a baker's van man, and they lived in Groves Lane, less than a mile from Margaret's lodgings on Haxby Road and her childhood home on Vyner Street. The adoption must have happened quite quickly, as Margaret did not have a child with her by August, when she moved into the lodgings on Huntington Road. It is not clear from the reports of the inquest whether Margaret's parents knew about this first pregnancy and their grandchild; or whether this was another stunning blow at a dreadful time for them.

For the rest of 1907 and early 1908, Margaret sought employment: though most of the approaches were made directly by Gramshaw. He recommended her to The Retreat, the Quaker-founded mental health institution in York that led the world in humanitarian care of its patients, as a probationary nurse. She was taken on at the hospital at the end of September 1907. At this time The Retreat had 164 patients, and 90 'nurses and maids' on its staff. Formal training for the hospital's nurses had only begun 10 years before, after significant changes in the approach to care of the mentally ill in asylums. Fifty years before, asylums had little-trained 'attendants', almost all male, to look after their inmates. But during the latter half of the 19th century, there had been increasing recognition of the need for training for these attendants, and by the beginning of the 20th century, both male and female nurses formed a trained, professional workforce that was aligned with, if not entirely integrated with, that of other forms of nursing.

The Retreat's training had originally been a three-year course leading to the award of a certificate. When Margaret joined, training had been extended to four years of practical experience and lectures, to be followed by an examination. This would result in certification by The Retreat, and also by the Medico-psychological Association, which offered a nationally-recognised qualification in mental health nursing. The main text used for training was known as the 'Red Handbook' and its contents demonstrate the demands that this course would have made on Margaret Brown as a probationer nurse. The syllabus covered anatomy and physiology, general nursing skills, understanding of the mind and mental disorders, the care of the insane and the general duties of attendants. The latter included obeying orders, promoting the objects of the institution and furthering the recovery of patients.

The practical demands of a nurse in training were no less arduous. The nurses' breakfast was served at 6.30am and they started their duty at 7.00am. They had a half-hour break at 10.30 – 'Sister and Nurse on the terrace' – then lunch for 30 minutes between midday and 1pm. After tea between 4.30-5.00pm nurses were on duty until 8.30pm when the night nurses came on. Supper was at 8.30pm then the day nurses had to be in their bedrooms by 10pm and 'lights out' at 10.30pm. Days off were one half day and one whole day on alternate weeks. A half-day off was given on two consecutive Sundays, and on the third Sunday, they had one hour off. Once every three weeks, they had four hours off on a Saturday or a Monday. Night nurses had one night off every three weeks.

As the introduction to The Retreat's Rules for Nurses put it:

'The Committee recognise that the work of nursing the insane is frequently arduous, and calls for much self-denial and patience. Mental disorder is one of the saddest forms of human affliction, and those who honestly strive to alleviate this suffering, and minister to the needs of the afflicted in mind, are undoubtedly performing true Christian service. The Committee extend to the nurses warm sympathy and encouragement in their work.'

Such a controlled and demanding environment, with every hour of the day organised and very little time off, might not have been very attractive to Margaret Brown in the throes of her affair with Sidney Gramshaw. Mental health nursing could have been a rewarding and secure career for life; but this was not to be. The Retreat's Matron, Charlotte Thompson, judged Margaret to be unsuitable for the role of nurse only two months into her probationary period. Her employment was terminated at the beginning of December. The management committee, which noted at each meeting 'Changes in the nursing staff', did not concern itself with probationers who did not make it to the status of Nurses. The committee discussed the building of a new recreation room for the nurses, the need to re-roof the gentlemen's verandah, complaints about the conduct of two male attendants, and the sad case of a patient who had been on an escorted visit to relatives when she evaded the nurse accompanying her, and hung herself in a toilet. Margaret's departure is not recorded.

Next Gramshaw answered the Thornton Watlass Rector's advertisement for a governess on Margaret's behalf. The Reverend Whitehead and his wife had four children aged between eight and eleven, so it was not an easy assignment, even with three other servants in the house. And it was a 'live-in' post in Thornton Watlass, a small village nearly 40 miles north of York, making it much more difficult for Gramshaw to visit and spend time with Margaret. She started work there in early February 1908, had holiday in March and April, but was due to leave in May because they had also found her – after only a few weeks in post – unsuitable for the work. The housemaid at the Rectory had reported Margaret's almost daily letters to and from Dr Gramshaw, the gifts of sweets, gloves and a veil, and the clandestine meetings with the 'gentleman friend' in Northallerton. Did Margaret fail to apply herself to this or any of the jobs found for her because she had hopes of better things? Did she believe that ultimately, the tall, 'fine-looking', respected doctor who was so interested in her would set her up in a life of leisure? Maybe she even told herself that he would leave his wife and family and marry her.

It is impossible to know for sure what was the basis of the affair on either side. Margaret may have been genuinely in love with Sidney Gramshaw, and desperately wanting a 'real' relationship with him. Or she might simply have loved the attention she was receiving from such a figure of authority and professional standing, and wanted to exploit his interest for all the material benefits it could provide – including removing the need to earn a living for herself.

Gramshaw might equally have been simply exploiting a willing young girl for some extra-marital excitement without any great commitment or affection. Or could he actually have been besotted with her, dazzled by her contrast with his middle-aged wife, and genuinely wanting a long-term relationship? If so, it was an obsession that must have started when she was a 12-year-old child, and his patient. However naïve, foolish, even conceited Margaret might have been in thinking she could manage this relationship, it was the older man's responsibility to stay away from her. And this was certainly no unique lightning strike of desire, a one-off aberration in his married life: Gramshaw was known to have had more than one affair in Stillington, with other women who were his patients. He was used to gratifying his desires as he wished and he had shown that he could procure extra-marital sex if he wanted it. He had no need to go after the teenager, either before or after she passed the age of consent. This had been set at the age of 16 since the amendment to the Offences against the Person Act in 1885 – but there were exceptions. One of these was for people in a 'position of authority or trust' in relation to a person under 18, in which case the age of consent was 18. This would certainly apply to Gramshaw as he was, or had recently been, the family doctor to the Brown girls. So his inappropriate sexual relationship with Margaret was probably also illegal.

The only known photograph of Margaret is a professional picture which shows her as a young adult. She has a round face with a determined chin and wide-set eyes. Her dark hair is piled elaborately on her head, and dressed with black, white and red flowers. She is wearing a Japanese-looking costume, with a wide black sash at the waist. She appears to be kneeling and she is holding a large fan across her front: she looks like a character from the chorus of The Mikado. This may be a clue to one of her shared interests with Gramshaw – musical theatre and plays – or simply a costume chosen to enhance the glamour of the photograph. Maybe she liked the Oriental look: when she arrived at the hotel in York for Easter in 1908, she brought her belongings in a 'Japanese basket'.

Whatever the nature of their relationship – however genuine or exploitative on either side – the two pregnancies

186

were pivotal moments in it. There were options for contraception at the turn of the twentieth century, and the doctor would have been well aware of them even if Margaret wasn't. Withdrawal was one; and the rhythm method, aimed at avoiding the time of ovulation, was also understood, though difficult to get right. Condoms of various kinds had been used for centuries. So it should been possible for the two lovers to at least try to avoid a pregnancy – though Margaret might have been secretly less concerned about the risk if she thought it might tie Gramshaw closer to her. And Gramshaw might have been more sanguine because he thought, as a doctor, he could sort out the problem should it occur. But the first pregnancy was allowed to run its course, and the child was given away for adoption.

There was about a year between the birth of this child and the start of the second pregnancy. When Margaret came to York in April 1908, saying (according to the letter received by Gramshaw but destroyed by him before it could be produced for others to see) that she wanted to consult him about her health, she was pregnant again. He came to see her at the Glynn Hotel on the day she arrived, the Wednesday before Easter. He visited her again on the Thursday. And on Good Friday, she lost her baby.

What was the conversation between them on that Wednesday and Thursday? Did Margaret hope the news of this baby would convince Gramshaw to set her up somewhere as his mistress, to bring up their child? If that was what she wanted, it may have been anathema to the doctor, if he had no intention of consolidating their affair into some parody of matrimony. In which case, did he, under the guise of examining her, ensure that the foetus would soon be aborted?

Or did Margaret herself ask him to do something to terminate this pregnancy as soon as possible? She had already experienced the pain of labour and childbirth, and then the wrench of giving away her first baby. Perhaps she was horrified to find herself in this position again and expected her lover to use his medical skills to resolve the problem safely and discreetly.

It is interesting that Margaret's dying declaration does not fit either of these scenarios. It was obtained by a magistrate after the intervention of the Chief Constable. The Chief Constable was acting after receiving an anonymous letter suggesting that he should look into the doctor's treatment of the girl. A dying declaration was taken under very specific circumstances: the key was that the person giving it was absolutely sure that they were going to die and no recovery was possible. Only with this conviction could it be assumed that they would tell the entire truth. Margaret had been told that she was dying so she had nothing to lose by telling the truth. Indeed, this was her one chance to cry out against the injustice of her situation, her physical pain and her anguish for the adult life she would never experience.

But she did not say: 'This man got me pregnant and he has aborted my baby against my will.' Nor did she say: 'I asked him to get end this pregnancy, and he did an operation on me that means I'm going to die.' Even though she was talking to a magistrate and her words were being taken down as a legal record to use after her death, Margaret said exactly what Gramshaw would have wanted her to say. She said she hadn't been sure she was pregnant and that she thought the 'bad fall' she had had at the Rectory had caused the 'premature birth'. She said nothing about a relationship with the doctor. She said nothing about an operation for abortion. It seems reasonable to question whether this was because the doctor was in the room with her while the deposition was being taken. After all, he was her doctor, she was dying, and the magistrate might have felt that it would be wrong to ask him to leave. The magistrate had no reason to suspect a sexual relationship between the patient and the doctor; so maybe Gramshaw was able to exert his silent pressure on the girl to say what he would have wanted her to say. Having taken so much from her and inflicted so much on her already, it is possible that, at the very end, he was once again using her in his own interests: hoping to protect himself from potential prosecution and disgrace.

It is also interesting that, in her dying declaration, Margaret talked about 'the child' being 'dead when born'; and the fall being responsible for 'the premature birth.' Unless this was a sanitisation of the statement by the magistrate, mindful that it might one day be read out in court, this would suggest that the pregnancy had progressed to the point at which there was a recognisable baby to deliver. Margaret had been living in at The Retreat from 30 September to 6 December 1907 and started living in at the Rectory on 8 February 1909. So the most likely opportunity for her and Gramshaw to conceive a child was during December and January, when she was out of work and available for clandestine meetings. If it had been conceived any earlier, her pregnancy would have been visible to her employers at the Rectory by April, and they would have cited this as a reason to dismiss her.

If conception happened early in December, she could have been 18 weeks pregnant by Easter in mid-April 1909. If she got pregnant late in January, she would only have been 10 weeks pregnant. The latter would fit better with her not being sure that she was 'in a certain condition'. But at 10 weeks, the foetus is only 4cm long, and it would be hard to describe delivery at this point as the premature birth of a baby: a lay person would call this a miscarriage. If she was in fact 18 weeks pregnant, the foetus would be around 14 cm from head to bottom, and weigh nearly 200g, with legs and arms, toes and fingers fully formed. This would fit better with the idea of the premature delivery of a child; and with Margaret expressly saying that the child was dead when it was born. It would also explain Gramshaw's liberal use of chloroform when he was attending Margaret in the hotel. Kenneth Allan had reported his uncle asking him to bring more chloroform to the hotel. Gramshaw himself had said that Margaret 'did not bear pain well' and had needed chloroform 'last time' – that is, when she was in labour with her first baby.

It does not fit, however, with her expressed uncertainty about whether she was pregnant. By 18 weeks, she would have missed four periods, and experienced numerous symptoms that, as a second-time mother, she would have recognised as signs of pregnancy. But she was dying when she made this statement, suffering from acutely painful peritonitis and a very high fever. It would not be surprising if she was confused and inconsistent in what she said to the magistrate.

It is unfortunate that the letter sent by Gramshaw to his nephew Kenneth Allan, asking him to bring a midwifery bag to the hotel, had been destroyed by Allan before the inquest. Maybe it would have said something about the stage of the pregnancy that he and his uncle were to attend to, or at least the instruments and drugs required to deal with it which might have provided clues. Maybe his uncle told him to destroy the letter to hide the true nature of the situation: that an operation had been performed, not to terminate an early pregnancy, or to deal with an early spontaneous miscarriage; but, at much greater risk, to terminate a pregnancy in the usually safe and stable middle months.

Chapter 17

DR SHORE AND THE TWO MRS SHORES

It might have been possible for Gramshaw, had he wanted to, to have taken Margaret Brown as his wife. A young woman called Annie Wakefield had found herself in a remarkably similar situation to Margaret's, twenty years before, and she had ended up marrying her doctor lover: though the end of her story was no less tragic than Margaret's.

Annie Wakefield was very young, like Margaret Brown: she was only twenty when she got married, though she told the Registrar that she was 23 and so of an age to marry without her parents' permission. So, like Margaret, she was only a teenager when she formed a relationship with an eminent medical man many years her senior:

Dr Offley Bohun Shore. Like Margaret, Annie was much lower in the social scale than her lover: she was working as a servant and barely literate. And there was a similar age gap between the couple: Annie was 20 at the time of her marriage and Offley Shore was 48, while the gap between Margaret and Sidney Gramshaw was seven years longer. Like Sidney Gramshaw, Offley Shore was also married with grown up children.

Unlike the situation in York, however, Shore does not appear to have met his new bride by having her as a patient. Annie worked as a servant for a farmer in a village near Spalding, in Lincolnshire. And while Shore had worked for the hospital at Stamford in Lincolnshire many years before, he had not done so for twenty years before his second marriage. It is not clear how Shore met Annie Wakefield, nor why he chose to marry her. Because, like Gramshaw, he had not lacked for extra-marital excitement during his marriage.

Offley Shore had married Anna Maria Leishman in Edinburgh in 1861, where he had undertaken his medical training. Her father was a 'Writer to the Signet' – a form of solicitor – and Anna Maria was his eldest daughter. The couple had three children: a son named Offley after his father and grandfather, and two daughters, Florence and Urith. Shore stopped practising medicine and speculated financially to the point that he was declared bankrupt. In June 1878, when their youngest child was just 13, the Shores separated. Offley Shore was then living in London and it was there that he was found to be having a number of affairs. The marriage ended in divorce, with the petition brought, unusually for those times, by the aggrieved wife.

Prior to the Matrimonial Causes Act of 1857, divorce was only possible by an ecclesiastical annulment of the marriage, or through a private (and very expensive) Act of Parliament, which had to be debated in the House of Commons. The Act recognised that marriage was a contract that came under the jurisdiction of the secular courts rather than a religious sacrament, and it removed divorce from the ecclesiastical courts. It established the Court for Divorce and Matrimonial Causes in London to deal with petitions for divorce: still an expensive business, but more readily achievable for women with some means. Mary Gramshaw might have been able to call on her family's money to pay for a divorce, because, like Anna Maria Shore, she had a father in a professional occupation: William Poole had been a banker.

However, the Act was not even-handed in its treatment of the divorcing couple. A man filing for divorce had to prove only that his wife had committed adultery: the sole grounds on which a divorce could be granted. But a woman seeking a divorce had to prove not only her husband's adultery but also that he was guilty of bigamy, desertion, cruelty, sodomy, bestiality or incest. Emily Pankhurst was reported to have commented on this difference saying:

'According to man-made law a wife who is even once unfaithful to her husband has done him an injury which entitles him to divorce her ... On the other hand, a man who consorts with prostitutes, and does this over and over again throughout his married life, has, according to man-made law, been acting only in accordance with human nature, and nobody can punish him for that.'

So Anna Maria Shore's petition for divorce cited both desertion and adultery:

> 'That in or about the month of June 1878 the said Offley Bohun Shore separated himself from your Petitioner and has never since cohabited with her and that he has deserted your Petitioner without reasonable excuse for two years and upwards …
>
> That on numerous occasions in and since the month of November 1885 the said Offley Bohun Shore has committed adultery with a woman whose name is unknown to your Petitioner at Number 23 Haymarket in the County of Middlesex.'

Shore's response to the petition probably came as a surprise to his wife. Nearly eight years after their separation, and in spite of her conviction that he was having an affair with another woman, he denied everything and asked the court to reject the divorce petition. Maybe he was concerned about his reputation and did not want to bear the stigma of divorce. Anna Maria had to amend her divorce petition to insert a new paragraph, before resubmitting it to the court:

> 'That on numerous occasions during the years 1883 and 1884 the said Offley Bohun Shore committed adultery with a woman whose name is unknown

to your Petitioner at Number five Jermyn Street in
the County of Middlesex.'

Presumably some searches and detective work had
taken place between the two petitions to find these new
accusations of adultery. Whether Anna Maria knew about
the other affair before, or if this came as a further shock
to her, is impossible to say. When the court convened
for the final hearing on the case, Shore himself did not
attend. The petition was considered sufficiently proved, a
decree nisi was granted, and costs were awarded against
Offley Shore. The divorce enabled Shore to marry again
just eight months after his decree absolute; though why he
chose to marry the young woman Annie Wakefield is hard
to fathom. She had no money, status, influential family
or friends, and no obvious hold over him. Maybe Offley
Shore was simply besotted by the girl; and maybe Annie
Wakefield was dazzled by his interest and saw the chance
for a much better life.

Could Gramshaw have done the same and married
Margaret Brown? He could not have initiated a divorce,
unless he had evidence that his wife Mary had committed
adultery, and there is no suggestion that this was ever
the case. Mary could have divorced him, providing she
could cite additional grounds to his adultery: he was still
living with her, so desertion would not work. But she
could perhaps have found grounds to claim cruelty. But
maybe Gramshaw did not want her to divorce him: he
had more to lose from the social scandal of divorce than
Shore had done. Offley Shore was a bankrupt, a speculator

who moved on from losing money in overseas companies to an unsuccessful scheme to mine for boron in Iceland. Sidney Gramshaw had a long-standing medical practice, Freemasonry, high offices in social and cultural societies, membership of medical organisations and civic dinners to consider. His reputation was far more valuable to him and being divorced by his wife would have been a massive blow to his credibility and respectability. And Mary Gramshaw might have had exactly the same considerations: she had a house, servants and a position in society; she attended civic dinners and hosted events in the city alongside her husband. Maybe she preferred not to expose the state of her marriage and not to have to start again as a divorced woman. Whatever she might have secretly hoped, Margaret Brown probably never had a chance of becoming the second Mrs Gramshaw.

The second Mrs Shore did not get the happy ending she might have envisaged either. By 1891, four years after the marriage, the two Shores seemed to be living separate lives in Holborn, London. Although sharing the same address as her husband, Annie is described on the census as 'Head of household' and 'living on own means.' In the same year, someone informed the Registrar that there was a 'mistake' on the Shore's marriage certificate. A hand-written correction to the certificate was added by the Registrar, and it was clearly a serious business to do so: the correction was made in the presence of the Superintendent Registrar and two witnesses – neither of them the parties to the marriage. The change is to the column for the ages of the parties, and the entry under Annie Wakefield's name reads: 'for 23 years, read 20 years.' At that time, the age at which a woman could marry without her parents' consent was 21. Whether Offley Shore did not know Annie's true age – she had inflated her years in previous census returns – or he did not expect to get her parents' consent to the marriage, is unknown. Maybe he was already regretting the marriage, and Shore himself was the informant, hoping that the evidence of deception would be grounds for an annulment. Certainly it seems that Dr Shore had quickly lost interest in his new wife. According to the family history, Shore met a man called Edwin Harris in The Oaks Club in London; and when Harris admired Annie, Offley Shore told him, 'If you like her, take her.'

Edwin Harris and Annie Shore became common-law man and wife. Harris was much closer to Annie's age, and in him she seems to have finally found someone who truly loved her. The two lived together in Streatham, London, until Annie's death in August 1906. Harris buried Annie in his family grave at Manor Park Cemetery, Forest Gate, Essex. The gravestone inscription reads: 'In loving memory of my devoted wife Annie who passed away 13th August 1906 aged 39 years.' A year later, Harris made a more formal marriage; but he kept a portrait of Annie Shore above his bed, which his new wife tried to pass off to a visitor as a portrait of her own mother. He also named his first daughter after Annie. When he died, he was buried in the same family grave as Annie Shore.

Harris's devotion is all the more touching because Annie Shore died of syphilis. It is unclear how the young woman contracted the disease, as neither Offley Shore nor

Edwin Harris seem to have suffered from it. But Annie lived with the ravages of the awful disease through to the dreaded tertiary stage, when the brain as well as the body is affected. Annie died of 'exhaustion due to general paralysis of the insane' in Camberwell House Asylum in London. In a final unhappy parallel with the Gramshaw family, one of them too would die in an asylum less than a year after the deaths of Margaret Brown and Sidney Gramshaw.

Chapter 18

THE WIDOW, THE DENTIST AND THE YOUNG LADY'S TEETH

It is hardly surprising that Mary Gramshaw left York as soon as she possibly could. She was labouring under a triple personal and social burden: the public exposure of her husband's affair with a teenager; his responsibility for the young woman's death and the abortion of their baby; and his suicide.

Social attitudes to suicide had changed radically in the preceding 50 years. It was no longer inevitably seen as an unforgivable sin against God, society and the family, according to a major study of suicide in Victorian and Edwardian England. From a practical perspective, the state no longer punished the family by confiscating all the dead person's possessions. Different circumstances and motivations for the act were recognised: four genres of suicide became familiar, described as 'the sad, the wicked, the strange and the comic'. Plays, songs and stories frequently used suicide as a plot device, making it common parlance for every class of society. Suicide was considered an escape from sexual dishonour for women and from worldly dishonour for men – and Gramshaw's suicide would fall squarely into this latter category. However, both he and the family he left behind paid the price for that. Although there was much greater understanding of, and sympathy for, the person who committed suicide in most cases, there was an exception. The study's author notes that:

> 'At the end of the 18th century, ordinary people condoned most cases of suicide and subscribed to "temporary insanity..." [but that] 'Outright condemnation was meted out to the rare case which forfeited sympathy by embarking on self-destruction in cold blood, or from self-interest, or as part of a chain of misdeeds ...'
>
> 'The investigation of suicide [in the early 20th century] had been taken over by professionals, and hand in hand with this and other less tangible changes, perhaps, had come the shrinkage of this way of death into an awkward topic best avoided instead of yet another familiar part of the human condition.'

No wonder Mrs Gramshaw wanted to get away from her life in York. Her friends and acquaintances, however shocked and sympathetic to her, would have struggled for some way to address the 'awkward topic', combined as it was with the equally awkward matters of adultery, illegitimate children, medical malpractice and (what could have been) manslaughter. She might have taken some comfort in the 1000-strong attendance at her husband's funeral; but that took place before the damning conclusion of the Margaret Brown inquest and its coverage by the local and national press. She could not count on public sympathy surviving long once the jury's verdict was out. After 39 years of marriage, and 35 years as the wife of the respected local doctor, singing in concerts and hosting receptions at his side, her life had changed irrevocably.

Mary Gramshaw fled south, moving in to live with her youngest son, Guy, in Basingstoke in Hampshire. Guy was 28, unmarried, and working as a travelling tea salesman when he took in his now-widowed mother and his older sister Amy. They lived together in Fairfield Road in Basingstoke – ironically, less than 80 miles away from Hurstpierpoint, where the Brown family had re-settled after leaving York. Meanwhile, back in the city, the Gramshaw's former residence at number 78 Bootham passed on to another medical man, Joseph Dawson, physician and surgeon. And the family solicitors, George Crombie and Sons, proceeded with the settling of the late Dr Gramshaw's estate.

The firm had long represented the Gramshaws. They had acted for them in the case of the assault on the Gramshaw's two eldest sons in 1892. They would have instructed the Queen's Counsel who defended Gramshaw in the action by the engineer to recover apprenticeship fees for Cecil Gramshaw. And Norman Crombie had represented Dr Gramshaw at Margaret Brown's inquest during the first two days of evidence. Then he had represented the widow and the family at Gramshaw's own inquest, all in the space of ten days. Now the firm was winding up his estate, starting with the provisions of his very detailed Will.

Norman Crombie himself was an executor of the Will, along with Dr Henry Foster, the friend who had tried to defend Gramshaw's actions at the inquest. To his widow Mary, Gramshaw left 'all the jewels, trinkets and ornaments worn or used by her during my lifetime'. He also left her all his books (except his medical books), prints, pictures, ornaments and musical instruments, as well as his 'solitaires' and 'the plain gold ring I am accustomed to wear': presumably his wedding band. In addition, his executors were to pay her 25 pounds. His other jewellery and valuables were divided amongst his children: Cecil, the eldest, was to have his gold watch and chain, his sporting gun and case, and his engraved onyx seal. William Gramshaw was left 'my signet ring presented to me by Mrs Harding and my wife', as well as a picture of Sidney Gramshaw's brother, Captain Leonard H Gramshaw, and the Captain's sword. The Captain, from the Royal Fusiliers, had died of a fever in Burma in 1890 at the age of just 34. The eldest daughter Amy received the carbuncle ring Gramshaw had been given by his father; and her younger sister Hilda received a gold signet ring. Both young women were also to be given 10 pounds.

Guy Gramshaw, the youngest sibling, was left his father's engraved Indian ring and a silver watch.

After these bequests, the rest of Gramshaw's belongings, including his medical books, medical appliances and all the household furniture with 'indoor and outdoor effects' were to be sold, and the money raised added to his personal estate. The two executors were then to invest these monies and divide the income from the investments equally between Mrs Gramshaw during her lifetime – 'if she shall so long remain my widow' – and Amy Gramshaw. If either of these women died, then their share would go to Hilda Gramshaw. After the deaths of both Mary and Amy Gramshaw, the trust should be wound up and the money divided equally between his surviving children.

There were two more important provisions in Gramshaw's Will. His medical practice was to be sold as a going concern; and 'all manuscripts, letters and like matter belonging to me shall immediately after my decease be destroyed by my trustees.' Was this simply good housekeeping; or was it intended to ensure that any letters he might have kept from Margaret Brown would not fall into the hands of his family after his death?

It is particularly significant that the date of Gramshaw's Will – revoking all previous Wills – is 3 May 1908: right in the middle of the Margaret Brown inquest proceedings. This was a Sunday, the day before the second session of the inquest. On the first day of the proceedings, Gramshaw's attendance on Margaret Brown (in two pregnancies), the landlady's suspicions of an illegal operation at the hotel and the anonymous letter to the police urging them to look into Gramshaw's conduct had all been exposed. Day two, due the day after the Will was signed, would hear from the Rectory housemaid, who could testify about the affair between the doctor and the governess, and from the doctors who carried out the post-mortem and would give their views on the cause of death. Before attending the second day of the inquest, Gramshaw got his solicitor to draw up a new Will for him and he signed it on the Sunday the presence of two witnesses: his nephew Kenneth Allan and the housemaid Eleanor Compton. So at the very least, his solicitor, his nephew and the housemaid – and possibly his friend Dr Henry Foster, the other trustee named in the Will – all knew that he had seen fit to write a detailed new Will that weekend. Yet all of them appeared to be taken by surprise when Gramshaw took an overdose of morphia less than 48 hours later, on Monday night, after the second day in court.

Unfortunately for Mary Gramshaw, her own jewellery, his wedding ring and an income for life was not all that Gramshaw left her. Over a year after the doctor's death, Norman Crombie was once again representing the family in court. This time it was to defend a claim against Mrs Gramshaw, as administratrix of her husband's estate.

'Echo of a York Case', read the headline in the York Evening Post. 'Doctor and the young lady's teeth.'

Recounting what it called 'a sequel to the famous York sensation, which caused such interest in York a year ago', the article set out the court case. Mr Alfred Segar, a dentist living in The Mount in York, was suing Mrs Gramshaw for £3 9s 6d 'for professional services rendered, at Dr

Gramshaw's request, to Miss M E Brown, now deceased'. The dentist claimed that Margaret Brown had been brought to him by Dr Gramshaw, who represented himself as the young woman's guardian, and promised to pay for the services rendered at each visit. Mr Segar had said that that would not be convenient, so it was agreed that Dr Gramshaw would pay for the work when it was completed. Gramshaw accompanied the patient 'on nearly every visit, and on one occasion administered an anaesthetic.'

Cross-examined by the defending solicitor, the dentist admitted that he had entered the work into his books in the name of Miss Brown. Then, in what was probably a heavily ironic under-statement, he added that 'If a lady were brought to him by a doctor under ordinary circumstances, he would not look to the doctor for payment, but this was an exceptional case.'

Questioned by the judge, Segar confirmed that he had only ever sent his account to Dr Gramshaw. He had not sent an account to Miss Brown 'because she had died before the time arrived for rendering it.' This is interesting timing: assuming the dentist did not normally wait for months before sending his account to a patient or their representative then the dental work on Margaret Brown must have taken place only a few weeks or months before her death. This would be during the time that she was working at the Rectory in North Yorkshire. It also adds to the many occasions that Gramshaw was seen in the company of the young woman: taking her to her lodgings in Huntington Street, visiting her there almost every day, meeting her in Northallerton, taking her to the dentist in

York. No wonder he cultivated the impression that he was her guardian: he could not have hoped to keep all of these occasions a secret from family, friends or acquaintances.

Norman Crombie stepped up once again to try to mitigate the troubles of the Gramshaws. He said that he did not dispute the amount of the claim but he did dispute the legal position. The whole course of the business relationship between the people involved, he proposed, showed that Alfred Segar was looking to Miss Brown for payment – a claim that ran directly counter to the dentist's account of conversations about paying for the treatment. Crombie also pleaded the statute of fraud, and contended that, whatever the merits of the case might be, there could be no question on the legal aspect, that the plaintiff was not entitled to recover his fees from his client.

The judge disagreed. His Honour said that, in his judgement, the plaintiff was entitled to recover the costs because 'There were peculiar circumstances in the case and he thought that Dr Gramshaw made himself absolutely responsible to pay in the first instance.'

He gave judgement for the dentist for the full amount, plus the legal costs. So, in a final humiliation, Mary Gramshaw had to pay the dentist's fees for the treatment provided to her husband's mistress. And the local press made sure that her old acquaintances in York knew about it.

Mary Gramshaw lived with her son Guy for the rest of her life. By 1920 they had moved to Basingstoke Road, Reading. And it was there that she died in 1921, at the age of 68. Her estate, such as it was – worth £47 11s 2d – was left to her eldest son, Cecil Henry Gramshaw, Engineer.

Chapter 19

AFTERMATH – THE SONS

The Gramshaw sons went on to have long and successful lives after their parents' deaths; unlike the Gramshaw daughters, who faced much darker fates. And some of the women associated with the Gramshaw sons might also have felt that fate had dealt them a harsh hand.

Cecil Gramshaw's career in engineering did not start well. When he was employed as an apprentice at the Electrical Engineering Corporation at the age of 17, the firm's premises in London burned down and the company folded. Transferred to Dublin as an apprentice to a consulting engineer from the former Corporation, Gramshaw felt that things were not properly explained to him, and that he was not learning anything. So he left his apprenticeship and took up a salaried post instead.

The consulting engineer took his father to court for the balance of the apprenticeship fees and won.

Cecil Gramshaw continued in the profession, however, and become a qualified electrical engineer, with a certificate from Finsbury Technical College in London. He was one of the first students at the College, which only opened in 1893, as part of the 'City and Guilds of London Institute for the Advancement of Technical Education' set up by 16 of the City's Livery Companies. In 1905, while he was living in York, he followed in his father's footsteps and became a Freemason in the York Lodge. He might have emulated his father in other ways too: he seems to have created some confusion about his age. He told the Lodge that he was 30 years old when he was initiated in 1905. This would put his date of birth as 1875. In fact, he was born in 1872, and was 32 when he was admitted, his 33rd birthday being late in the year. Perhaps he just wanted to appear to have achieved entry to the Lodge at a younger age than his father, who had been 31 when he joined the Lodge in 1885.

Like his mother, Cecil seems to have left York in the wake of his father's death in 1908 since his record of fees paid to the Lodge ends in that year. In October 1916, Gramshaw married Marie (or Mary) Sampson in Lambeth. In the 1911 Census, however, Gramshaw completed and signed the form showing himself as having been married for two years: that is, married in 1909, the year after his father's death. He records that he is living with his wife Marie, who is aged 34 to his 39 years, and there are no children of the marriage. Gramshaw was working as an electrical engineer in the oil industry, while Marie was employed in 'manufacture'. Whatever the circumstances of their relationship, in 1911 the couple was living in Earlsfield, Wandworth, in south west London. They stayed in London for a while, living in Lambeth and Wimbledon before moving out to Twickenham by 1918. During the First World War, Cecil Gramshaw was a Captain in the City of London Police Reserve, as Officer Commanding 'C' division. There is a picture of him in 1917, with other officers from the Reserve, wearing the uniform of a double-breasted coat over white shirt and dark tie, leather gloves and peaked cap. He is of average height and stands slightly round-shouldered: like most of his fellow-officers, he has a neat moustache.

By 1920, Cecil Gramshaw and his wife had left London and were living in Western Elms Avenue, Reading. This was the same city that was home to his mother and younger brother Guy, who had moved from Basingstoke to live on Basingstoke Road, Reading. Their houses were less than three miles apart. The couple stayed in Reading until at least 1925, before moving back to west London in the 1930s. Since the electoral rolls (which, from 1918, showed all the adult members of the household, both male and female) do not show Marie Gramshaw with Cecil Gramshaw at any of his addresses throughout the 1930s, it seems likely that they had parted company. Where she went and why remains a mystery: but it seems that she died in Nottingham – the county of her birth – in 1963 at the age of 85. Marie and Cecil Gramshaw left no children from their marriage.

In 1929, Cecil Gramshaw applied to be made a Freeman of the City of London 'by redemption' (that is, upon a payment), with his profession listed as 'Electrical Engineer' and premises at 75b Queen Victoria Street, EC4 – although he is not listed as a member of the Institution of Electrical Engineers. The Freedom of the City is awarded to people who have achieved success, recognition or celebrity in their chosen field, and Gramshaw could have been admitted as a Freeman of a Livery Company relevant to his profession. He would need to obtain the Freedom of the City in order to proceed to be 'clothed in the livery' of his Company. However, 'by redemption' means that he paid a fee for the application, which would not be the case if he was presented by his Livery Company; so it is not entirely clear what his motivation was for seeking the privilege.

Gramshaw remained in London for the rest of his life. He lived in Fulham for several years, in Ruskin Mansions. In 1933, he was at number 9 Ruskin Mansions. At number 8 lived a Miss Clara Bryant and Mrs Evangeline Maconachie. In 1938, the electoral register shows that Gramshaw was now living at number 8 Ruskin Mansions with Clara Bryant and Mrs Maconachie. Later he moved to Floriston Gardens in Stanmore, Middlesex. During the Second World War, he was a Captain in the Home Guard whilst in his 70s, working as a liaison officer and earning the right to the War Medal and the 1939-45 star. He died in Rupert House nursing home in Edgware in May 1951 at the age of 78. Interestingly, he wrote a new Will, revoking all previous Wills and codicils, on 29 April 1951, just two weeks before he died. In it he left his interest in the house at Floriston Gardens to Miss Clara Bryant, suggesting that they had been co-habiting since the 1930s when he moved in with her and Mrs Maconachie at Ruskin Mansions. He left a ring with the family crest – the demi-griffin segreant – to his brother William: this may have been the ring on which his father had failed to pay excise duty; or, more likely, since Sidney Gramshaw did not leave a signet ring to his eldest son, Cecil may have bought his own ring with the family crest. The rest of his estate, valued at just over £344 (worth around £11,726 today), was strangely left not to Clara Bryant, but to 'my friend Alexander Norman', a Company Director who was also the sole executor of the Will.

Guy Gramshaw too left Reading after his mother's death. He had a peripatetic occupation as a commercial traveller selling tea, so he may have had first-hand knowledge of many parts of the country. Interestingly, in 1891, when Guy was still living at home in Stillington at the age of eight, his parents had a boarder at their house called Richard Hilhouse, who was a retired tea merchant. Maybe he had influenced the young boy with his stories of the tea trade – a thriving business in the late nineteenth and early twentieth century. In 1851, when almost all the tea in Britain came from China, annual consumption per head was less than 2lbs. But by 1901, with cheaper imports from India and Sri Lanka (then called Ceylon), consumption had trebled to over 6lbs per head. Tea was so important to Britain that during both world wars, the Government took over importation of the product to ensure it continued to be available.

So Guy was in a successful and stable occupation. He chose to settle in Devon, which was the birthplace of his wife, Elsie Parish, whom he had married in Reading in 1917. Sadly, Elsie died in 1924 at the age of 31. Two years later, Guy married again. His second wife was also a Devon woman, called Olive Hannaford, born in Totness. By 1939, the Gramshaws were living in Paignton, and Guy had changed his profession: he was now a credit broker, a job that required less time away from home. Their marriage lasted 40 years, until they both died in 1966. He too seems to have left no children.

The third Gramshaw brother, William, was a company man. In 1943 he celebrated 50 years' service with his firm, putting a notice in the local paper thanking friends and acquaintances for their congratulations. The company was George Harker and Co, Ltd, of London, established in 1826; and William Gramshaw had started there in 1893 at the age of 18. The company was originally a drysalters and stationers operating in dried fish, oil and spices. Later it extended its interests, becoming a specialist importer of rice, pulses, dried fruit, canned goods, spices, nuts and foreign produce generally. The company even owned its own ship that coasted between London and Scotland. It had 'retail agents' in all parts of the country, and its representatives toured the country in horse drawn coaches; they could be absent from the London offices for up to three months at a time.

William himself lived in Exeter and listed his occupation as 'Commercial traveller', so he was likely to be one of the firm's retail agents. He was sufficiently senior however to represent the firm at the funeral of Walter Hibberd, who was the senior director of a similar company of wholesale provision merchants in Exeter. William became a regular attendee at meetings of the Exeter Commercial Travellers' Association. His wife, Clara, meanwhile, featured frequently in the local papers playing in, and often winning, croquet tournaments.

William was not unusual in being a long-serving employee of George Harker and Co. In 1926, its centenary year, the firm hosted a dinner to celebrate the anniversary at which it lauded the contribution of 38 employees who between them had 1422 years of service – the average length of service being 37 years. As a newspaper reported admiringly:

'If their total years' service were carried back from present to past, the first man would have started less than 100 years after the Romans left Britain … Some of them have retired on pension. Others who still work include Mr B. Hallett who has 61 years' service and still carries on as a traveller at the age of eighty-four. The veteran of the warehouse, Mr A. Clarke, aged 82, has been with the Company for sixty-six years. A number of others have been employed more than half a century.'

William Gramshaw had married Clara Carter, who was 10 years his senior, in 1903. Seven years later, they were living in Exeter with Clara's sister Minnie also in the household; and they had no children. Like his brother Cecil, William served as a Special Constable during the First World War. He was sworn in in July 1915 and in January 1917, at a special reception at Exeter Guildhall, he and many others received badges and armlets in recognition of their service. Alderman Campion, Chairman of the Watch Committee, described the events leading up to the creation of the badges:

'In August, 1914, to provide adequately for all eventualities, the Watch Committee authorised the Chief Constable to enrol and organise an entire force of special constables. Up to the end of 1914 the number enrolled was 100 ... and at the end of 1915 127 were performing beat duty for three hours a day on two days a week ... Almost the whole of those who had joined the force had undergone some instruction in police duty, and each batch before being placed on duty had been inspected and addressed by the Mayor. A short time ago it was suggested by a special constable that some little mark of service should be awarded, and on the recommendation of the Chief Constable the Watch Committee decided to institute a service bar for each 50 attendances on duty, and also to award with the first service bar earned a new coat badge which could be worn when off duty by those who desired to do so ... the bar and badge were by no means valuable in themselves, but in the City at least they would distinguish their wearers as men who had done and were doing honourable and necessary service during the present war.'

Amongst the 110 men who were presented with their badges and armlets that evening, William received a badge and one bar, showing that he had been on special duty at least 50 times.

Like his younger brother Guy, William married twice. Clara Gramshaw died in January 1936 at the age of 74. Later that year, William re-married. By the time he was celebrating his 50 years with the company, he was married to May Sharrocks, who was 22 years younger than him. William died in Exeter in 1965, one year before his younger brother. As neither he nor Guy Gramshaw seems to have left a Will, it is impossible to know what happened to the family's signet ring with the demi-griffin crest, which Sidney Gramshaw had left to William.

The Yorkshire Evening Post, covering the death of Dr Gramshaw, reported that he left a widow and three sons, 'one of whom had served in the South Africa War.' This war, also called the Second Boer War, took place between October 1899 and May 1902. So it would not have been Guy who went to fight – he was only 16 years old when it started, and barely 18 when it ended. Cecil and William were 26 and 24 years old in 1899 – of an age to choose to volunteer if they wished. And a few years earlier, in 1891, there was a second boarder in the Gramshaw household in Stillington, in addition to the retired tea merchant who might have influenced Guy. The other boarder was William Gourlie, a 40-year-old who had been pensioned out of the army due to 'injuries received in South Africa.' So maybe he fought in the first Anglo-Boer War, between December

1880 and March 1881; and maybe he influenced the older Gramshaw boys with his war stories.

Neither Cecil nor William Gramshaw appears in the 1901 UK census return, suggesting that they were both out of the country when it was taken in April that year. It is possible that William was in South Africa, as his company had four employees who served in this conflict. But William does not appear on the list of those who received a campaign medal for the war, nor does he appear as an officer or 'other ranks' in the records, so it is more likely that his absence was due to reasons other than the war. However Cecil, the eldest of the Gramshaw sons, is in the records: he did go to South Africa and received a campaign medal for doing so.

The medal is listed in the records of the South African Constabulary (SAC), which had been formed in October 1900, and was fully ready and trained with 7,500 men by May 1901. The SAC was established by Major General R S Baden-Powell (who went on to form the scouting movement in the UK) and was originally intended to be the police force in the Transvaal and Orange River Colony, as it was thought that the hostilities would soon be over. However, it used military ranks and initially drew on men already in the military to form its force, later also recruiting men from England and Canada. As the war continued, the number of the Constabulary was increased to 10,000 and a Reserve Division was also raised: it was this unit that Gramshaw joined. The force's actions in its first two years' service were more military than civilian policing:

'From the time the Force was raised until the end of the War it was not able to undertake Police duties, but was employed as a Military Force under the Commander-in-Chief, and was constantly engaged in field operations and on Blockhouse lines. 9 Officers and 85 men were killed in action or died from wounds, and 213 Officers and Men were wounded, whilst 274 Officers and Men died from sickness.'

Cecil Gramshaw joined the Reserve Division in 1901 under the command of Major H W Wilberforce. He held the rank of Lance Corporal – the second of three 'other ranks', above private but below corporal – and wore the khaki uniform and Stetson hat designed by Baden-Powell. All recruits to this 'police' force were given 'a certain amount of military training. The drill in use by the Mounted Infantry was taken as a standard, and all ranks were instructed in simple movements, riding, the use of the rifle, Maxim gun, and semaphore signalling.' In June 1901, when Gramshaw was in South Africa, the SAC had 229 Officers and 8349 men in the ranks. There were also nine nursing sisters, two civilian clerks and 712 'natives'. The records also keep a tally of the horses, mules and oxen, reflecting their strategic importance to the force: in 1901, numbers were 5122, 512 and 693 respectively.

Gramshaw was discharged from the Constabulary in September 1901, after less than a year in the force. This may not have been by his choice: questions were asked in the British Parliament about the down-sizing of the

Constabulary, and the discharge of men who had signed up in 1901 for three years' service, but found themselves dismissed earlier 'with only the cost of their railway fare to Capetown.'

For his service in South Africa, Cecil Gramshaw was entitled to the Queen's South Africa (QSA) campaign medal, with clasps for Belmont and Transvaal. The South Africa medal had been ordered by Queen Victoria and after her death, approved for use by the new King. Struck from silver, with the Queen's head on the front and Britannia on the reverse, it was issued to all British and Colonial soldiers as well as ancillary support staff such as nurses, who met the criteria of serving in South Africa after October 11th, 1899. Altogether around 450,000 to 500,000 QSAs were issued.

Clasps are metal bars bearing the name of a particular town or military engagement, worn on the ribbon above the medal. Gramshaw's entitlement to the two clasps helps to define the time he spent in South Africa and sheds light on his other roles in the country. The Belmont clasp was for 'all troops under Lieutenant-General Lord Methuen's command who were north of Witteputs (exclusive), on November 23rd, 1899.' This very specific condition suggests that Gramshaw must have been in the country very soon after the start of the war in October 1899 – if not earlier – and prior to his joining the South African Constabulary Reserve Division. Practical preparations for the war had been underway from very early in 1899, with troops in the country preparing the infrastructure necessary to support the soldiers and deal in due course with prisoners and civilian detainees. An account of the work of engineers in these preparations says:

'They included the preparation of camps for the original concentrations, for permanent garrisons, and for prisoners of war; the erection of huts for cantonments, for prisoners of war, for hut hospitals, and for the accessory buildings of general hospitals (under canvas); the erection of storehouses and sheds for every purpose, of stables, remount establishments with all their accessories, such as kraals, sick lines, dipping troughs, etc., etc., and of quarters and offices. In this direction accessory buildings were put up for hospitals for 20,000 and hut wards for 6,000 beds; hut barracks were erected for 7,500 men and for 8,500 prisoners of war; 210,000 square feet of floor space of covered storage was arranged, also sheds and stabling for 10,000 horses, kraals, watering and feeding arrangements for 53,000 horses and mules. All this construction work included water supply, drainage, sanitary services and maintenance. The lighting, largely electric, was carried out by the search-light sections and the Electrical Engineer Volunteers.'

It seems likely that Cecil Gramshaw, with his training in electrical engineering, was one of these volunteers in South Africa. The Electrical Engineer Volunteer Corps came from all over the UK and were attached to the Royal Engineers. Cities such as London, Newcastle and Durham sent several corps of engineers; and the major counties of Scotland and England, including Aberdeenshire, Cheshire, Gloucestershire, Hampshire, Lanarkshire, Northamptonshire and West Yorkshire, sent more. Gramshaw had started his electrical engineering apprenticeship in London and could have joined one of a number of engineering corps from the city.

The relevance of 23 November 1899 is that it marked the midpoint of a campaign led by Lord Methuen. He had been ordered to take his troops from the Orange River to the Modder River, establish communications with the town of Kimberley, and hold the line so that the army could bring up heavy guns and stores to pass into Kimberley. The units under his command included 'certain Royal Engineer details'. The march to Kimberley began on 21 November: Belmont (for which the clasp was named) and Witteputs (the marker for those who were eligible) were two of the villages along the railway line that marked the path of the advance towards the Modder River. On 28 November the troops attempted to cross the river but met fierce resistance from the Boers. The Battle of Modder River led to the loss of 70 British men and officers with more than 400 wounded. Gramshaw must have been involved in this expedition – though the engineers were not in the front line – to earn the Belmont clasp. A separate 'Modder River' clasp was issued to men who were actually with Lord Methuen at the river on 28 November.

Just over a year later, sometime in 1901, Gramshaw joined the new South African Constabulary Reserve Division. To be eligible for the Transvaal clasp, Gramshaw was required to have been in the Transvaal region between 24 May 1900 and 15 July 1901. As the Transvaal was one of the two regions (with the Orange Free State) which the SAC was intended to patrol, it could be his SAC service that earned him this recognition; or he could have been there in his engineer capacity.

As well as his medals, Gramshaw was also entitled to some pride in his final unit, the South African Constabulary, as it was lavishly praised in the House of Commons after the end of the war. Joseph Chamberlain, Secretary of State for the Colonies, said in a speech in the House in 1903:

'I attach the utmost importance to the South African Constabulary, to the new Force, as a great civilising and uniting influence. (Hear, Hear) It may have been regarded in the past exclusively from its military capacity, and indeed during the War, it distinguished itself under military command, and some of the most gallant little actions of the War conferred the greatest credit on the members of the Force.'

When the Constabulary was wound up in 1908, to be replaced by two separate police forces, the High Commissioner for South Africa wrote to the Inspector General of the SAC to praise 'its record of unstained honour and public utility' and predicted that 'its fame will long remain in South Africa.'

Cecil Gramshaw's successful two years in South Africa marked something of a watershed for him: because when he set off for the continent, he left behind a wife and child in Dublin; and when he returned, he seemed to have lost all interest in this family.

Chapter 20

THE FAMILY IN MERCHANT'S QUAY

Robert Ladley was having a hard life even before he met Cecil Gramshaw. He was a widower living in Hamilton Street in Dublin's Merchant's Quay district in the 1890s. He was bringing up seven children, with 17 years age difference between the eldest and the youngest, on his own. Four were daughters, who might have difficulty once they were adults finding respectable occupations to contribute to the family income; and three were sons. Ladley worked for a distillery as a commercial clerk, quite possibly Jameson of Malahide, which was a major employer in the city. Possibly adding to their daily tensions, the family was Presbyterian at a time when only two percent of the city's population shared that religion.

Dublin was not a thriving city at this time. The traditional industry of ship-building had declined almost to nothing by the end of the 19th century, though other local industries – biscuit-making, coach-building and brewing and distilling – still survived. Even so, there were estimated to be 24,000 men, one quarter of the adult males of the city, dependent on casual and seasonal labour, and many went months without work. Like other capital cities, Dublin had extensive slums and the decline spread from the back streets to include main streets and squares, until by 1911 Dublin had the worst housing conditions of any city in the United Kingdom. Ladley's struggle to keep his large family fed, clothed and housed must have been monumental: and then his eldest daughter Florence met Cecil Gramshaw.

It was the fate of an engineering company in London that brought the two together. The Electrical Engineering Corporation Limited had been formed from the merger of two other companies that had been wound up after going bankrupt: the United Electrical Engineering Company Limited of Lambeth, and J G Statter and Company Limited, based in West Drayton, Hillingdon, London. Mr Statter became a director of the new company, while the managing director was a well-known consulting engineer, Mr Manville. The Electrical Engineering Corporation Limited was formally constituted in February 1890 with share capital of £150,000. The Corporation also had another valuable asset: it held the patent for 'A new process of producing and dividing Electric Light and Apparatus therefor [sic].' The discovery had been made by Paul Jablochkoff, previously the owner of one of the defunct companies, and now living in Paris: the potentially valuable patent had transferred to the new Corporation with the take-over of his company.

With these strong foundations, the Corporation set up business on the West Drayton site at Trout Lane, Yiewsley. They advertised for more staff – blacksmiths 'used to general engineering work' and pattern makers – and obtained permission to extend the premises and build new offices. But the business had an inauspicious start when there was a fatal accident on the site in the first month of the company's operations. Sydney Myers, a 16-year-old pupil at the works, was killed in a particularly gruesome incident. At the inquest into his death, the works manager, John Cushney, described what had happened:

'On Wednesday last Myers had occasion to enter the room where the dynamos were tested for the purpose of marking some 'resistance coils'. To reach those coils, which were hung upon rectangular frames fastened to the wall, it was necessary he should stand on some boxes near a revolving shaft, which made 170 or 180 revolutions a minute. Witness presently noticed the deceased "doubled up and going round with the shaft." Wires which he had been marking, and probably holding in his hands, were bound round the boy and the shaft. He was tied tightly to the shaft by the wire. The steam was shut off, and he was extricated as soon as possible.'

Mr Cushney and one of the company's directors went on to clarify the company's policies which, if followed, would have prevented the awful tragedy – no doubt mindful of the fact that the local Inspector of Factories was present at the inquest and was intending to examine the shaft:

> 'Before he began his work of marking, Myers should, by the rules of the establishment, have stopped the shaft, which he could easily have done by simply pulling a handle. Mr Statter, a director of the company, said if the deceased had told the foreman that he had work to do behind the shaft, the foreman would have stopped it.'

Sydney Myers was taken to St Mary's Hospital, where he died shortly afterwards from internal haemorrhage resulting from his fractured ribs and other injuries. Whether he knew that he should have stopped the shaft and ignored the rule, or no-one had told him this, or he did not dare ask to interrupt the work by shutting it down, will never be known. Probably, as a young pupil of only a few months' experience, he should have been better supervised. Regardless of whose failings were involved, Myers paid a terrible price for them.

In spite of this accident and the attendant publicity, the company continued to grow until it employed more than 150 people, and the directors set their sights on business across the sea in Ireland. The managing director, Mr Manville, was also engineer to the Dublin Corporation (amongst others), which he must have hoped would give him an advantage in obtaining contracts in the country. In November 1890, the company's representative Mr Garvey was in County Cork, giving a detailed presentation to the Fermoy Town commissioners about the 'feasibility and advantage' of introducing electric lighting to the town. He allayed their fears about safety by assuring them that 'the system of lighting in England and Ireland is very different to that in America' (where they had heard of many accidents) because '... all works must be carried out under the regulations of the Board of Trade'. He explained that 'there was very much less risk than in using gas, especially as regards fire. Insurance companies insure premises lit by the electric light at a lower rate than those lit by gas.' He came away from the meeting with the promise of information about the number of lights required, and whether the plan would be for the town only or private housing as well, so that he could produce an estimate for the work. Still pursuing Irish contracts, the company also advertised in the Irish Times, offering 'to submit plans and estimates for electric lighting and every description of work to which Electrical Motive Power is applied.'

But the Electrical Engineering Corporation's growth and development came to an abrupt halt after less than a year. In January 1891, the works at West Drayton were badly damaged by fire. It had started in the woodwork above the boiler, though how it began was never established. Most of the premises was gutted by the blaze, with only the pattern shop and the offices being saved. The papers reported that the fire had caused £14,000-16,000 worth of damage and 'the occurrence has thrown 150 men out of employment.'

The fire also destroyed the viability of the company, which went into voluntary liquidation. Its assets were sold off in June that year.

Cecil Gramshaw had been a pupil at the West Drayton works. He had been taken on by the Electrical Engineering Corporation as an apprentice engineer at the age of 17; so he probably knew young Sydney Myers, his fellow pupil at the works who died in the tragic accident with the shaft. The closure of the West Drayton works and liquidation of the company could have left him untrained and unemployed: but Mr Manville, the managing director, took him on personally as an apprentice and sent him to continue his apprenticeship at the works of the Dublin Corporation. In April 1891, Cecil was with his family in Stillington, so it was probably later in the year that he went to Dublin. Sometime in the next two years, Cecil left his apprenticeship and 'took a situation at a small salary.' In December 1893, Mr Manville sued Cecil's father at the High Court in London for the balance of the apprenticeship fees that should have been paid to him. A total fee of 200 guineas had been agreed, to be paid in four instalments of 50 guineas each. But Dr Gramshaw had paid only the first instalment after Cecil went to West Drayton and repeated letters from Mr Manville asking for the next payment had been ignored. When the court found in Manville's favour, Dr Gramshaw had to pay the remaining 150 guineas.

In court, Cecil Gramshaw claimed that he had abandoned his apprenticeship because 'the working of the apparatus was not properly explained to him' – was he remembering Myers' accident and thinking this would be a damning indictment of the Corporation? – and he 'left because he learned nothing.' This was despite evidence from other electricians that he would have gained valuable experience if he had stayed. But perhaps it wasn't a lack of information or experience available that made him leave his apprenticeship for a paid post. Maybe he needed to be earning his own living because he wanted to be able to afford a household of his own with Florence Ladley. Although Florence was 22 years old in 1893 (one year older than Cecil) and so of 'full age' for marriage, her father would no doubt have looked more kindly on Cecil as a potential son-in-law if he was earning a living.

Cecil did travel to England on occasions while training and then working in Dublin – he was in Stillington in 1892 when he and his brother were set upon by a group of young labourers – but he must have spent significant time based in Ireland. The relationship between him and Florence Ladley blossomed over the years. On 4 March 1897, when he was 25 and Florence was 26, they were married in the Ormond Key Presbyterian Church in Dublin: a large and impressive building standing on the north quay of the River Liffey by the Grattan Bridge. There were three formal witnesses' names, rather than the usual two, on the marriage certificate: Robert Ladley, the bride's father; Catherine, the bride's sister; and another Ladley. No-one from the groom's family was a formal witness to the occasion.

Robert Ladley must have been delighted for his daughter and also relieved for himself. With one daughter safely married, he had one less person to support and worry about. His other grown-up daughters, Mary and Catherine, were 20 and 18, and could continue to undertake the domestic duties in the house after Florence's departure. His younger sons Robert and George, at 16 and 15, would soon be old enough to go out to work, leaving the youngest children, Alexander and Eileen, still at school. His burden as provider for the family was to be lightened a little by Florence and Cecil's marriage.

Cecil and Florence set up their marital home at 45 St Alban's Road, Dublin, still in the Merchant's Quay district and less than ten minutes' walk from her family home. Just less than 18 months into the marriage, on 30 August 1898, the Gramshaws had a baby son. Cecil registered the birth of Harold Victor Gramshaw in December that year. Then, at some point the following year, Cecil Gramshaw signed up to go to South Africa for the Anglo-Boer War. He was clearly there by 23 November 1899, because he was eligible for the Belmont clasp. Many of the men involved in that campaign were reported to be 'newly-arrived from England', and suffering from their three-week sea journey. So at the very latest, Gramshaw had left Dublin some time in October 1899, when the baby was just over a year old. But if, as seems likely, he left earlier, to join up with a volunteer corps of electrical engineers and receive his basic training, then he could have left much earlier in his young son's life. The boy and his mother moved back in with her family at Hamilton Street. In the 1901 census of Ireland, Florence Gramshaw is described as a 'boarder' in her father's house, implying that she was not intending to stay there permanently. Harold is an infant of two years old. Presumably, once Cecil returned from the war, the Gramshaws intended to move out again into a household of their own and continue to build their shared life and their family. After all, Cecil still had a job in Ireland: between January and March 1901, the General Electric Supply Company of O'Connell Street, Waterford, was advertising that it was 'prepared to undertake all branches of Electrical Engineering including Electric Bells, Telephones, etc', with the important notice that:

'The Plant erected by this Firm will be guaranteed to comply with the Fire Insurance Rules, which is most important, as the Insurance Companies will only recognise a Certified Engineer's Report in a case of fire, which Certificate our Electrical Engineer, Mr C H Gramshaw, holds from Finsbury College, London.

C H Gramshaw, Electric Engineer and Manager.'

If a return to family and the manager's job was the plan, it did not last long. Cecil Gramshaw was discharged from his duties in the South African Constabulary in September 1901. The earliest he could have been back in Ireland would have been in mid-October that year. Whether he went back to Dublin to re-join his wife and his three year old son is unclear: if he did, he left again in just a few short years. By early 1905, he was living in York and being initiated into the York Lodge of Freemasons. He paid the annual Lodge fees there until 1908, although he was working for the General Electric Company at their premises in Queen Victoria Street, London. By 1911, he was living in Wandsworth, London; and when he completed the census form that year, he said that he had been married to Marie, also resident at the address, for two years.

Florence Gramshaw remained at her father's house. In 1911, she was once again described as a 'daughter' of the head of the household – not a boarder – and as married for 14 years. Her father, Robert Ladley, now 70 years of age, was still working as a buyer for the Dublin distillery. He was supporting not only Florence, but his other daughters, Mary, Catherine and Eileen, all of whom were still living at home and unmarried. Two of his sons were also still single and living at home, though they were working: George was an assistant clerk at the Government valuation office and Alexander was a commercial clerk, so there was some additional income for the household. Harold Gramshaw, Robert's grandson, was twelve years old and at school.

It must have been a huge shock and disappointment to Florence when her marriage broke down. She had married a young engineer, a fine-looking man (if he took after his father) with a job in Dublin, who could have supported them both very well. He had volunteered to support his country in the war in South Africa, using his engineering skills and earning medals for his service. Then in a very short space of time, he had left her with a young son to look after and gone back to live in England. What were Florence and her family to make of this decision? Did her father try to insist that his son-in-law fulfilled his responsibilities to his young wife and continue to support her? Clearly Cecil Gramshaw wanted to forget about this marriage: he was setting himself up with a new 'wife' in London. But he may have been wary of his father-in-law's potential to cause trouble for him. Gramshaw dated his claim of 'marriage' to Marie from 1909 but he did not actually marry her until October 1916. This was just a few months after Robert Ladley had died in May 1916. Did Gramshaw hear of his death and believe that the danger that his desertion of Florence would be exposed was now gone? Was he not concerned that anyone else in the Ladley family might pursue him?

There is also the question of Gramshaw's own family. Had he told them about his marriage and child in Dublin? Sidney and Mary Gramshaw had been grandparents for nine years by the time of Sidney's suicide in 1908: were they aware of this and in touch with their daughter-in-law and grandson? It is hard to imagine how – or why – Cecil would have kept the marriage secret in the earlier, happy days of the union. Were his family not concerned when he returned to England alone in the early 1900s, or when he re-married in 1916 without any evidence of a divorce from his Irish wife? His mother or his siblings could have exposed him at any time, had they known of the Dublin marriage. Perhaps, if they knew about it, he took a risk and told them that his wife had died, to explain his return and his freedom to re-marry.

When he married Marie, Cecil declared his status as 'bachelor' to the Registrar and this was recorded on his marriage certificate. This had not been true since the date of his 1897 marriage: if he had obtained a divorce from

Florence in the meantime, he should have recorded his status as 'the divorced husband of Florence Ladley'. The truth seems to be that he was still married to Florence when he went through the ceremony with Marie Sampson at Lambeth Registry Office, which may explain why the marriage was 'by certificate' rather than after three public reading of 'the banns'. Whether Marie knew this, or what explanation Cecil had given her for being unable or unwilling to marry her before, and how he explained his change of heart, is open to speculation.

Given that divorce was very expensive and still mostly socially unacceptable, bigamy was not an unusual solution to problems in a marriage. It was of course illegal – the Offences Against the Person Act 1861 made it a specific crime:

> 'Whosoever, being married, shall marry any other person during the life of the former husband or wife, whether the second marriage shall have taken place in England or Ireland or elsewhere, shall be guilty of felony, and being convicted thereof shall be liable … to be kept in penal servitude for any term not exceeding seven years…
>
> Provided, that nothing in this section contained shall extend to any second marriage contracted elsewhere than in England and Ireland by any other than a subject of Her Majesty, or to any person marrying a second time whose husband or wife shall have been continually absent from such person for the space of seven years then last past,

and shall not have been known by such person to be living within that time, or shall extend to any person who, at the time of such second marriage, shall have been divorced from the bond of the first marriage, or to any person whose former marriage shall have been declared void by the sentence of any court of competent jurisdiction.'

The useful exception to the charge of bigamy, for a person whose spouse had been absent for seven years and 'shall not have been known to be living within that time', was much relied upon. When Norman Weekes was charged with bigamy in Leeds in 1919, his defence was that he thought his first wife, whom he had married in 1912, was dead. In a story that paralleled Cecil Gramshaw's, Weekes was also an engineer who was engaged by a city corporation, and who met and married a young woman in the city where he worked. When the war began, he left home and was stationed in Ireland and in York. After the war, like Gramshaw, he was not inclined to return to his wife. He met his new love, a 'lady transport driver', in Leeds. His wife became aware of a cooling in their relationship, but he denied having any new love interest. At the beginning of 1919, Weekes told his new fiancée that he had only lived with his first wife for six months, and that she had died of double pneumonia. The couple was married in April and set off for America where Weekes had a new job. By this time, the new wife's family were suspicious, and the couple was enticed back from America on the pretext that the woman's father was seriously ill. Weekes was arrested when their ship docked at Liverpool.

Like Weekes, Cecil Gramshaw waited seven years after he had parted from Florence (presumably around 1902) before he began calling Marie his wife in 1909. He was still taking a risk, however – he would have been hard pressed to claim that he thought his wife was dead, when Florence was still living in her father's house in Dublin and he could have communicated with her at any time to know that she was still living. Presumably it was her father's death in 1916 that gave him the courage to convert his common-law relationship into a bigamous marriage. But a steady stream of newspaper stories of people convicted and sentenced for bigamy must have kept Gramshaw at least a little on edge about his actions. Another Leeds-based engineer was sentenced to nine months' hard labour for having married bigamously: his first wife had re-appeared and 'there was a scene.' A self-styled doctor who had married no less than six times whilst still legally married to his first wife was also found to have committed 'an ingenious fraud'. His defence was that 'all he had been anxious to do was get a home and settle down.' He received ten years' penal servitude. And Halifax stonemason John Thornton was convicted of making two bigamous marriages to two different barmaids – he also said that he had not seen his first wife for nine years and he thought she was dead.

Marie Gramshaw lived with Cecil until at least 1925 when they both appear on the electoral roll at their home in Reading. But from the early 1930s onwards, Marie is not at the same address as Cecil. They may have just become disenchanted with the marriage and parted company. Or perhaps Marie found out then, for the first time, that her 'husband' had a previous, and still living, wife, and that her marriage was a sham. The former may be more likely, as when she died in Nottingham in 1963, Marie was described as a 'widow' – Cecil having died 12 years before – so she had not completely renounced their union.

Florence Gramshaw, the deserted wife, lived at her father's house in Hamilton Street, Dublin for the rest of her life. She never re-married and died in the family home from a stroke at the age of 73 in 1945. Interestingly, her sister Catherine, who registered the death, described Florence on the death certificate as a widow. Had the family been told at some point – maybe after their father's death in 1916 – that Cecil Gramshaw had died, in a bid to discourage them from looking for him? That could explain why he had the confidence to marry again.

Florence and Cecil's son Harold did not wait in Dublin to see if his father would return. He was just 16 years old when the First World War started but at some point he joined the Leinster Regiment – Leinster being the province in the east of Ireland that included Dublin. Formally known as the Prince of Wales's Leinster Regiment (Royal Canadians), the regiment had been created from the merger of two other regiments, one of them originally raised in Canada in response to a rebellion in India. In 1875, the Canadian regiment had been recognised as the successor to the 100th Regiment of Foot (Prince Regent's County of Dublin Regiment). In 1881 it merged with the 109th Regiment of Foot to create the Leinster Regiment – the Royal Canadians. From this regiment, Harold Gramshaw joined the Army Cyclist Corps as a private. The Corps had been created in 1915 to cover 14 cyclist battalions that were part of the Territorial Force, and mostly used for coastal defence and reconnaissance. Some of the army cyclists were sent to the Western Front, though the ground conditions made them unsuitable for front line activity and they were mainly used behind the lines for reconnaissance. Walter may have been in France, as he was at one stage listed by the War Office as 'wounded and missing', though his mother and her family would have been relieved that the report was later amended to 'neither wounded nor missing'. For his service, he was entitled to the Victory Medal with the 1914 or 1914-15 star and the British War Medal.

Perhaps influenced by his experiences with the Royal Canadians, at the age of 21 Walter emigrated to Canada. He arrived in Quebec from Liverpool in July 1920 aboard the 'Victorian'. On his immigration form, he said that his intended occupation was 'farmhand' and his object in coming to the country was 'to learn farming'. To the question of whether he intended to remain permanently in Canada, he answered unequivocally 'Yes.' His contact in the country was listed as a friend called Wallis W A Weston. There was a W Weston who also served in the Army Cyclist Corps; maybe he was a Canadian who inspired Walter to come to his country after the war. Walter had one hundred Canadian dollars in his possession, and, it was noted, he could read and write. His passage appears to have been paid for him. The form also confirmed that he was not mentally or physically defective, had not had tuberculosis and was not an anarchist. With these assurances, he was accepted into the country.

Once settled in Canada, Harold Gramshaw moved on from farming into a more lucrative profession. By the time he married a Canadian woman, Edythe Castle Teasdale, in the County of York, Ontario, in 1935, he was working as a 'collector'. Later he was recorded on the Toronto voter list as an accountant, then a book-keeper, before he retired. On his Canadian marriage certificate, Harold was required to state his parents' names and his father's place of birth. He recorded Cecil Henry Gramshaw, born in England, and Florence Ladley. Whether he had any recollection of meeting the former is very doubtful: if Cecil ever went back to Dublin after his time in South Africa, he had left again before the boy was five years old.

There were to be two more interesting marriages in the Gramshaw family shortly after Dr Gramshaw's death; and one more appalling tragedy.

Chapter 21

HILDA GRAMSHAW AND KENNETH ALLAN

There was a surprising absentee from Sidney Gramshaw's funeral. While the mourning party included his widow, his three sons and his daughter Amy, Gramshaw's other daughter, Hilda, was not present.

Edwardian mourning customs, though no longer quite as strict as those at the end of the 19th century, were still very specific. For a child mourning a parent, the mourning period was six months in 'full mourning' clothes, followed by three months in 'half-mourning'. Complete seclusion from society lasted for six weeks, and absence from balls and dances lasted six months. An article in Vogue in the 1920s suggested that mourning dress lasted longer than this: 'for a member of the immediate family, meaning a parent, a sister or brother, or a child, a year of deep mourning and a year of second mourning is the strictly correct usage'.

Hilda's mourning for her father took an unusual form – just nine days after his death and six days after the funeral that she did not attend, she got married. Hilda's new husband was Edward Lister Newman, 35 years old and a 'gentleman'. She was 29, ten years older than her father's dead mistress. Both parties gave the same address as their residence at the time of the marriage: number 11, Esplanade, Whitby. They were married in the church of St Hilda in Whitby with Gertrude Newman, Edward's widowed mother, and a Mr Wilkinson as their formal witnesses. No-one from the Gramshaw family was a formal witness to the marriage.

If Hilda was not at her father's funeral because she was ill or too distraught to attend, it seems unlikely that she would have proceeded with her wedding just six days later. It is more likely that her absence from the funeral and her choice to continue with her wedding plans were because she was furious with her father after the inquest revelations and his suicide; and so she refused to observe the traditional mourning behaviours that would have indicated the respect and grief expected of her. Whether any of her family broke with mourning tradition to attend the wedding is not clear; but surely if her mother or one of her brothers had been there, they would have signed the register as witness to the marriage in place of Mr Wilkinson.

After the wedding, John and Hilda Newman moved to the village of Sleights in the impressively-named parish of Eskdaleside cum Ugglebarnby, near Scarborough. Two years later they were living on their own private means and had no children. In 1926, after only eight years of marriage, Hilda died at the age of 47: the second of the Gramshaw daughters to have her life cut short.

Kenneth Allan, Dr Gramshaw's medical student nephew, was a member of the mourning party at the doctor's funeral, although he had as much reason as anyone to be angry with the man. His uncle had deliberately involved him in the aftermath of an illegal operation, which could have blighted his medical career before it had even started. But he seems to have come out of the events of April 1908 professionally unscathed. He completed his medical degree at Durham University and was entered onto the Medical Register the following year: the fifth generation of the family to join the medical profession. He did not however remain in the country for very long. In 1910 he obtained a certificate from the London School of Tropical Medicine; and by 1911, after a short period as a house surgeon at the Norfolk and Norwich Hospital, he was working as a doctor for the West Africa Colonial Office in Gambia, as part of the Colonial Medical Service. This was a section of the British Government Service which administered most of what were then Britain's overseas possessions. In 1916, he returned to England and joined the Royal Army Medical Corps attached to the King's African Rifles, reaching the rank of Captain. For his service in the First World War between 1916 and 1919, he was eligible for the Victory Medal and the British War Medal.

Shortly after the war, in 1921, Kenneth too got married. His bride, Hermione Anna Victoria Bouvier, came from an interesting background. Her father and mother, her three older sisters and two older brothers had all been born in Prussia and were German nationals. Hermione, the youngest of the family, was the only child born in England and holding British citizenship. Her father Otto was a former Army officer with the rank of Captain. When the family came to England in 1885, Captain Bouvier became the manager of the Chilworth Gunpowder Company, close to their new home in St Martha, a parish of Guildford in Surrey. It was his employment here that provided young Hermione with what must have been a formative experience in her early life.

Gunpowder was an important business in Chilworth. There had been gunpowder mills in the area since the first was established by the East India Company in 1626. Ten years later the proprietors, Collins and Cordwell, were appointed sole powder makers to King Charles I and the Chilworth mills became the only authorised gunpowder factory in the country. The Chilworth Gunpowder Company itself was formed as the subsidiary of a German company, which may have been a useful connection for Captain Bouvier. Using steam and water-driven turbines, it produced different grades of gunpowder for military use, for blasting in mines and quarries, and for sporting guns. The company was always aware of the significant dangers of working with the explosive. In Bouvier's time, safety features included a roof-level lever system which meant that an explosion in one chamber of a mill triggered a drenching mechanism in all of its bays to contain the spread of fire. Many of the buildings were also protected against the effect of explosions by semi-circular blast banks, made of earth and corrugated iron: these were known in the industry as 'Chilworth mounds'.

Unsurprisingly, there had always been accidents around gunpowder. Three of the notorious 'gunpowder plot' participants of 1605 had been badly injured when they tried to dry out their gunpowder in front of a fire and it exploded. At the Chilworth works in the 1860s, John Farnworth was killed in an explosion in the press house, where the powder was compressed to improve its explosive power. Tragically, his father had also died as a result of his work at the gunpowder mill. He had gone home after work and sat down in front of the fire in his working clothes. The powder remaining on his clothes ignited and he was killed. The danger of even such fine dust residue was illustrated again on a horrific scale when Captain Bouvier was in charge of the works in February 1901. On the frosty morning of Tuesday 12 February, the premises were rocked by two explosions that left six workers dead.

The foreman, William Bragg, had been employed at the works for 15 years without witnessing a single accident. He described what had happened that February morning at the inquest into the men's deaths. He had gone to work at six o'clock in the morning, as usual, and changed from his own clothes to factory clothes. This was a safety precaution: working around gunpowder, it was essential that clothes had no metal buttons and no pockets in which dangerous items might be carried into the works. His first act on duty was to inspect the 36 men going on shift with him to ensure that their working clothes conformed to these rules. He sent them on to their various departments, then repeated the inspection after the 8.30 breakfast break in the mess room. Three of the men went back to their work as 'tram-pushers': moving the tram carrying barrels of gunpowder dust between the end of the tram tracks and the 'corning' house, where the cakes of gunpowder were broken into different sizes and graded. Three other men were sweeping up. Bragg had just turned away and was about 20 feet from the tram when the first explosion occurred. He told the inquest:

> 'I was struck on the head at the same time as I heard it and knocked down. I lost my senses for a few seconds only, and when I looked round the corning house seemed to be up in the air, and the tram had disappeared … I could feel the burn from the fire here [indicating a large scar on the back of his head] … I remember crawling round behind the wall when the pieces were falling down.'

Bragg had been lucky. The second explosion, of the corning house, had been larger than the first, which was the tram exploding: and the force of the first explosion had pushed the tram tracks several inches down into the frozen ground and thrown a heavy brass handle more than 200 feet over the top of the corning house. One of the workmen had been thrown 30 feet against a brick wall.

Captain Otto Bouvier was also fortunate. He had been on site and had just left his office at 8.40 when the explosions occurred: he was only 300 feet from the corning house, containing 500lbs of fused pressed gunpowder cakes, when it exploded. At the inquest, he explained that the company conformed with every regulation and requirement of the Home Office, in addition to making improvements of their own. The Government Inspector of Explosives, Major Cooper Kay, endorsed this. The company had been rated 'excellent' on every inspection since the 1880s, he told the Coroner, and he had noted at his last inspection that the corning house was 'more clear of dust' than any other he had inspected. In his view, one of the workmen carrying the barrels of dust to the tram had slipped, some dust had been jarred off the barrel, and had been ignited by a spark from the man's hob-nailed boot striking a steel rail or a stone on the frozen ground. He considered it 'an accident, pure and simple', and had no criticism to make of the Chilworth Gunpowder Company:

'He confessed that the arrangements by which a space of five yards in that case of the ordinary surface of the ground had to be crossed by men carrying powder barrels, with hob-nailed boots on was not so safe as it might be. But the sole reason for that was the endeavour of the company to improve on the regulations laid down by the Home Office. According to the term of their licence with regard to the tramway, the rails of such tramway within three yards of the corning house should be of wood, brass, or other suitable metal. In order to improve on that the Company said they would not have any tramway at all within five yards of the building. He thought on the whole that it would be preferable to have had tram-rails of brass or wood right up to the platform of the building, so that the men in the building, who had proper over-shoes, should have the loading of the tram from the platform. He had been speaking to the representatives of the company, and they said not only would they do that but they would also provide the tram-pusher – only one would be needed – with special shoes.'

The Inspector went on to lavish praise on the company and its practices, and the Coroner repeated this in his summing-up, calling the company 'a paragon of perfection so far as gunpowder works were concerned.' The jury retired for only 15 minutes and returned to say that the men had met their deaths through 'an explosion of gunpowder at the tram, which caused the corning house to explode; and that no-one was to blame for the accident.' The Coroner translated this into a verdict of 'accidentally killed by an explosion of gunpowder.'

With the company exonerated of any blame, Captain Bouvier led the company's response to the tragedy. The directors had agreed that the company would pay all the expenses of the funerals for the six dead workers: and Captain Bouvier attended each funeral service, along with his wife and daughters. Hermione, the youngest, was just thirteen when she attended the first funeral, of William Marshall, at St Martha's churchyard. This was followed by three interments in one day: the double funeral of William Prior and George Smithers at Shalford, and the burial of William Sopp at Merrow. Walter Abbott's funeral took place at Shramley Green, then Robert Flower Chandler was buried at Stoke Cemetery near Guildford. Such a series of solemn events, and exposure to the grief of so many widows and fatherless children (seven of his children attended William Prior's funeral), must have had a big impact on the young girl.

Hermione was 33 years old when she married Dr Kenneth Allan at Tonbridge in Kent in 1921. He had arrived back in England from the First World War in 1920, and then returned to his work for the Colonial Medical Service. It is not clear how long, or where, they actually lived together; but by 1925, he was living in Gambia in Africa, and the marriage was in trouble. Through his solicitors, Allan placed an announcement in various newspapers:

'We the undersigned BLYTH & HORNOR as Solicitors and Agents for Kenneth Bruce Allan of Bathurst, Gambia, West Africa (Colonial Medical Service) hereby give notice that the said KENNETH BRUCE ALLAN hereby expressly withdraws all and every authority which his wife HERMIONE ANNIE VICTORIA ALLAN now residing at 6 Grosvenor Gardens, Tunbridge Wells, Kent, may have at any time either expressly or by implication or otherwise acquired to contract for him or in his name or as his agent or in any way to pledge his credit and that she has for some time past been and still is in receipt of a sufficient allowance from the said KENNETH BRUCE ALLAN for the purpose of providing herself with all suitable necessaries and that the said KENNETH BRUCE ALLAN will not be responsible for her debts whensoever or howsoever incurred.

Dated this 5ᵗʰ day of September, 1925.'

Such a disclaimer was not uncommon when a couple was separated but not divorcing: it drew a clear line between their finances and their separate lifestyles. Sadly, this notice came only nine months after the birth of the Allan's son and only child, Ronald.

Allan's permanent residence was recorded as 'Nigeria' when he paid a visit to the UK in 1932. By 1939, both Kenneth and Hermione were living in England, but not together. Kenneth Allan was retired from medical practice and living with a housekeeper in Bexhill, Sussex. Hermione was living alone in Banstead in Surrey. In 1945, Allan remarried to a woman named Ena Maud Henrietta Brett-Gardner; and in the same year he changed his Will to leave everything to her.

Kenneth's first marriage had clearly been troubled from very early on; and Hilda Gramshaw's marriage had been cut short by her untimely death. But all of their troubles pale in comparison with the awful fate that had claimed the eldest of the Gramshaw sisters, Amy.

Chapter 22

AMY THE ART STUDENT

Amy was the third child and eldest daughter of the Gramshaws. As such, she was the 'Miss Gramshaw' who stood at her parents' side hosting the soirée for the York and District Field Naturalists' Society, when her father was the Society's President. She was a young woman with all the accomplishments expected of her class and gender. At York School of Science and Art, she won prizes for her drawing and helped to organise the annual art students' dance. In Stillington, she sang in choirs with local schoolchildren and in concerts alongside her parents. Her achievements and her social appearances are all the more impressive because Amy Gramshaw had epilepsy.

By the start of the 1900s, when Amy was a young woman, great strides had been made in the understanding of epilepsy – what they called 'epileptology' – by the medical profession. Doctors knew that the disease involved abnormal electrical activity in the brain, although they had no way of routinely measuring or recording this activity until the invention of the electroencephalograph in the 1920s. They also recognised that there were two main types of epileptic seizure, then called 'grand mal' epilepsy (now 'generalised seizures') and 'petit mal' epilepsy (now 'focal seizures'). In the former, the sufferer loses consciousness during seizures involving convulsions with violent muscle contractions and sometimes incontinence. Focal seizures are less obvious episodes, sometimes called 'absences', in which the sufferer looks blank and is unresponsive but does not usually lose consciousness, fall or convulse. The first brain surgery aiming to treat epilepsy took place in 1831, with the removal of an abcess which was causing fits by affecting the electrical activity of the brain. Medical treatments were limited to various herbal and chemical substances until the middle of the 19th century, when the anticonvulsant and sedative traits of potassium bromide were discovered. This was the main treatment for epilepsy until 1912, when phenobarbital was discovered.

The medical profession might have got to grips with epilepsy at the start of the 20th century but for the general public it remained a frightening and very stigmatised disease. As late as the early 19th century, people with epilepsy were treated as either lunatics or possessed. Even now it has been said that 'there is general agreement that stigma and exclusion are common features of epilepsy'; and that 'The history of epilepsy can be summarised as

4000 years of ignorance, superstition and stigma, followed by 100 years of knowledge, superstition and stigma'. Reflecting this, epilepsy was sometimes called the 'burning disease', the 'falling sickness' or the 'shameful disease'.

Social rejection, denial of education and isolation from society were common responses to people with epilepsy when Amy was growing up. It is likely that she had the less obvious form of the disease, with focal seizures, since otherwise it is hard to imagine that she could have gone to school and been out in society in the way that she evidently was. And while Amy was out and about, at the same time in England there was a sad example of how a young person could be isolated and imprisoned by epilepsy even in the highest of high society.

Prince John was born into the British Royal Family in 1905, the youngest child of King George V (who was Prince of Wales when John was born) and his wife, Mary. The young prince was found to have epilepsy at the age of four. The public was never told and he was isolated at Sandringham for the rest of his short life, although he did appear in public at times in the earlier years before his condition worsened. He died at Sandringham in 1919 at the age of 13, following a severe seizure. The British Epileptic Association has said that, 'There was nothing unusual in what [his parents, the King and Queen] did. At that time, people with epilepsy were put apart from the rest of the community. They were often put in epilepsy colonies or mental institutions. It was thought to be a form of mental illness.'

The recent discovery of a letter about the boy's death, written by his brother the then Prince of Wales, later King

Edward VIII, to his lover, painfully reflects the attitudes of the day:

> 'I've told you all about that little brother darling and how he was an epileptic and might have gone west any day. He's been practically shut up for the last two years anyhow so no one's ever seen him except the family and then only once or twice a year and his death is the greatest relief imaginable and what we've all silently prayed for.
>
> But to be plunged into mourning for this is the limit just as the war is over, which cuts parties etc right out. No one would be more cut up if any of my other three brothers were to die than I should be. This poor boy had become more of an animal than anything else.'

After her father's suicide, Amy moved with her mother to live with her younger brother Guy at Fairfields Road in Basingstoke. That first Christmas, after all the shocks and upheavals of the past year, must have felt very strange to Amy. At Christmas 1907, she had been living with her parents and sister in the big house at Bootham in York, attending civic dinners and balls, with the status of coming from a respectable professional family that boasted a local doctor at its head and two Freemasons amongst its members. By Christmas 1908 she and her mother had been publicly humiliated by the exposure of her father's affair with a woman 10 years younger than his daughter, his illegitimate children and the illegal operation for an abortion he had carried out, resulting in the death of his mistress. Then they had had to cope with the shock and stigma of his suicide and attend his funeral. Now the big house on Bootham was the home of Dr Joseph Dawson, Physician and Surgeon; Amy's sister Hilda had left the family to get married without even attending her father's funeral; and Amy and her mother were living over 200 miles away in the unfamiliar south of England. Perhaps the stress of the festive season in new surroundings added to the strains of their awful year, and it all became unbearable; because in January 1909, nine months after her father's death, Amy went suddenly and violently mad.

Dr Macpherson from New Street House in Basingstoke was called to the Gramshaws' house to see Amy on Tuesday 26 January. He reported:

'I found her suffering from acute mania, struggling violently and screaming at the top of her voice. It required three men to hold her and she refuses all food and drinks. I also saw her [later] and the condition was the same.'

It was left to Amy's mother to tell the doctor what had happened in the previous terrible 24 hours. She said that her daughter had got up early on Monday morning and attacked her and her son Guy, attempting to tear their clothes off. She had continued to be violent ever since and it took three men to restrain her. She was suicidal and, even more frighteningly, she was homicidal: she had tried to strangle her mother. Her condition, after more than 24 hours of such intense and violent activity, fighting with the people restraining her and having had nothing to eat or drink, must have been dreadful. Dr Macpherson made the only decision possible: that, in her own best interests and for the safety of her family, Amy would have to be removed to an asylum.

The Lunacy Act of 1890, responding to public concern about instances of wrongful confinement in a mental institution, required more than just a medical opinion before a patient could be admitted. Although two doctors had previously been required to sign the certificate to admit a patient, there was a view that two obliging doctors might be found by a family that was keen to offload a member into an asylum. Under the new Act, a Reception Order, signed by a Justice of the Peace, a County Court judge or a magistrate, was needed in addition to the medical certificate. Henry Jackson, a JP for the Borough of Basingstoke, 'having called to my assistance Dr J F Macpherson, a duly qualified medical practitioner', completed the form certifying that 'Amy Isabelle Gramshaw is in such circumstances as to require relief for her proper care and maintenance ... [she] is a lunatic and a proper person to be taken charge of and detained under care and treatment', and signed it. 'Lunatic' at this time meant someone with a temporary mental illness and 'idiot' was used for someone who had had mental impairment from birth: although these terms are jarring to modern ears, both were intended to be descriptive rather than pejorative.

George Slater, the Relieving Officer for the Union of Basingstoke, also signed the necessary paperwork – the

Statement of Particulars – confirming that the Union would pay the necessary fees to the asylum for Amy's care. The particulars included information about Amy – that she was single, aged 32, a member of the Church of England and 'of no occupation' – and about her illness. It noted that this was her first attack of mania, she had had no previous admissions for care and treatment as a 'lunatic, idiot or person of unsound mind' and that the current attack had lasted for one day. The 'supposed cause' of her mania was listed as 'epilepsy'; and to question of whether she was subject to epilepsy, Slater wrote 'yes'.

Epilepsy is not a mental illness, it is a neurological one, and people with epilepsy will not necessarily ever have a mental illness. But people who suffer from epilepsy can also suffer from intellectual disabilities or from autism, if for instance the intellectual impairment and epilepsy both result from birth trauma. Depression, anxiety and cognitive disorders such as poor memory can result from injury to the relevant part of the brain, from side effects of medication, or as a result of living with the condition. Different to any of these is a rare condition called 'post-ictal' (meaning after a seizure) mania, or post-ictal psychosis. Only two per cent people with epilepsy will suffer from this and it is usually a short-term condition in which the patient displays symptoms of acute psychosis, including insomnia, hallucinations, delusions, extreme changes of mood, euphoria, and distractibility. Amy's prolonged attack of mania does not sound like post-ictal psychosis.

Psychiatric symptoms occurring after an epileptic seizure, or between seizures, were cited by doctors in admission notes for many patients at the Hampshire County Lunatic Asylum, where Amy was to be admitted, according to a comprehensive study of patients treated between 1861 and 1899. Eliza Bedford was 50 years old when she had her first admission, after a manic period following a seizure. She went on to have five more admissions. Edward Atkins' tragic story started when he was a baby and was badly burned on the head in a fire. He had 'fits' from the age of two and was admitted twice to the asylum because of his unmanageable behaviour between seizures; he died at the age of 13. George Dacre's epilepsy was blamed for causing his dementia, which brought him to the institution for care. George Mott was admitted at the age of 38 after his 'fits' made him violent. Hannah Neal was said to have 'delusions and epilepsy'. Whether these cases were true post-ictal mania or unrelated mental illness co-existing with epilepsy, it is impossible to say.

Equally, it may be that Amy's epilepsy, though cited as the 'supposed cause' of her first episode of mania, had nothing to do with it. Her mother had not reported that her sudden illness followed a seizure; though since it started early in the morning, it is possible that Amy had had a generalised seizure in her bedroom before starting her violent rampage that day. Whatever the cause, the doctor, Justice of the Peace and Relieving Officer all agreed that she needed to be admitted to the Hampshire County Lunatic Asylum for treatment. Although only one in five of the asylum's patients was admitted after less than 10 days' mental illness, Amy certainly qualified to be one of these very urgent admissions.

The asylum, in the village of Knowle near Fareham, was in the very south of the county, nearly 40 miles away from Amy's new home in Basingstoke, which was in the north of the county. Opened in 1852, the asylum occupied a 100-acre site which included farms, laundries, workers' cottages, a chapel and a cemetery. It even had its own railway station, Knowle Halt. With over 1,100 patients and around 100 nurses and attendants at that time, the asylum was like a small village. Its buildings included accommodation for the key staff of the institution. There was a 14-room house for the medical superintendent, occupied by Dr Henry Kingsmill Abbott, his widower father and his unmarried sister; an 11-room house for the asylum's chaplain, William Richard Williams and his wife Harriet; and a six-room house for the asylum engineer, Frederick Harvey and his family. There was also a separate house for the head attendant, occupied by Harry Kyle and his wife.

Public asylums like Hampshire's had begun to be established following the 1808 County Asylums Act; and the Lunacy Act of 1845 had accelerated this public provision by requiring the construction of asylums in every county. All were to have written regulations and a resident qualified doctor, and all were subject to regular inspections. The Act also improved the status of mentally-ill people by recognising them as patients who required treatment, and created the Lunacy Commission to ensure that the various provisions of the Act were put into practice. These were all very practical actions intended to reflect the sea-change in attitudes to people with mental illness between the 18th and 19th century, that acknowledged them as human beings with a temporary disturbance in their health rather than uncontrollable animals. There was now a focus on benevolence and social reform, and scientific and medical progress in their treatment, rather than just containment. This concern to provide good places of care with respectable standards of living is illustrated in a minor, pragmatic way by the advertisements for suppliers to the asylums. Warwick County Lunatic Asylum published:

'Persons desirous of Contracting to supply this Asylum with Fine Flour, Soap, Grocery, Eggs, &c., from the 30th day of September, to the 31st day of December next, are requested to send to the Asylum, free of expense, Sealed Tenders for the same, signed by the party tendering ... Particulars of the Articles required are stated in the Forms of Tender, to be had on application at the Asylum, where samples of such of the Articles as it is practical to show may be seen ... The Committee do not pledge themselves to accept the lowest, or any Tender.'

So the asylum wanted a good supply of groceries and would not simply accept the cheapest offer from tradesmen: their patients were not 'out of sight, out of mind' and were not to be given only the most basic provision. The Devon County Lunatic Asylum went further, when advertising for a supplier of 'best ox and heifer beef, best ewe and wether mutton.' They also asked for tenders to supply, amongst other things, salt, cheese, butter, manure, white lead and coffins; and they warned that 'they must be delivered free of expense and will be returned by officers of the asylum if their quality is not equal to the sample.'

With the legal and medical paperwork in order, the Hampshire asylum automatically admitted Amy Gramshaw as one of the 242 patients taken in that year: more than half of whom were women. Patients were often accompanied to the asylum by their Borough's Relieving Officer so Amy may have travelled south with George Slater, with or without her mother. She was admitted on 26 January, the day Dr Macpherson first saw her at home in a state of uncontrollable mania, so perhaps Mrs Gramshaw stayed at home to recover when her daughter was taken away. Some peace may have been restored to the household in Basingstoke; but there was to be no peace for Amy.

Chapter 23

'MAY THEY REST IN PEACE AND RISE IN GLORY'

The regime at the Knowle Hospital was probably as good as any to be found in a public asylum. For a start, the hospital stood in an ideal environment, on a hill, in the countryside, with views over the sea and the Isle of Wight. The tendency to build public asylums in rural surroundings was due, in part at least, to the belief that a natural, rural environment with its surroundings of fields, woods and other natural landscapes, was itself therapeutic, helping to calm and restore the patients. The other, less altruistic, reason for the choice of these locations was sometimes the objections of local people to idea of building an asylum close to their homes and towns.

Knowle Hospital had 100 acres around it, and the farms and workshops which helped towards self-sufficiency for the organisation also provided meaningful work for those of the patients who were able to do it. The concept of 'moral treatment' of people with mental illness – based on gentleness, care and respect for the sufferer as a human being, and a therapeutic relationship between doctor and patient – had been pioneered at The Retreat in York in the 18th century. The approach had spread into the wider psychiatric community and was adopted in the County asylums set up in the 19th century. So where possible patients with learning difficulties would be taught to look after themselves and work if they could; and people recovering from acute mental illness could also be provided with meaningful tasks as well as social activities to support their recovery.

Within the walls of the asylum, regimes had also improved markedly in the 50 years before Amy's admission. The use of restraints for violent or self-harming patients was radically reduced. The Lincoln asylum banned them altogether, following the death of a patient who had been restrained for a long period, and both it and the Hanwell asylum in London which followed suit, managed well enough without them. Where restraints were used, their use had to be noted in a special record book for regular review. The training of staff and the professionalisation of the former asylum 'attendants' into 'nurses' was encouraged by the provision of a special qualification for attendants offered by the Medico-psychological Association. This took time to become the norm: at the time of Amy's admission, only a quarter of the male attendants and about one sixth of the female attendants at Knowle Hospital had obtained this qualification. But qualified or not, all the attendants had to abide by a strict set of Rules for work in the asylum which set out the standards of behaviour and conduct expected of them both in their personal lives and in their treatment of patients. Attendants could be – and were – sacked for being unkind, rough or dishonest with patients or for taking advantage of them. When Amy was there, the staff-to-patient ratio was one attendant to every eleven patients: a workforce described as 'of moderate strength' in the Annual Report. Overseeing them and their work was a committee of Justices of the Peace and lay Visitors – externally-based people whose role was to keep an objective, disinterested eye on everything that happened in the asylum.

In charge of the patients at the Hampshire County Lunatic Asylum on a day-to-day basis was the Medical Superintendent, Dr Henry Kingsmill Abbott. Born in Dublin, he had qualified as a doctor after studying at the University of Dublin and arrived at Knowle Hospital as Assistant Medical Superintendent in 1890. Mental health was his chosen area of work: he never worked in another field and his expertise was such that he became an Examiner in Mental Diseases for the University of Dublin. He took over the role of Medical Superintendent at the asylum in July 1906. Unlike the hospital's chaplain, engineer and head attendant, Dr Abbott never married and he lived on site at the hospital for the rest of his life. When he died in post at the age of 59 in 1922, he was buried in the hospital's cemetery, his coffin carried there by some of the male nurses. It was said that 'he carried out the duties with rare skill and ability and with wonderful patience, sympathy and conscientiousness, and had won the complete confidence and esteem of the Visiting Committee and all associated with the Institution.'

Although the route of entry to a County asylum was a legally-based one, linked to the Poor Law system and requiring signatures from a Justice of the Peace and the Relieving Officer as well as a doctor, the asylums considered themselves part of the medical system rather than simply a better class of workhouse. The Hampshire County Asylum described its purpose as:

'to restore, relieve and protect those who are afflicted with the greatest of all visitations that befall the human race' and 'to soothe, alleviate and cure the sufferings and mental diseases of those unfortunate individuals who crave our warmest sympathies and also promote their early recovery.'

To this end, in its Annual Reports, the asylum regularly reminded doctors and families to seek admission early in a patient's illness not as a last resort, to give the greatest chance of a cure. The truth was, however, that in spite of great increases in medical and scientific knowledge, there was still very little therapeutic treatment to be offered to their patients at the start of the 20th century. The care given by the attendants was largely personal rather than clinical; and the opportunity to eat better, to rest and sleep, and have 'asylum' in the sense of refuge from the trials of everyday life, formed a large proportion of the treatment available.

The casebooks of the Hampshire asylum's patients reflect the common view that both emotions and insanity were related to the state of the organs of digestion and that all bodily functions needed to be restored to normal if sanity was to be restored. Hence the emphasis on good food and regular meals in the asylum regime as a key part of recovery; and the regular weighing of patients, since weight gain was seen as a sign of recovery.

The problem was that Amy was refusing all food and drink when she was admitted. She had not eaten or drunk between the Sunday night and Tuesday morning when Dr Macpherson saw her at home; and at least another half day had elapsed while she was transported to the asylum. During this time she had been very physically active, attacking her mother and brother, fighting the three men trying to control her, and screaming continuously. By the time she was admitted to Knowle Hospital she must have been dehydrated and hungry, but too violently agitated to recognise her own needs.

For a patient who was manic, violent and uncooperative, and in urgent need of sustenance, asylums had only one option: force-feeding. Also known as forced alimentation, or more neutrally as 'artificial feeding', the practice had been used in asylums since the late 18th century. It involved firstly restraining the patient either by the use of straps or a straitjacket, or by a number of attendants holding the patient down. (Although the use of restraints for other purposes had to be recorded in the asylum's restraint record, restraining a patient just for the purposes of force feeding was not considered 'mechanical coercion' and so did not need to be recorded.) Then a thin tube was inserted, usually through the nose or mouth; if the latter, then a wedge or gag was used to hold the jaws apart. The food – often milk or beaten eggs – was poured down the tube using a funnel. This could take a few minutes or much longer, depending how much was to be given. Finally, the tube was removed, though the patient might continue to be restrained for a while to minimise the chance of immediate regurgitation. The whole procedure might be repeated several times a day. There were other methods of artificial feeding: German asylum physicians preferred rectal feeding to using a tube through the mouth or nose, inserting butter, port wine and beef tea by this route. Meanwhile a French physician favoured the use of electrical charges to the neck which both opened the mouth and promoting swallowing. Neither of these approaches found favour with British asylum doctors.

Although the process, even by the oral or nasal route, sounds brutal, in the context of asylums and patients whose food refusal was due to their illness, it was not intended to be punitive. It was considered a medical treatment: simply a mechanical means to ensure that patients could receive the good nutrition that was considered essential to their recovery. The term 'fat and well', appearing frequently in patients' case records, was used to indicate a satisfactory state of convalescence from mental illness.

But however good the intentions, forcibly feeding a patient was dangerous. A misplaced tube using the nasal route to the stomach could end up in the lungs; and a struggling patient was liable to vomit during or after the procedure and then inhale food substances into the lungs. The result was often pneumonia, an infection in the lungs which, in pre-antibiotic days, could often prove fatal. And this, sadly, was Amy Gramshaw's fate. Just nine days after her admission to Knowle Hospital, Amy was dead. Her death certificate, signed by the asylum's medical superintendent Dr Abbott, records 'lobar pneumonia supervening on acute mania'. She was 32 years old.

There is no certainty that it was force feeding that caused her to develop pneumonia, as there are no case notes about Amy: she had not been in the asylum long enough for anything other than her admission notes to be recorded. But given that she was in a state of acute mania and refusing food and drink on admission, it seems likely that she would have been forcibly fed in the first few days of her stay. If she inhaled some food during those first terrifying experiences of force feeding, the timescale is right for pneumonia to develop and overwhelm her by the tenth day after admission.

Five days later, in the chill of a particularly snowy February, Amy was buried in the asylum cemetery. Her family had the option of taking her body away for burial elsewhere; but if the family did not make arrangements, it was the responsibility of the governing body of the institution to do so. The Lunacy Commissioners did not really approve of asylums having their own cemeteries.

They felt that having a burial ground so close to the asylum could be a health risk; that it was bad for the patients' morale to see what could be their final resting place on a daily basis; and also that it stigmatised the patients by keeping them separate from other members of society even in death. Interestingly, The Retreat at York addressed this last objection by opening up its burial ground to members of the Society of Friends – Quakers – who had not been inmates of the hospital.

The Church Commissioners were involved in the development of some asylum cemeteries and in consecrating these burial grounds. They recorded the conveyance of land for the Hampshire asylum cemetery in their Annual Report of 1856. So Amy was buried in consecrated ground when she was laid to rest in the Hampshire County Asylum cemetery. Families could attend these burials, but there is no record of whether Amy's mother and brother, or any of her other siblings, came to Knowle Hospital for the ceremony. It was quite common for asylum patients to be buried without relatives present and to lie in an unmarked grave, which would be understandable for the families of 'pauper lunatics' who had been long-term patients, for whom the cost of travel and of a headstone might be prohibitive. For Amy, who had been a patient for less than two weeks, and whose main family lived only 40 miles away and had the means to travel, it would have been more unusual if she had gone to her grave alone.

In one of the stranger aspects of Amy's story, it appears that no inquest was held into the circumstances surrounding her death. She was a young woman who was physically well when she entered the asylum. She died less than 10 days later with no medical notes made about her condition in the interim. With these factors, her death would seem to fall firmly into the category of 'unexpected' and 'unexplained' deaths that should be referred to the local Coroner. The fact that she was an asylum patient when she died did not matter: there were many instances of inquests into the deaths of such patients being held in public, as required, with the Coroner and jury seeking diligently to establish what had happened to the individual. There had even been an inquest into the death of an ex-patient of the Hampshire asylum, at which Dr Abbott was called to give evidence. John Fielder had committed suicide by cutting his throat ten days after being allowed to leave the Hampshire County Asylum. He had been at the asylum from November to the end of January suffering from depression. The papers reported on Dr Abbot's statement to the inquest:

'He [John Fielder] remained till the 30th January, and was under my observation almost every day. He was very depressed, but never talked about suicide, or shewed any tendency to it. He was very deaf, and not easy to converse with. Deceased got very much better towards the end of December, and his friends were anxious to have him out. After they had signed a certain undertaking I considered it was quite safe to let him out on trial. The order for his release was not made until he had been carefully observed. I did not look upon threats of suicide so seriously as I did on attempted suicide by a patient, and in my opinion deceased's mental condition was such as he might safely be allowed out for a month on trial. Deceased was very anxious to leave. I have had sixteen years' experience, but had only had one similar case to this. I did not think there was any risk of suicide.'

The jury returned a verdict of suicide during temporary insanity; and they gave their opinion that 'the authorities at the asylum were in no way to blame for liberating Fielder.'

John Fielder had died whilst living out in the community. But inquests into deaths that took place within the asylum walls were also not unusual. Later in the same year in which Amy died, the Gloucester Coroner held an inquest into the death of Ann Williams, a 98-year-old woman who was a 'pauper lunatic' and who had died in Gloucester County Asylum. She had been admitted three years earlier with senile dementia and it would have easy to assume that age had finally caught up with her. But the Coroner made enquiries because she had complained of pain in her shoulder on the day before her death. The asylum doctor had diagnosed a fracture and put her arm in plaster. Thereafter she 'suffered considerable pain and shock from the injury and, gradually sinking, died on Monday afternoon'. Guided by the doctor, the jury decided that death was due to 'senile decay, accelerated by a fractured shoulder accidentally sustained, how the fracture was sustained, there was no evidence to show.' An earlier case from the same asylum was also referred to the Coroner because the death followed an accident. Hannah Baldwin, who was 71, had fallen out of her bed in the asylum. Although she said she was not hurt and she was subsequently nursed entirely on bedrest, she grew gradually worse and died 12 days later. At post-mortem examination, she was found to have a fracture to her neck and a broken right femur as well as long-standing heart disease. The verdict was that her death had been due to the heart disease but accelerated by the fractures.

Another trigger for an inquest into an asylum death, apart from accidents, was death soon after admission. Charles Popplewell was a 42-year-old coal porter who had been taken to the Essex County Asylum on a Monday at five in the afternoon and died less than two hours later. The doctor testified that Popplewell had been in poor physical as well as dire mental health before his admission: he had been taken to the asylum infirmary with difficulty breathing and a raised pulse rate. The cause of death, confirmed by post-mortem, was heart failure.

Amy Gramshaw would have fallen into this category of death soon after admission. The difference was that she had been perfectly well when she was admitted so her fatal illness must have been acquired during her stay. Her case was more akin to that of William Hayes, an ex-Army man, who was admitted to the Buckinghamshire County Asylum with acute mania, like Amy, and who then acquired erysipelas and died. Erysipelas is a bacterial infection of the skin which extends into the subcutaneous lymph vessels.

In Hayes' case, the infection entered through abrasions on his face caused by his violent behaviour during his mania. The asylum doctor said at the inquest:

> 'He was very much excited and was put into a padded room, and afterwards into a strong room. He caused bruises and abrasions on his body by striking himself and rolling about the room, but none of them were serious, and most of them soon disappeared. On Wednesday he noticed marks of erysipelas on the right side of the face, which started from a small abrasion at that spot. That became very severe during the next three days, and at time the maniacal excitement continued, but in a lesser degree, owing to the weakness of the deceased. He gradually became more and more exhausted, and died on the previous Sunday night about 8.15. Witness had made a post-mortem examination, and ascertained that the immediate cause of death was exhaustion from mania and erysipelas, due to the abrasion on the eye caused by the deceased himself.'

Amy too had been admitted in a state of mania and had then acquired pneumonia. Her death certificate however gives pneumonia as the main cause of death, coming on top of ('supervening on') her mania. She did not, according to this certificate, die of 'exhaustion' from her mania, which would have been an expected outcome of mental illness. So there should surely have been an inquiry into the cause of the pneumonia, a condition unrelated to her mental illness. Yet there seems to have been no referral to the Hampshire County Coroner and no inquest. Perhaps her death was simply unnoticed amongst others in the Hampshire asylum that year, when a total of 98 inmates died, eight of them from an outbreak of colitis – an inflammation of the bowels causing diarrhoea – that affected 80 of the patients. Another 113 patients were discharged in the same year. However the same level of activity was likely to have prevailed at the Gloucester, Essex and Buckinghamshire asylums yet they still reported any inmates' 'unexplained' or 'unexpected' deaths to the Coroner.

It is possible that a post-mortem was carried out on Amy's body in the five days between her death and her burial. This was a time when medical and scientific advances were being made in the understanding of mental illness; and when there was conflict between physicians who believed that there must be visible changes in the brain in mental illness and those who thought that the illness of the mind might not be visible in the physical brain. So most asylums had their own mortuary – or 'dead house' – and in some asylums up to seventy per cent of inmates who died were subject to a post-mortem examination. The post-mortem aimed to clarify the cause of death of the individual, to increase knowledge about mental illness for the medical profession, and to produce more accurate mortality statistics for public health purposes. Consent from the deceased's family was not required; they had to actively object to a post-mortem to withdraw consent that was otherwise assumed. If Amy's body was examined in this way, there is no remaining record of the findings. But as anatomised bodies were often buried in multi-occupancy graves, this may explain why Amy's grave number is 778.2, possibly indicating that she was not buried alone.

Knowle Hospital is now closed and the cemetery, after some years of neglect, is now a woodland looked after by Wickham Parish Council. There is a memorial stone which records that five and a half thousand people were buried in the former asylum cemetery. Beneath this is a simple inscription that seems particularly appropriate after the tragic end of Amy's life: 'May they rest in peace and rise in glory.'

Chapter 24

CRIMES AND LIES

The jury at the inquest into Margaret Brown's death could not have stated their verdict more clearly. The young woman's death, they concluded, had been due to 'acute peritonitis caused by septic poisoning introduced into the system by wounds caused by an operation for abortion'. The doctor involved in the illegal operation, Farbrace Sidney Gramshaw, had been sitting in court with the jury for the first two days of the inquest. However, unlike in the case of the Nottingham midwife, Emily Jennings, the inquest jury's conclusion was never tested in a criminal court because Dr Gramshaw committed suicide before the inquest verdict was known. It is possible, as with Jennings, that the second jury might have completely exonerated Gramshaw. But his suicide precluded any criminal action being brought, leaving him adjudged by the Coroner's court to have caused Margaret Brown's death by carrying out the abortion – but never convicted of this in a criminal court.

Had his case gone to trial, what charge might he have faced for the death, in addition to the charge of procuring an abortion? Emily Jennings, who did not seem to have any intention to kill Harriet Brown when she did whatever she did when examining the pregnant woman, was still charged with murder. A charge of murder, according to the Crown Prosecution Service, requires that the accused:

> 'is of *sound mind and discretion* (i.e. sane); *unlawfully kills* (i.e. not self-defence or other justified killing); *any reasonable creature* (i.e. a human being); *in being* (i.e. born alive and breathing on its own … *under the Queen's Peace* (i.e. not in war-time); *with intent to kill or cause grievous bodily harm* (GBH).
>
> The necessary intention exists if the defendant feels sure that death, or serious bodily harm, is a virtual certainty as a result of the defendant's actions and that the defendant appreciated that this was the case.'

As an experienced and qualified doctor, Gramshaw no doubt believed that he could carry out a termination of the pregnancy without killing the young mother. So it is unlikely that it could be shown that he 'felt sure' that death or serious bodily harm was 'certain' as a result of his actions. However, his actions in carrying out the abortion did lead to Margaret Brown's death, so a charge of manslaughter might have been brought against him. Manslaughter can be committed in one of three ways:

'Killing with the intent for murder but where a partial defence applies, namely loss of control, diminished responsibility or killing pursuant to a suicide pact.

Conduct that was grossly negligent given the risk of death, and did kill ("gross negligence manslaughter"); and

Conduct taking the form of an unlawful act involving a danger of some harm that resulted in death ("unlawful and dangerous act manslaughter").'

The latter – a form of 'involuntary manslaughter' – would seem, to the layperson at least, to fit the case. The abortion was unlawful and involved the danger of harm – infection, perforation, haemorrhage – which did transpire in the form of peritonitis and caused the death of the patient. But Dr Gramshaw never faced any charges for the death that he caused. Only his actions and admissions, and the inquest jury's findings, suggest strongly that his most egregious crime was the killing of his young lover and his own unborn child in the illegal operation he carried out at the Glynn Hotel at Easter 1908.

As part of his affair with Margaret Brown, Gramshaw also broke the law governing the age of consent for sexual intercourse. Although the age of consent was 16 in most circumstances, where an individual was in a 'position of authority or trust' in relation to a person under 18 years of age, the age of consent was 18. Gramshaw had been in the position of family doctor, admitting at the inquest that 'he had attended them all', referring to the Brown sisters. Under today's law, this would be an 'abuse of a position of trust' under the Sexual Offences Act.

From a professional perspective, any of these crimes – performing an abortion, manslaughter, abuse of trust by sexual activity – would most likely have ended Gramshaw's medical career. The General Medical Council would consider each of them to indicate professional misconduct and remove him from their Register, making it impossible for him to practise. With his professional, personal and family life all facing ruin, Gramshaw must have seen suicide as his only option. Suicide, illegal until 1961, was his final crime.

His other crimes, much earlier in his life, were minor by comparison. He evaded the excise taxes due on his use of the Gramshaw arms, and his employment of menservants, resulting in fines from the court of petty sessions. He failed to pay school fees and apprenticeship fees for his sons' education: and while he evaded the first charge on a technicality, on the latter he had to pay back the sums owed after losing a case at the High Court. And he misrepresented his medical qualifications and experience to his employers (and for many years to patients in a public directory advertising his services) by falsely claiming a medical degree from the University of Pennsylvania and experience as resident medical officer at the Nottingham Dispensary.

Gramshaw was also habitually dishonest. He lied to the Census takers (on several occasions), the Apothecaries Hall and various employers about his age. It is unlikely that Dr Huthwaite would have allowed his assistant to attend the critically-ill Harriet Brown if he had known that Gramshaw was only 15 at the time. The examiners of Apothecaries Hall, Dublin, would not have allowed him to sit for their Licentiate if they had known he was only 19, not over 21, at the time; particularly as this meant he had not had time to achieve the years of experience in different specialities required to sit the exam.

But Gramshaw was not unique in any of these infractions. Many people failed to pay their excise duties; and many people were flexible about their age, both at Census time and on key occasions such as marriages. Equally, it has never been unusual for people to exaggerate their experience and expertise in order to secure a job. Ultimately, Gramshaw gained an enormous amount of experience as a local doctor in 35 years in the role. The fact that 1,000 people from York, Stillington and surrounding villages turned out for his funeral testifies to the respect and gratitude he generated in local families by attending to their births, illnesses, accidents and deaths. Even if some of those present were drawn by sheer curiosity following the scandalous newspaper stories, there was still a solid show of support for 'the village doctor'. Until the fateful decision to undertake an illegal abortion on Margaret Brown, Gramshaw had been, in the eyes of his patients, his profession and his community, a good doctor.

Nor was Gramshaw unique in being a doctor brought down by his own shocking crime. He was not the first nor the last doctor to use his medical skills illegally; and many of the medical men who did so committed more, and considerably more heinous, crimes than Dr Gramshaw.

Dr William Palmer was one. He and Gramshaw shared a number of interests: both were keen on horse-racing and both were prone to womanising. The difference was that Palmer also gambled heavily on the horses and often desperately needed money to service his debts. At the age of 17, he was dismissed from his medical apprenticeship for embezzlement. He was said to have left another training post when it was discovered that he had been running an abortion service on the side. Once he had managed to qualify as a doctor, in 1846 at the age of 22, he set up his practice in Rugeley in Staffordshire and got married. Then the activities that earned him the nickname 'Palmer the Poisoner' began. His mother-in-law, Ann Thornton, died while visiting the Palmers and her money passed to Palmer's wife, also called Ann. Four of the couple's five children died in infancy between 1851 and 1854. In 1854 Ann herself died shortly after her husband had taken out a £13,000 assurance policy on her life and while he was having an affair with their housemaid, who bore his child. Palmer also insured his brother Walter's life; and Walter subsequently died in 1855.

In November of the same year, Palmer went to the races in Shrewsbury with his friend John Parsons Cook.

Afterwards they went out celebrating together in a pub and then returned to Rugeley to the Talbot Hotel. Cook was already complaining of feeling ill; and a chambermaid at the hotel sampled a portion of the broth that had been prepared for John Cook, and which Palmer had insisted his friend should eat, and also fell ill. On 21 November, John Cook died in the agony of tetanic convulsions, which contorted his body so that at times only the back of his head and his heels were touching the bed. His death came just three days after the Palmers' youngest child also died. Meanwhile Dr Palmer had collected Cook's winning on the races. His own betting had been massively unsuccessful.

John Cook's stepfather demanded a post-mortem examination of his stepson's body. In spite of Palmer's attempts at the post-mortem to upset the container containing the stomach contents, and then to bribe a postboy to overturn the carriage carrying the container, antimony – a toxic, semi-metallic element – was found in Cook's stomach. This finding, together with the evidence about the compatibility of Cook's symptoms with strychnine poisoning and the fact that Palmer had bought strychnine shortly before Cook's death, led the inquest jury to a verdict of 'wilful murder'. They had formed the same conclusion at the inquest into Walter Palmer's death. The bodies of Palmer's wife Ann and his brother Walter were exhumed and re-examined, but there was not enough evidence to be found in these post-mortems to add their deaths to the criminal charge against Palmer. He was charged only with the murder by poisoning of John Cook.

William Palmer's trial took place at the Central Criminal

Court – the Old Bailey – in London, where it had been moved under the provisions of a new Act of Parliament because it was felt that he was unlikely to have a fair trial in Staffordshire. No fewer than 26 doctors and four eminent professors of chemistry or anatomy gave evidence, principally about tetanus, tetanic convulsions, and whether they should expect to find strychnine at post-mortem if a person had died of poisoning by the substance. Unfortunately for the jury, their evidence, based on experiments on dogs, cats and rabbits as well as their individual recollections of human cases they had treated, was contradictory. They agreed that Cook had died from tetanic convulsions but could not agree on what caused the convulsions. The prosecution focused on poisoning by strychnine, claiming the antimony which was found in his body had been used to 'soften up' Cook's system so that he would succumb to the strychnine (which was not found). The doctors for the defence claimed his death was 'incompatible' with strychnine poisoning and repeatedly pointed out that none of the substance was found in his body. They suggested idiopathic (of unknown cause) tetanus, tetanus resulting from syphilis, 'epileptic convulsions with tetanic complications', or convulsions caused by some 'gritty granules' found in Cook's spine. They even proposed that Cook's symptoms were indistinguishable from those of angina.

While the jury grappled with the daunting volume and complexity of the medical evidence, they also had to grasp Palmer's complicated financial activities. They heard evidence that he had forged his mother's signature in order to draw money from her account. They were told about his debts, high-interest borrowing, rapidly-cashed insurance policies, and dire need for large sums of money at the time of Cook's death. Palmer's local solicitor, who had been enlisted by Palmer to help set up the insurance policies on his wife and brother, was not helpful in court. He dithered desperately to try to avoid confirming his signature on various documents that he had clearly both written and signed. And he found himself repeatedly having to deny that he had had a 'relationship of impropriety' with Palmer's mother, in whose house he admitted he had stayed for two or three nights a week, in the absence of Palmer or his brothers, in spite of having a house of his own only a quarter of a mile away.

Along with the professors, doctors and solicitors from Rugeley, Birmingham and London, the trial brought numerous other witnesses in front of the jury. From Palmer's home town of Rugeley came the police inspector, the postmaster, a number of doctors, the bank manager and his clerk, a butcher and a saddler, three staff members from the Talbot Inn, and the apothecary and his assistant. From Staffordshire county were called the police superintendent, the Coroner and some farmers. A police inspector from London, a woman who had had tetanus and survived, and the Secretary of the Jockey Club added to the mass of evidence that the twelve jurymen needed to consider, as they tried Dr Palmer for his life. The defence did its best, even venturing to ask the judge to amend his summing up to the jury, which seemed to favour the prosecution's case. This seems to have instilled confidence in the accused: at one point, Palmer passed a note to his solicitor saying that he was confident that the jury would return a 'not guilty' verdict.

The trial lasted for 12 days and the jury was out for just one hour and 17 minutes. In spite of the purely circumstantial evidence they had heard, they returned with a verdict that Palmer was guilty of the murder of his friend John Cook. The judges put black cloths on their wigs and Lord Campbell pronounced the sentence of death. In part of his address to the prisoner, he said:

'Whether this be the first and only offence of this sort which you have committed is only known to God and your own conscience. It is seldom that such a familiarity with the means of death is made the means of committing a crime … the Act of Parliament under which you have been tried, and under which you have been brought to the bar of this Court, gives leave to the Court to direct that the sentence, under such circumstances, shall be executed either within the jurisdiction of the Central Criminal Court, or in the county where the offence was committed. We think, for the sake of example, that sentence ought to be executed in the County of Stafford. I hope that this terrible case will deter others from committing such atrocious crimes, as it will be seen that whatever may be the skill, science or experience for accomplishing such an offence, it will be detected and punished.'

Around 30,000 people turned out when Palmer the Poisoner was hanged at Stafford Gaol in June 1856 and buried in the prison grounds. The case was so notorious that an apocryphal story says that the people of Rugeley petitioned the Prime Minister to change the name of the town to dissociate it from the scandal. Supposedly the PM responded that the name could be changed as long as the town was named after him. His name was Palmerston. Whether the poisoner's contemporaries William Palmer, teacher of flute, singing and the pianoforte, or Professor William Palmer Forte, who had a Chair in Chemistry at University College London, or the Reverend William Palmer of Magdalen, felt it necessary to dissociate themselves from their unfortunate namesake is not known.

Amongst all the accusers surrounding William Palmer at the time of his trial, there was one person who came forward to speak in defence of the accused's character. Dr Alfred William Warder was a general practitioner living and working in Chelsea in London. Like Palmer, he was a family man, with a wife and four children. In addition to his medical work with patients, he was also a researcher in toxicology and a lecturer in medical jurisprudence – legal aspects of medicine – at the school of medicine attached to St George's hospital in London.

But if a character witness is expected to be of unimpeachable integrity, then Palmer was relying on the wrong man. Lord Campbell might have hoped that William Palmer's conviction would act as a deterrent to others. On the contrary, as a newspaper commented later: 'To Warder, however, the [Palmer] case seems not to have been a warning, but simply a study...'

Chapter 25

THE THREE WIVES OF DR WARDER

Dr Alfred Warder was a methodical man: an organiser and a planner. On Monday 9 July 1866, he took the train up to London from Brighton with two tasks to accomplish. First, he went to a druggist shop and bought some prussic acid. Then he took a hansom cab to the house in Brompton where his four children were staying with his sister-in-law, Miss Gunning. He did not go into the house to see her or the children: he had come prepared with a letter already written and he simply sent this into the house by one of the servants. Then he returned to the station and caught a train back to Brighton. Arriving at nine o'clock, he returned to the furnished apartment in Bedford Square where he and his wife Ellen had been staying for the last two months.

Dr Warder told the landlady of the Bedford Square apartment, Miss Charlotte Lansdell, that he had already dined and did not require anything. He asked her to make up his account for the rooms he and his wife had been occupying. When the landlady and her servant retired to bed that Monday evening, they left Dr Warder in the sitting room. Once they had gone, at about 11.00pm, Warder let himself out of the house, leaving the door on the latch, and walked to the Bedford Hotel on Cavendish Place where he had already booked himself a room for the night. He was carrying a black bag and the staff there believed that he had just arrived from London on the late mail train. He said he would go to bed immediately and he was shown up to his room.

The Warders normally lived in Penzance in Cornwall. They were visiting Brighton where Ellen Warder's brother, Mr Richard Brannell, was a local surgeon and where her sister Jane also lived. Their marriage, three months before the visit, had been a surprise to the Brannell family. Ellen Brannell was the youngest sibling of a respected family from Penzance who had finished her education in Paris and worked as a governess in 'superior' families. Now that she was suddenly married for the first time at the age of 37, the couple was visiting relatives so that Alfred could be introduced to his new in-laws. It had been his idea to have a quiet wedding without telling the family; they were married in January and he wanted to keep it from their friends until midsummer. Ellen Brannell had agreed to the quiet wedding without telling her family; but once they were married, she let her relatives and friends know of her new state. Her new husband, who was almost ten years her senior, was a general practitioner who had worked in Chelsea as well as in Devon and Gloucestershire, lectured in medical jurisprudence at a London University, and been the medical officer for St Luke's workhouse in Chelsea; she was no doubt very proud of him.

Ellen's marriage might have been secret but it was not precipitate. She had known Alfred Warder for some time before the wedding as he had previously been married to her best friend, Jane Ann de Valerie, the daughter of a Royal Navy commander, whom Ellen had met in Paris. In fact, Ellen had signed her name to Alfred and Jane's marriage certificate as a witness in December 1864. Jane had died the following year. Ellen had married the widower on 26 January 1866, and they had arrived in Brighton at the end of May to introduce the groom to the bride's brother and sister.

In the house at Bedford Square on the morning of Tuesday 10 July, the servant went up to the Warders' rooms sometime between seven and eight o'clock to deliver the account as Dr Warder had requested the night before. When she reported back to Miss Lansdell, the landlady went up to the Warders' apartment herself. She looked in the sitting room and the bedroom and found no sign of the doctor. His bed had not been slept in and both rooms were in the same state as they had been the previous day. She was not particularly concerned, however: she had seen that the front door was on the latch and assumed that the doctor had gone out for an early walk.

At the Bedford Hotel, it was also noted that Dr Warder had not come down for breakfast. The chambermaid looked in on him several times during the morning and saw him lying in bed, his feet poking out of the covers. His continuing absence became the talk of the servants. When he had still not stirred by two o'clock in the afternoon, the maid went into the bedroom. Then it was quickly apparent why he had not arisen that day: he had been dead for many hours. A Dr James Pickford who lived on the opposite side of Cavendish Place was called in to see the body. He thought the doctor had been dead for twelve to fourteen hours, meaning that he had died in the early hours of the morning. On the bedside table was a small blue bottle with the capacity to hold ten fluid drachms; it now held only four drachms of Scheel's prussic acid. Scheel's mixture contained four per cent of the pure acid, twice the strength of an ordinary medical mixture. Dr Pickford noted the 'easy position of the body' and the undisturbed bedclothes and deduced that the dose Dr Warder had taken would cause almost instantaneous death, without convulsions. He seemed to have planned his own demise with meticulous organisation and care. Strangely, in the pocket of the dead doctor's trousers, Dr Pickford found a well-worn bottle containing two opium pills, each of four grains' strength, which seemed to have been carried in the pocket for a long time. This, Dr Pickford thought, was Dr Warder's long-standing suicide kit; though in the end, when he had decided to take his own life, he chose what was probably a quicker and more certain method. Also in the hotel bedroom with the body was a letter, addressed to Miss Lansdell of Bedford Square and marked 'To be forwarded immediately.'

The inquest into Alfred Warder's death began the following day at the Bedford Hotel where he had died. Miss Lansdell from the Bedford Square lodgings and the staff of the Bedford Hotel in Cavendish Place gave evidence of the circumstances leading up to the discovery of the doctor's body; and Dr Pickford described what he had found in the hotel bedroom. The Coroner then read out the contents of the letter that the doctor had left beside his deathbed to be sent on to Miss Lansdell:

'My dear Miss Lansdell – you have already suffered enough through me and mine, and another death in your house would of course be worse. When you receive this, have the kindness to telegraph to Miss Gunning, 7, Sydney Street, Brompton, London SW, to whom you give up [sic] what I have left in your house. I have left on the table the cash for the bills, and 3 pounds in addition as some compensation.

Believe me truly yours, A W Warder.

P.S. Inquire for my keys and watch.'

The surgeon Richard Brannell, Dr Warder's new brother-in-law, also gave evidence at the inquest. He said that the deceased doctor had married his sister Ellen Brannell about five months before, without the knowledge of any member of the family: 'He was a perfect stranger to me until he came to Brighton about the end of May last.' The last time Richard Brannell had seen Alfred Warder was on the Saturday, four days before, when they had both attended Ellen Warder's funeral. Questioned by the jury about this encounter, the surgeon did not mince his words. He said: 'I did not speak to him at the funeral of my sister, because the circumstances of her death rendered it disagreeable for me to do so: in fact, I believe him to be her murderer.'

This would not have come as a complete shock to the jurymen. An inquest into the death of Ellen Warder had already begun and was adjourned awaiting the results of tests being carried out on her internal organs. Suspicion was already rife that her death on 1 July at the age of 37, only five months after her marriage, had not been a natural one.

Ellen had fallen ill almost as soon as she arrived in Brighton. Her brother had called in a local doctor, Richard Taaffe, who prescribed for hysteria, and the patient improved. Her husband, Dr Warder, however, said that she was suffering from great pains in the bladder for which he was administering a tincture of aconite in a dose of 20 drops. Dr Taaffe objected to this treatment and the dose, and substituted henbane, tincture of castor, valerian and laudanum and water fomentations. These remedies seemed to be working. But after a while Dr Warder informed his colleague that his wife had 'got tired' of these medicines and could not take them. So Dr Taaffe changed his prescription: but he did not fetch the medicines himself, leaving Warder to do so.

Ellen Warder was cared for by her husband and Dr Taaffe never saw her by herself. Her husband alone took her food and administered her medicines. As the woman's health continued to fluctuate, Dr Taaffe became suspicious that 'something was being administered to her improperly'. He consulted with her brother and they agreed to call in a third medical man, Mr Frederick Jowers. This was on Saturday 30 June and the decision was too late to save the ailing patient. On the following day, at six o'clock in the morning, Ellen died in the apartment at Bedford Square. Her brother arrived just as she died.

Richard Brannell knew that his sister had brought a substantial sum of money to her husband on her marriage; and with the suspicious circumstances of her death, he demanded a post-mortem on the remains. The examination was carried out by Dr Taaffe, assisted by Dr William Moore and Mr Jowers, and parts of Ellen Warder's stomach and intestines were sent for analysis to Dr Alfred Swaine Taylor of Guy's hospital: the same expert who, ten years earlier, had examined the organs of John Parsons Cook for the trial of William Palmer. Alfred Warder asked Dr Taaffe for a death certificate after the post-mortem; but Dr Taaffe refused to give it, even when Dr Warder pointed to the appearance of his wife's liver and brain as sufficient cause of death (he had been present at his wife's post-mortem). He pressed Taaffe, saying he thought the body should be buried immediately 'as it would not keep in this hot weather.' The funeral eventually took place on Saturday 7 July, almost a week after Ellen's death.

The inquest on Ellen's body was opened then adjourned until 13 July, to allow time for Dr Taylor's report to be provided; and Dr Warder was summoned to appear at the resumed inquest. Mr White, the Chief

Officer of the borough police, went so far as to issue a subpoena to the doctor, fearing he would not attend the proceedings voluntarily. And, while the circumstances were not sufficient to warrant the doctor's arrest, the police kept up a covert surveillance on his movements, including his visit to London. They were aware that this followed an unsuccessful attempt to buy aconite from a druggist in Brighton.

The police had further reason for suspicion against Dr Warder when they received some startling information from Devon. In a letter dated 10 July – the day the doctor was found dead in his bed at the hotel – the Superintendent of the Devon police wrote to his counterpart in Brighton with some local intelligence:

> 'A Dr Warder, stated by the inhabitants to be the same Dr Warder that had lived at Ottery St Mary, in the district, about two years and a half ago, had a wife who died under similar circumstances to those of which the wife of Dr Warder had died in Brighton. There was no post-mortem examination as the death was not reported to the Coroner or the police. No part of the body was ever sent to a professor or chemist to be analysed; but it was left with Dr Warder to be buried in a very quiet way. He left Ottery St Mary very shortly afterwards, sending his children away.'

This was a reference to the death of Alfred Warder's first wife, Alicia, to whom he had been married for 19 years. The marriage had not been untroubled: she had left him several times to live apart. Then, during one of their periods of co-habitation, she had died. The couple had four children, three girls and a boy who were aged between eight and 16 years old when their mother died in 1863. Afterwards the children were initially sent to live in Italy, though they had since returned to live with their maternal aunt in London. As the inquest into Dr Warder's death continued, his sister-in-law Miss Gunning, through the presence of her solicitor Mr Eland, provided evidence of more of Warder's methodical planning: he had written three letters to her, providing detailed instructions about his children's futures. The first, dated 3 July, two days after his wife's death, said:

> ' "… as, in the event of anything happening to me, you would be the nearest relative to the children, I thought it desirable to give you a list of what I now possess …". There followed a minute list of property ranging from 100 acres of land in New Zealand to many kinds of stocks and investments, specifying where each was deposited, and the possible prospects of each. He also apportioned each to the children, and finally commended the children to the care of Miss Gunning.'

The second letter was dated 9 July and was the one he had hand-delivered to a servant at Miss Gunning's house during his trip to London. It said: 'In my present state of difficulty I thought it best to leave a little property in your hands to take care of. I will write to you again.' The third letter bore the same date and this too was read at the inquest and reported by the press:

' "I write to you, I believe, for the last time, as when you shall receive this I shall be no more." It went on to request that the children should "not be told all" – tell them merely that his "death had been sudden". He then wrote, "And now to business" following this up with an explanation that he had changed a deposit note for £2,300, and had thought it best to do so, and leave the cash at her house in the box which she had received. He reviewed at length the prospects of one of his sons, and begged Miss Gunning's influence with a member of the peerage (whom he named) on his (the son's) behalf. Towards the end he alluded to the approaching marriage of one of his daughters to a German gentleman, who expected to get a professorship, and said he had written to her the same night (Monday), and had sent her £100, which would last her six months, by which time Miss Gunning would have settled on what she would do for the future. The directions given in this letter were most minute and circumstantial, and dealt clearly and lucidly with a very large amount of property, widely distributed in investments &c. Mr Eland [Miss Gunning's solicitor] added that there were some grounds for believing that insanity was hereditary in the family of Dr Warder.'

Dr Warder's organisation and planning rather discounted the possibility that he had been insane around the time of his death. And Dr Taaffe gave evidence that he had had numerous conversations with Warder about his wife's condition and never saw any sign of insanity. The post-mortem on the doctor's body had found nothing organically wrong with his brain and had confirmed the presence of prussic acid in his stomach. The solicitor's hopeful reference to insanity in the family was a last-ditch attempt to give the jury grounds for the often-used verdict of suicide whilst temporarily insane.

In this case, however, the jury did not take the easy way out. They returned a verdict of *felo de se*: suicide. At this time, this would still mean the deceased's property and possessions being forfeited to the Crown. Mr Eland fought a rearguard action against this, suggesting to the Coroner that Warder had in fact already given his property on trust to his client, Miss Gunning, in his letters and he claimed it on her behalf for the benefit of the deceased's children. The Coroner recorded this claim in his report but left it to the Crown to decide how to dispose of the property. He did however comment that the Crown often passed the property back to the family of the deceased. Then he ordered that the body of the deceased should be disposed of in accordance with the verdict of *felo de se*. So Dr Warder's body was taken to Brighton Cemetery at ten thirty at night and buried in unconsecrated ground by the light of the policemen's bulls-eye lamps. On his coffin was the plain inscription 'A W Warder 1866'.

Chapter 26

THE THIRD MRS WARDER

Ellen Warder suffered terribly, both mentally and physically, before her death. When the inquest on her death resumed for the second time on Monday 16 July at the Olive Branch Inn, the medical evidence was finally available. Dr Taylor, the expert from Guy's hospital, had delivered a very long report which was summarised in the press:

'The chemical and physiological tests concurred therefore in showing that there was no aconite and no alkaloidal poison remaining in the contents of the stomach and intestines of the deceased at the time of her death. The result was, however, quite consistent with the death of the deceased from poison especially poison such as aconite. The only chance of finding it in the contents of a stomach would be in those cases where a comparatively large dose had been swallowed by the deceased shortly before death. If small doses had been given at intervals – a fact to be indicated by symptoms – and none had been given within two or three hours before death, none would be found in the contents of the stomach; but in all cases, whether poison remains in the stomach or not at the time of death, the cause of death can only be determined by a knowledge of the symptoms from which the deceased suffered while living, and in the appearances found in the body after death.'

So although he had not found poison in the body, Dr Taylor believed that death by poisoning could not be ruled out and a decision on this would depend partly on information on the patient's condition and symptoms before death. This information he heard from the doctor who had attended her for the full five weeks of her illness: Dr Taaffe. The expert questioned Dr Taaffe closely and reached his conclusion, at the same time setting out for the jury the extremes of physical distress that had afflicted the victim:

'I have heard the evidence of Dr Taaffe, and the depositions of all the other witnesses, and from what I have myself seen, as well as from the statements of Dr Wilkes, I have formed an opinion upon this case. I have come to the conclusion that the symptoms are those of death from some poison, aconite most probably. My reasons for this opinion are these; the parched condition of the throat, thirst, constriction of the throat, frequent and severe vomiting without any natural cause to account for it, the cessation and recurrence of the symptoms without any natural cause to explain it; the sickness not yielding to the usual sedative remedies, but coming on at intervals, showing great irritability of stomach such as irritant poison would cause; all food and liquids being instantly rejected although no ulceration was afterwards found to explain it; the severe griping pains in the bowels and no purging; the great depression of the heart's action as denoted by the feeble pulse; and the muscular weakness. Then the recovery and relapse without apparent cause form a striking difference between cases of poisoning and of disease. Taking the symptoms as a whole, they are not consistent with any disease I have seen, read or heard of, but they are consistent with such as would be produced by tincture of aconite at intervals in small doses. Some other vegetable irritant might have produced the effect, but I think it most likely aconite.'

Questioned by the jury, Dr Taylor said that Dr Warder had been connected with the Grosvenor Place School of Medicine, and 'no man better understood how to administer aconite, or any other medicine, either healthfully or mischievously, than he did.' He added that, at the time of Dr William Palmer's trial ten years before, 'Dr Warder was one of the school who came forward strongly to defend him': no doubt implying that Warder could have been influenced – or inspired – by Palmer's undetected use of poison for several years before he was caught.

Unlike the objective medical evidence, the testimony of Ellen Warder's relatives and friends painted a more personal and painful picture of the suffering the dead woman had endured. Her sister-in-law Jane Brannell said that Ellen had been a healthy person until she married. Jane had seen Ellen in London at the end of April, when her sister-in-law complained of several attacks of illness affecting her bladder, with the first attack being the most violent. Ellen reported that her husband did not seem to be too concerned: he had said 'he supposed it would wear itself out.' Jane also visited Ellen when she was ill in Brighton, seeing her last on the night before her death. Then Ellen had appeared to Jane to be like 'someone recovering from a bilious attack', and Jane had no inkling that her sister-in-law would be dead in the morning.

Throughout her illness, Dr Warder appeared to be a most attentive husband:

'Dr Warder's attentions were, apparently, of the most devoted kind. For 14 days he rarely quitted the bed or sofa-side of his sick wife, performing unremittingly the duties of the most careful nurse. Mrs Warder's friends had never seen such devotion. She was not allowed to move from the sofa, lest pain or inconvenience might be caused; and her husband was even seen to wash his wife's face and hands, and comb her hair, when too weak to do this herself.'

In spite of this loving attention, Ellen Warder had her own fears about her husband's treatment. As her sister-in-law Jane Brannell told the inquest:

'I recollet my sister saying in London "It is but the one thought of my life that this is the same illness as poor Annie died of." Annie was the name of Dr Warder's previous wife. She did not tell me in London what medicine he was giving her; but she once took up the small phial in her bedroom, and said, "This is aconite, a most deadly poison. I would not touch it for the life of me but he drops it [i.e. ensures the correct number of drops for the desired dose] for me."'

Did she really have an inkling that her illness was not being treated by her husband, but caused by him? She remembered her best friend Annie, Warder's second wife, who died after just eight months of marriage; was the awful truth dawning on her when Warder gave the final dose of aconite to bring about her death? She was never alone with Dr Taaffe, or with her friends and family members, so she never had an opportunity to ask for help or voice her suspicions. Her fear and anguish must have been overwhelming, alongside her physical suffering.

At the end of that third day of the inquest, the Coroner summed up the case. He asked the jury to decide on two questions: 'whether the deceased met her death from poison, and, if so, whether or not that poison was administered by her husband.' The jury did not take long to come to their verdict:

'The jury consulted but a very few moments, and then returned a verdict of Wilful Murder against Dr Warder (who committed suicide on Monday week). The foreman said the jury were of the opinion that the deceased died from poison given to her by her husband, most probably aconite in small doses.'

With this accusation against the dead man formalised, the papers went on to speculate about the deaths of Warder's first two wives. They could not find a financial benefit to him from his first wife, Alicia's, death: but maybe he was just tired of her after 19 years of marriage and wanted a new wife. He married again after just over a year, to Jane Ann de Valerie, a woman whose life was insured and who lived only eight months after her marriage. Once she was dead, he gave up his medical practice, so the press deduced that he then had plenty of money. He married Ellen, his third wife – who brought £500 to the marriage – less than a year after 'Annie's' death, and she lived less than six months after that. Each of the women died from the same symptoms so it is highly likely that Warder poisoned each of his three wives. His indifference to the prolonged suffering of the women before death is in stark contrast to his concern that his own death should be very swift and painless; hence the use of prussic acid rather than the less certain morphia overdose. His callousness in killing those closest to him also contrasts with his polite concern for his Bedford Square landlady. For her benefit he removed himself to a hotel to commit suicide, and added three pounds to his bill payment 'for the inconvenience' he had caused by murdering his wife on her premises. It also contrasts with his concern for his children by the first wife he had killed: he cared about his daughter's imminent marriage, her financial security and his son's future prospects.

Palmer and Warder were both 19th century poisoners. But the abuse of medical knowledge to commit murder did not end at the turn of the century. Two years after Gramshaw's death, in 1910, Dr Hawley Harvey Crippen poisoned his second wife Cora and was hung for the crime. Dr John Bodkin Adams, a genial and popular GP from Eastbourne, was thought to have poisoned more than 160 of his elderly patients between 1935 and 1956 in order to benefit from their Wills. He was acquitted of the two murder charges brought against him, however. The most prolific medical killer of all is also the most recent: Dr Harold Shipman is thought to have killed more than 200 of his patients by injecting them with an overdose. He was found guilty of 15 murders and sentenced to life imprisonment. He committed suicide in prison.

Dr Gramshaw's crimes were very different to these. He never intended to kill Margaret Brown; he did not plan a murder. He only wanted to solve their shared problem by ending a pregnancy. He used his medical knowledge to do something illegal, and he should have foreseen the risk of serious harm, so he may well have been found guilty of manslaughter had he stood trial. But like many of his medical forebears, he chose to end his own life rather than let justice take its course.

That could have been the end of Gramshaw's story. But seventy years on, a surprising new development opened the book again.

Chapter 27

SEEKING DR GRAMSHAW

In 1989, the York Press carried a brief article headed 'Lost Image'. It said:

'A retired York nurse is trying to find a photograph of her father more than 80 years after his death.

Dr Farbrace Gramshaw practised in Stillington for 30 years, then moved to Bootham, York, before killing himself with an overdose of morphia as a scandal blew up in his private life. Now a child born out of wedlock is searching for a photograph of the man she never saw.

Inquiries to the medical schools in London and Dublin, where he trained, and to the Philosophical Society, of which he was a member, have proved fruitless. Dr Gramshaw was a Past Master in the York freemasons, but his 82-year-old daughter has been unable to discover whether the lodge has a photograph in its archives.

If any readers have a photograph or think they could find one, please ring Mary on York [telephone number].'

This was Mary Ronayne, Margaret Brown's first child, whose birth in February 1907 was both attended and registered by Dr Gramshaw, hoping to find a picture of her father. Margaret had given up the baby for adoption very soon after the birth; she was certainly adopted within six months, as Margaret did not have a baby with her when went to The Retreat as a nurse in September 1907. In fact, the hospital must have been unaware that Margaret had ever had a child, or she would not have been accepted as a nurse probationer. It was very difficult to find work as a single mother with an illegitimate child, so many mothers were forced to give up their child one way or another.

The most formal way of passing on responsibility for a child was by arranging for him or her to become the 'ward' of someone else. This gave the guardian custody of the child, although not full parental rights. Wardship was granted by the Chancery Court, so it was not much used – and certainly not by impecunious young unmarried mothers.

At the other end of the social scale there was 'baby farming'; still remarkably prevalent in the 1900s when Margaret had her first child. This was, at best, a form of fostering or 'boarding out' in which a woman paid another family to look after her child. Sometimes this was a temporary arrangement paid for week by week; but often the mother left her child for good in this way, having made a single payment to the family taking in the child. At worst, however, children in baby farms were neglected or badly treated, and sometimes killed, leading to the passage of the Infant Life Protection Act 1887. Under this legislation, if more than one child was adopted for money, and for more than 48 hours, the home had to be registered and regularly inspected. This was intended to ensure that they were in suitable accommodation and appropriately fed and clothed. However, there were weaknesses in this protection. It only applied until a child was five years old, and it did not cover people who were serial adopters – for money – of one child at a time. It also did not require any notification of the removal of an adopted child, so it could not detect frequent child deaths in a household. Children who died in baby farms could simply be disposed of – in one reported case, a woman burned the corpses on the kitchen fire while telling others in the household that the undertaker had been to take them away.

In spite of the Act, and revisions to tighten up the tracing of children in 1897, scandals and criminal cases associated with baby farming were frequent throughout the first decade of the 20th century. In 1905 a Grimsby couple was being sought by the police after the deaths of three of the seven children they were looking after, without having registered their home. They had insured the lives of the children and claimed the payout as their parents. In Dorset in 1904 there was a 'horrible case of child cruelty':

'At the Dorset Assizes yesterday, Mr Justice Ridley heard an exceptionally bad case of cruelty to children. The accused was Emma Hooper, of Stoborough, Fareham, a widow who eked out a living by baby farming. In October 1902 she undertook charge of Dorothy and Ethel Jackson, the illegitimate twin daughters of Bessie Jackson, a domestic servant. The mother paid £2 6s a month for the twins and an older child.

The evidence for the prosecution disclosed gross neglect and ill-usage. A box filled with straw served as a cradle, and the children were never taken out into the fresh air. When discovered on May 9th they were much emaciated. The Rontgen rays [x-rays] revealed that the right shoulder blade of the child Dorothy and both the bones of her legs had been fractured. The broken ends of the bones had grown together irregularly without surgical aid. The prisoner, at the time, said to the Inspector, "If I had had a doctor I should have had to pay him."

The prisoner was sentenced to twelve months' hard labour, the Judge describing it as a really dreadful case.'

In Leeds, a woman who not only ran a baby farm but also a private maternity home that performed illegal operations – abortions – was sentenced to five years' penal servitude in 1906. For the most shocking cases of baby farming and child cruelty, sentences could be even harsher: they included the death penalty. Ada Williams was 24 years old when she was hanged at Newgate prison in 1900 for killing a baby of 19 months old called Selina Jones:

> 'The woman lived at Barnes, and for a premium adopted the infant, whose body was some time afterwards found in the River Thames, tied by means of a sash cord. Medical evidence given at the trial showed that the child had been stunned and then strangled. The woman's husband was tried with her at the Old Bailey, but acquitted.'

Three years later, there was a rare double execution at Holloway prison at the conclusion of the 'Finchley baby farming case'. Annie Walters, aged 54, and Ameila Sach, 29 – a nurse and a midwife – had been found guilty of the systematic trafficking of young children and the murder of a newborn baby. They were hanged together and buried in the prison precincts.

Not all baby farming was badly done. Miss Isabel Smith, an Inspector for the London County Council, reported that, for every unsatisfactory instance she had come across in seven years' experience …

> '…there were a dozen clean and industrious women, careful and even skilled nurses, who were, in order to help to meet the cruel London rents, giving to their helpless charges for the paltry remuneration of five or six – in rare cases, it is true, seven, eight, or even ten – shillings per

week not only the necessary food, shelter, and laundry, but, with the full consciousness of the heavy responsibility entailed, far more anxious and careful attention day and night than they had probably bestowed on their own children, or that the poor little "unwanteds" were likely to have ever received from their own kith and kin.'

Nevertheless, the Government set up a Select Committee of the House of Commons in 1908 to consider whether the provisions of the Infant Life Protection Act should be extended to households which had taken in a single child. The wording of the Act was not entirely clear and a Glasgow judge had tried to clarify it in a case two years earlier:

'He had come to the conclusion that, while the phraseology of the Act was somewhat peculiar, it was only intended to apply to a person who got more than one infant at a time, and not to a person who on successive occasions got one infant at a time. It seemed to his Lordship that the theory of the Act apparently was that as one swallow did not make a summer, so one baby at a time did not make a baby farm.'

This interpretation would have excluded many households from the necessity for registration and inspection, and permitted serial (though not simultaneous) abuse, neglect or murder of single looked-after children without any intervention from the authorities. Pressing the need for a change to this situation, the General Secretary of the Scottish National Society for the Protection of Children told the Committee that, in his Society's experience, single child adoptions were very common. He was not very complimentary about the way this practice was often carried out:

> 'So far as one could judge, the motive for adoption was frequently a desire for company. Working class people often adopted a child in much the same way as childless women in other classes of society adopted cats, or dogs, or parrots. In the second place, they seemed to do it not altogether in a professional manner, but more to supplement their living. In cases where only one child was kept the liability to neglect was greater.'

He may also have lacked a basic understanding of the world in which his Society operated, since it seems far more likely that the need to make a living through fostering was the pre-eminent motivation, with the desire for company coming a long way behind.

Following the Select Committee's report (and a number of other committees' work), the Government passed the Children Act 1908. This had a much wider scope but included the reforms that had been called for to the Infant Life Protection Act following recent court cases. So the registration of foster homes was extended to cover those taking in only one child at a time; the age limit for the children whose care was regulated was raised from five to seven years; any deaths amongst these looked-after children had to be reported to the Coroner, who then usually had to hold an inquest; and the person taking in the child was forbidden to be a party to any insurance on the child's life.

Margaret Brown had to decide what to do with her illegitimate daughter Mary the year before these reforms were made. She chose a middle path between the exclusive and expensive route of wardship and the perils of the baby farm: adoption. While there was no formal or legal mechanism to have a child adopted in 1907, arrangements could be made locally and this is what Margaret did. She handed her child to a local couple who took on her care and upbringing, and became her family.

George and Frances Flatt, aged 30 and 34, lived in Groves Lane, York, only half a mile from Margaret's childhood home on Vyner Street and the flat where Mary had been born on Haxby Road. They had been married for two years and had no children of their own when they took Mary Brown into their home. Frances Flatt was a York woman, whose parents and brothers lived close by in Nelson Street; her husband George came from Suffolk. He had come up to York and married Frances in 1905, and he was now working as a baker's van man. Their adopted daughter Mary seems to have been the Flatt's only child; by 1911, she was four, and still listed on the census under her birth name of Mary Brown, with her relationship to the head of the household 'adopted child'. The only other occupants of the house are her adoptive parents, the Flatts, and a lodger.

The close proximity between Margaret Brown's old home, her temporary lodgings and the adoptive family's home opens up two interesting possiblities. One is that Margaret might still have been in touch with her daugther during the first year of the youngster's life, visiting her at her adopted home. She might even have hoped to reclaim the girl if she could settle down somewhere and be maintained by her well-off doctor lover. If so, this plan came to a tragically premature end with Margaret's death in 1908. The second possiblity is that it could have been Dr Gramshaw who found the childless couple to adopt Margaret's baby. He had been in practice in York for four years when Mary was born, and was in a position to know people who might want a child but be unable to have one of their own. In search of a solution for his young mistress's difficulty, and under the usual pretext of being her guardian, he might have introduced Margaret to George and Frances Flatt. Given that Mary Brown grew up knowing that Dr Gramshaw was her father, however, either Margaret Brown or Gramshaw himself must at some point have told the adoptive parents this. Since both died in 1908, when the child was only just one year old, it can only have been the Flatts who told Mary about her paternity.

Sadly, Mary Brown did not have her adoptive parents for most of her adult life. Her mother Frances died in 1927 at the age of 54, when Mary was just 20 years old. And her father George died five years later at the age of 55. He did live long enough however to see his daughter become a nurse, and get married in 1928. Her bridegroom was

John Bradley, five years her senior and a 'motor driver' by profession. His father worked as a carriage gasman for the London and North Eastern Railway, where Mary's father was also working as a labourer. So it is possible that the two young people were introduced through their fathers' acquaintanceship at work. Interestingly, Mary's unusual middle name seems to have evolved over time. On her birth certificate it was recorded as Ronayne. By the 1911 census, when she was four years old, it was 'Roumania'. And her death registration has 'Mary Romania Bradley.'

Mary went on to have a daughter of her own and lived to be 90 years of age. She died in 1997. There was no follow-up to the newspaper article about her search for an image of her natural father, Dr Gramshaw. It is likely that she did not find any photographs, since none seems to exist except a single poor reproduction of a picture used in a newspaper at the time of his death. The York Medical Society has a photograph album with excellent posed portrait photographs of its members in the late 19th and early 20th century; but F. Sidney Gramshaw is not amongst them. The other groups and societies of which he was a member – the York and Ainsty Hunt, the York Philosophical Society, the York and District Field Naturalists' Society, the York Lodge of Freemasons – also seem to have no photographs of this particular member. For a man so socially active and consious of his position in society, Gramshaw appears to have been remarkably camera-shy. Or maybe there were photographs – professional or personal – which his family either did not keep, did not pass on, or chose to keep private. In the absence of a good photograph, the image which lingers in the mind in relation to the life and crimes of Dr Gramshaw is that of the faded lead-lettering on his gravestone which reads, appropriately: "In hope of the mercy of God".

*The house in Stillington where the Gramshaws lived for 30 years,
then called The Villa*

Dr Gramshaw's last house at 78 Bootham, York,
then called Dunholme

St Nicholas's Church, Stillington, where Dr Gramshaw served on the vestry committee and where his funeral was held.

Grave marker for Dr Gramshaw. It reads 'Farbrace Sidney Gramshaw
MD FRCS He practised his profession for thirty six years in this county
and died 7th May 1908 aged 54. In hope of the mercy of God.'

The house at 36 Vyner Street, York,
where Margaret Brown grew up.

The premises at 169 Haxby Road, York,
where Margaret Brown had her first baby.

The former Glynn Hotel on Micklegate, York,
where Margaret Brown died.

Grave marker for Margaret Brown.

A WORD ABOUT SOURCES

Where possible, I have used official sources to recreate the story of Dr Gramshaw and his family. These include the births, deaths and marriages index; information from local archives such as street directories, parish records and hospital casebooks; information from national records such as army medal rolls, probate and Will records and company shipping lists; and the training and membership records of medical Royal Colleges. Unfortunately, for some aspects of the story, formal records no longer exist. None of the formal inquest papers relating to Sidney Gramshaw or Margaret Brown remain in local or county archives, for example.

So much of the material for these aspects of the book was found in newspaper coverage of the events. This coverage is often extensive – it is always a bonus to find verbatim reporting of what witnesses said at a trial or inquest – but also sometimes contradictory. Different reporters cover the same story in different ways, and report direct quotations from key players, or even individuals' names, differently. I have taken the approach of combining information from a range of newspaper stories to try to arrive at a reasonable account of what happened, what was said, and by whom.

In the following pages I have identified the sources of the story in each chapter, whether official record, online information, research by others, or archived newspaper coverage. I hope this will help the reader to understand how the story was recreated, and where background information has come from.

References/sources

Chapter 1

https://premium.weatherweb.net/weather-in-history-1900-to-1949-ad/

British Newspaper Archive

Chapter 2

Births, Marriages and Deaths Index accessed online

Medical Register online

British Newspaper Archive

Will of William Farbrace Gramshaw: The National Archives PROB 11/1976/223

Stillington and District Community Archive

www.nhshistory.net

Archives of the Apothecaries' Hall Dublin at The Royal College of Physicians of Ireland

The Medical Directory 1873

Kelly's Directory North Riding of Yorkshire 1872

https://www.genuki.org.uk/big/eng/YKS/NRY/Stillington/Stillington90

Chapter 3

British Newspaper Archive

Stillington and District Community Archive

Chapter 4

Royal Society of Physicians of Ireland, archives of the Society and of Apothecaries' Hall

Tracing your medical ancestors, by Michelle Higgs, published by Pen and Sword Family History, 2011

National Newspaper Archive

A History of the York and Ainsty Hunt, by William Scarth Dixon, published by Richard Jackson, Leeds, 1899

http://www.legislation.gov.uk/ukpga/1875/55/pdfs/ukpga_18750055_en.pdf

The Letters of Lady M W Montagu during the Embassy to Constantinople, 1716-18, Vol 1

Anti-Vaccination Leagues, Archives of Disease in Childhood, 1984, 59, 1195-96

https://vaccine-safety-training.org/history-of-vaccine-development.html

The History Of Vaccines And Immunization: Familiar Patterns, New Challenges. Alexandra Minna Stern and Howard Markel, Health Affairs>Vol. 24, No. 3: The Vaccine Enterprise

The Royal College of Surgeons of Edinburgh

Chapter 5

University of Pennsylvania Catalogue 1869-70,1870-71 and 1871-72 on www.archives.upenn.edu

Archives of the Apothecaries' Hall Dublin at Royal College of Physicians of Ireland

Nottinghamshire Archives DD/ND/6/3, DD/ND/6/4, DD/ND/1/2

The Royal College of Physicians of England

The Dispensaries – Healthcare for the Poor before the NHS. Britain's forgotten healthcare system, by Michael Whitfield, Author House, 2016

The Public and Private Faces of Eighteenth Century London Dispensary Charity, by Bronwen Croxson, Medical History, 1997

Bosworth, Ennis C. (1998) Public healthcare in Nottingham 1750 to 1911. PhD thesis, University of Nottingham.Access from the University of Nottingham repository http://eprints.nottingham. ac.uk/11306/1/243761.pdf

British Newspaper Archive

UK Medical Directories 1895, 1900, 1905

UK Medical Registers online 1875, 1879, 1887, 1899, 1903

The Royal College of Surgeons of Edinburgh

Chapter 6

British Newspaper Archive

Arms and the (tax-)man: The use and taxation of armorial bearings in Britain, 1798–1944. Dissertation by Philip Daniel Allfrey

Stillington and District Archive

www.measuringworth.com

Registry Minutes, Stillington STN 24 at the Borthwick Library, University of York

Chapter 7

British Newspaper Archive

Kelly's Directory of York and the North Riding of Yorkshire 1900, 1902, 1905, 1906

www.yorktheatreroyal.co.uk

The History and Development of York County Hospital, by Chris Dowell, published 2007, Studio Two Printers

Petticoat Government – the story of the York Home for Nurses, by Rosemary Cook, published in 2019 by Troubadour

The Genesis of Freemasonry, by David Harrison, published 2009 by Lewis Masonic

Archivist, Zetland Chapter, York Lodge of Freemasons, personal communication

United Grand Lodge of England Freemason Membership Registers

https://www.masonic-lodge-of-education.com/lodge-officer-duties.html

www.masonicperiodicals.org The Freemason May 7 1887 p14

York Medical Society archives at The Borthwick Library, University of York YMS1/1/1/3, YMS1/1/1/4, YMS1/4/1

www.historyofyork.org.uk

Wikipedia – Bootham Park Hospital

Chapter 8

Bodies of Evidence – medicine and the politics of the English inquest, 1830-1926, by Ian A Burney, published 2000 by the Johns Hopkins University Press Baltimore and London

British Newspaper Archive

The Coroners' Society of England and Wales
www.legislation.gov.uk
AMERICAN JOURNAL OF PHARMACY – Volume 53, #5, May, 1881 Page 12 The Southwest School of Botanical Medicine http://www.swsbm.com

Chapter 9

Kelly's Directory of York and the North Riding of Yorkshire 1902 and 1905

Leading the Police: A History of Chief Constables 1835-2017. Ed. Kim Stevenson, David J Cox and Iain Channing, published by Routledge 2017

Bodies of Evidence – medicine and the politics of the English inquest, 1830-1926, by Ian A Burney, published 2000 by the Johns Hopkins University Press Baltimore and London

British Newspaper Archive

https://en.wikipedia.org/wiki/Dying_declaration

Chapter 10

British Newspaper Archive

Chapter 11

British Newspaper Archive

https://www.visit-nottinghamshire.co.uk/blog/read/2019/09/the-fantastic-history-of-goose-fair-b5961

UK Medical Registers online 1879

Morris and Co´s Directory of Grantham, Chesterfield and Gainsborough 1869

Chapter 12

British Newspaper Archive

https://www.historyextra.com/period/modern/a-brief-history-of-capital-punishment-in-britain/

Chapter 13

British Newspaper Archive

https://www.yorkstmarys.org.uk/about-us/history-of-york-st-marys/

John S Haller Jr, PhD. Opium usage in nineteenth century therapeutics https://www.ncbi.nlm.nih.gov/pmc/articles/PMC1807799/pdf/bullnyacadmed00022-0039.pdf

https://www.history.com/topics/crime/history-of-heroin-morphine-and-opiates

Opium Addiction Among Medical Men, by J. B. Mattison, Medical Record, Vol. 23 (June 9, 1883), 621-23.

A large quantity of morphia (twelve grains?) taken hypodermically with suicidal intent; recovery. Percy Pope, M.R.C.S. ENG., L.R.C.P. EDIN. Published: March 17, 1894 DOI: https://doi.org/10.1016/S0140-6736(01)67629-3

Chapter 14

Burial of Suicide Act 1823 (4 Geo. IV) from https://forest-of dean.net/fodmembers/index.php?id=11312

https://www.thevintagenews.com/2016/12/27/in-early-english-common-law-suicide-was-a-punishable-crime/

HC Deb 21 May 1823 vol 9 cc397-432 Sir J. Mackintosh

Chapter 15

Archives of the Easingwold Advertiser and Weekly News, British Library Boston Spa

Death, Grief and Poverty in Britain, 1870-1914, by Julie-Marie Strange, published in 2005 by Cambridge University Press

Parish records of Stillington – Register of Burials 1868-1954 STN 7 at the Borthwick Library, University of York

Crockford's Clerical Directory 1874, published in London by Horace Cox

Chapter 16

British Newspaper Archives

Cemetery Records, York Cemetery: Genealogists, Friends of York Cemetery

Public & Second Class Graves Trail leaflet by Friends of York Cemetery

The Professionalisation of Mental Health Nursing in Great Britain, 1850 – 1950, by Michael Arton. A Dissertation submitted for the Degree of Doctor of Philosophy, History of Medicine, University College London, 1998

The Retreat archives at the Borthwick Library, University of York RET/5/7/1/4 Rules for Nurses at the Retreat, York Approved by the Committee of the Retreat May 13th 1902 (York 1902) – accessed online via Wellcome Library

Crockford's Clerical Directory 1908, published in London by Horace Cox

York Family History Society

www.abortionrights.org.uk

Birth, Marriages and Deaths Index

British Census records 1891, 1901, 1911

https://case.edu/affil/skuyhistcontraception/online-2012/
  Rhythm-method
www.nhs.uk/start4life/pregnancy/week-by-week

Chapter 17

British Newspaper Archive
The Nightingale Shore Murder, by Rosemary Cook,
  published by Matador, 2015
Birth, Deaths and Marriages Index
Divorce petition and papers for A M Shore v. O B Shore
  1886, The National Archives Ref J77/350/549
British Census records 1891, 1901
Personal communication from Professor Raymond Davis,
  grand-child of Edwin Harris

Chapter 18

Suicide in Victorian and Edwardian England, by Olive
  Anderson, published by Clarendon Press, Oxford,
  1987
British Newspaper Archive
https://www.gov.uk/search-will-probate   re   Will   of
  Farbrace Sidney Gramshaw
Electoral Roll 1920
Births, Deaths and Marriages Index
National Probate Calendar 1921

Chapter 19

British Newspaper Archive
Births, Deaths and Marriages Index
United Grand Lodge of England Freemason Membership
  Registers

Electoral Rolls 1914, 1918, 1919, 1920, 1925, 1933, 1946, 1950

London, England, Freedom of the City Admission Papers, 1681-1930

http://www.herberthistory.co.uk/cgi-bin/sitewise.pl?act=det&p=849 re Finsbury Technical College

http://www.liverycompanies.info/fellowship-of-clerks/freedom--apprentices/freedom-by-redemption.pdf

https://www.gov.uk/search-will-probate re Will of Cecil Henry Gramshaw

https://www.tea.co.uk/history-of-tea

1939 Register

https://demos-uk.com/george-harker

https://www.in2013dollars.com/uk/inflation/1950

UK Military Campaign Medal and Award Rolls 1793 – 1949 National Archives of the UK; Kew, Surrey, England; Class: WO 100; Piece: 271; and WO100/162

Review of the South African Constabulary, 1900 – 1908 by Colonel R S Curtis, accessed via www.angloboerwar.com (includes speech by Joseph Chamberlain)

The war in South Africa, 1899-1902. Chapter IV The Engineer Work accessed via www.angloboerwar.com

History of the War in South Africa. Chapter XII Advance from the Orange River accessed via www.angloboerwar.com

https://api.parliament.uk/historic-hansard/commons/1903/jul/02/south-african-constabulary#S4V0124P0_19030702_HOC_60

Chapter 20

British Newspaper Archive

The National Archives of Ireland – births, deaths and

marriages, calendar of Wills and administration, Census 1901, 1911

http://www.census.nationalarchives.ie/exhibition/dublin/religion.html

http://www.census.nationalarchives.ie/exhibition/dublin/commerce.html

http://www.legislation.gov.uk/ukpga/Vict/24-25/100/crossheading/bigamy

https://search.ancestry.co.uk/cgi-bin/sse.dll?indiv=try&db=CanadaOceanArrivals&h=255844

The National Archives Service Medal and Award Rolls Index WO 372/8/95783

https://www.forces-war-records.co.uk/units/282/leinster-regiment

https://www.forces-war-records.co.uk/units/4659/army-cyclist-corps

www.forces-war-records.co.uk

Chapter 21

British Newspaper Archive

Births, Deaths and Marriages Index

https://www.edwardianpromenade.com/etiquette/mourning-in-edwardian-and-post-war-england/

https://historicengland.org.uk/listing/the-list/list-entry/1018507 (Chilworth Gunpowder Works)

The Medical Register online

www.forces-war-records.co.uk

The 1939 Register

Chapter 22

British Newspaper Archive

Births, Deaths and Marriages Index

Highlights in the History of Epilepsy: The Last 200 years. Emmanouil Magiorkinis, Aristidis Diamantis, Kalliopi Sidiropoulou and Christos Panteliadis. Epilepsy Research and Treatment, Vol 2014, Article ID 582039

Epilepsy stigma: Moving from a global problem to global solutions. Hanneke M de Boer. Seizure: British Epilepsy Association. DOI: 10.1016/j.seizure.2010.10.017

Bringing Epilepsy Out of the Shadows. Rajendra Kale, BMJ 1997;315:2-3 (History of epilepsy quote)

https://www.epilepsy.org.uk/news/news/king-edward-viii-hidden-brother-epilepsy-was-animal-64829

https://www.epilepsysociety.org.uk/seizure-types#.XhMc7kf7SM8

https://www.epilepsy.com/article/2016/11/epilepsy-and-psychological-disorders

https://www.ncbi.nlm.nih.gov/pmc/articles/PMC6248685/ – Sukaina Rizvi, Faiza Farooq, Shanila Shagufta, Ali M Khan, Yasir Masood and Hina Saeed (2018) Postictal Mania Versus Postictal Psychosis Cureus. 2018 Sep; 10(9): e3338. doi: 10.7759/cureus.3338

Susan Margaret Burt (2003) "Fit Objects for an Asylum" The Hampshire County Lunatic Asylum and its Patients, 1852-1899", University of Southampton

Hampshire Record Office 48M94/B1/13, 48M94/B6/A58 – Knowle Hospital Admission Register, Reception Order

Chapter 23

Takabayashi A. Surviving the Lunacy Act of 1890: English Psychiatrists and Professional Development during the Early Twentieth Century. Med Hist. 2017;61(2):246–269. doi:10.1017/mdh.2017.4

Susan Margaret Burt (2003) "Fit Objects for an Asylum" The Hampshire County Lunatic Asylum and its Patients, 1852-1899", University of Southampton

https://www.sciencemuseum.org.uk/objects-and-stories/victorian-mental-asylum

www.irishexaminer.com/breakingnews/views/analysis/the-violent-history-of-brutal-and-intrusive-procedures-890160

Encyclopaedia of Asylum Therapeutics, 1750-1950s. Mary de Young. Published by McFarland, 2015

https://emotionsblog.history.qmul.ac.uk/2012/06/fat-and-well-force-feeding-and-emotion-in-the-nineteenth-century-asylum/

https://www.netweather.tv/weather-forecasts/uk/winter/winter-history

Hampshire Record Office 48M94/B11/1, 48M94/E2/2 – Knowle Hospital Register of Deaths, Register of Burials

Troubled proximities: asylums and cemeteries in nineteenth-century England by Chris Philo. First published February 27, 2012 Research Article https://doi.org/10.1177/0957154X11428931

Andrews J. Death and the dead-house in Victorian asylums: necroscopy versus mourning at the Royal Edinburgh Asylum, C. 1832-1901. Hist Psychiatry. 2012;23(89 Pt 1):6–26. doi:10.1177/0957154X11432242 https://www.

ncbi.nlm.nih.gov/pmc/articles/PMC4112573/#__ffn_
sectitle
British Newspaper Archive
UK Census 1891, 1911
Hampshire Record Office 48M94/A9/8 Knowle Hospital
Annual Report 1909

Chapter 24
https://www.cps.gov.uk/legal-guidance/homicide-
murder-and-manslaughter
https://www.cps.gov.uk/legal-guidance/rape-and-sexual-
offences
The British Newspaper Archive
http://staffscc.net/wppalmer/?page_id=198
https://murderpedia.org/male.P/p/palmer-william.htm

Chapter 25
The British Newspaper Archive
The Births, Death and Marriages Index
https://murderpedia.org/male.W/w/warder-alfred.htm

Chapter 26
The British Newspaper Archive
https://murderpedia.org/male.S/s/shipman-harold.htm
https://murderpedia.org/male.A/a/adams-john-bodkin.
htm
https://murderpedia.org/male.C/c/crippen-hawley.htm

Chapter 27
The British Newspaper Archive
The Births, Deaths and Marriages Index

https://reviews.history.ac.uk/review/806 re adoption in early 20th century

https://www.thetcj.org/child-care-history-policy/%E2%80%98the-hope-is-in-children-the-times-671908 re the Children Act

Acknowledgements

Many thanks to the volunteer genealogists at York Cemetery who have been unfailingly helpful and interested, and who have restored the grave of Margaret Brown so that it is once again visible as a memorial to her life.

Thank you to the archivists at the Borthwick Library, Hampshire Record Office, Nottinghamshire Archives Research Service, The British Library at Boston Spa, the Royal College of Physicians of Ireland, the Royal College of Surgeons of Edinburgh and York Explore Archives, without whom the local and family history elements of this book would have been impossible to uncover.

Thanks also to the local societies who helped with information: the Stillington and District Archive and the York Family History Society.